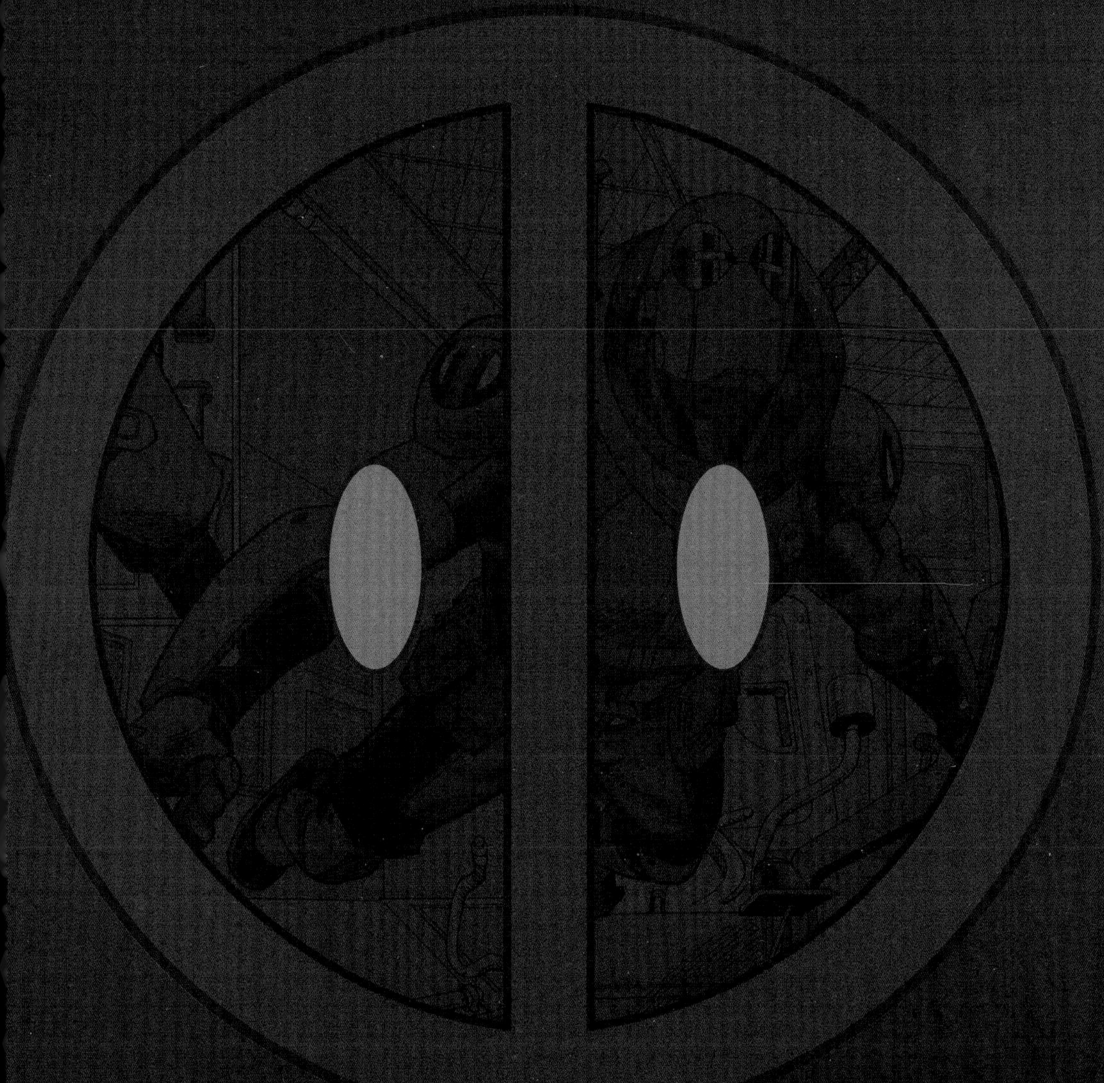

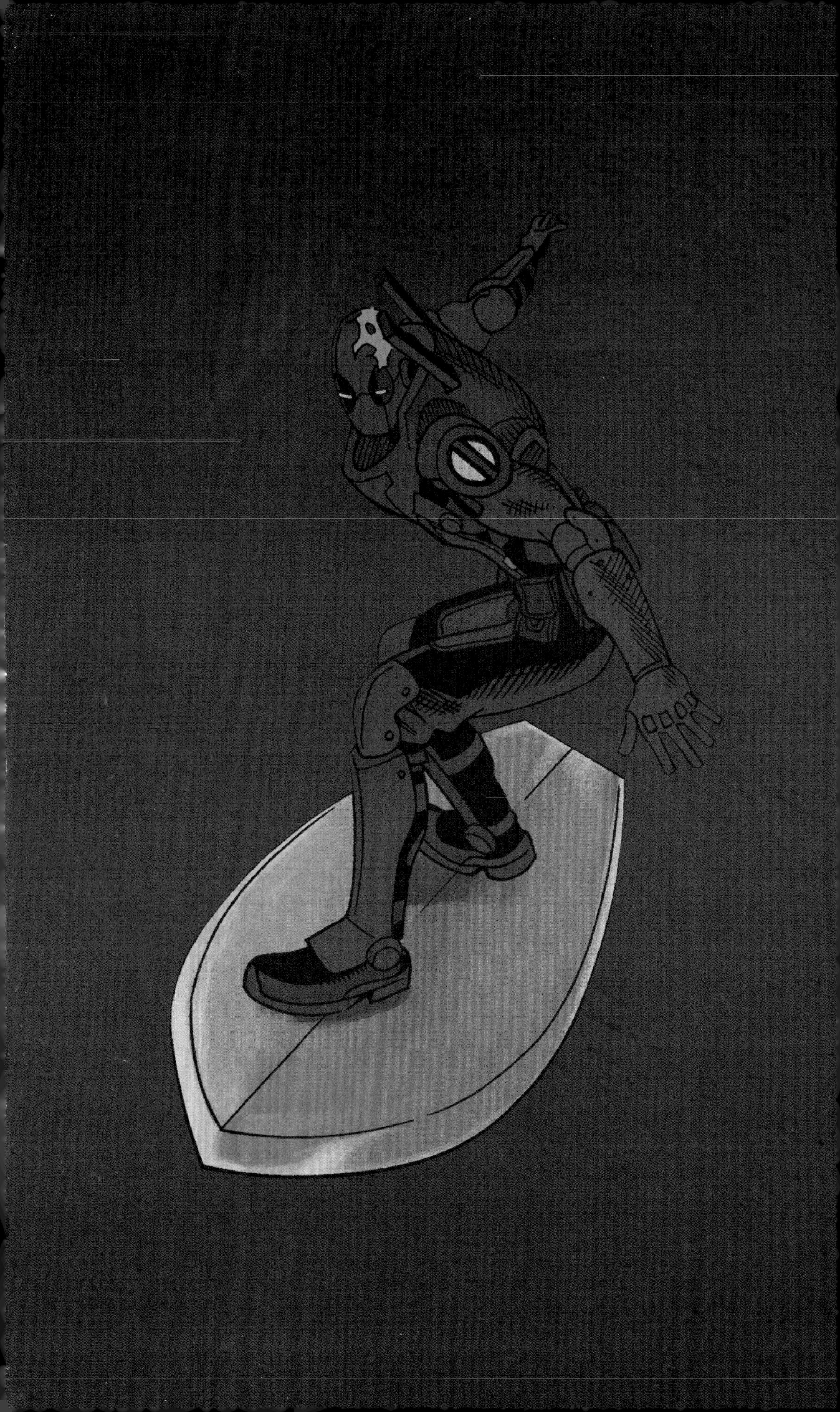

THE WORLD'S GREATEST COMIC MAGAZINE!

DEADPOOL

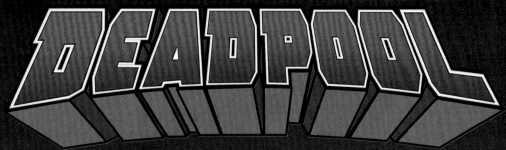

DEADPOOL IN SPACE

GERRY DUGGAN
writer

MIKE HAWTHORNE
penciler

TERRY PALLOT
inker

JORDIE BELLAIRE
colorist

VC's JOE SABINO
letterer

MIKE HAWTHORNE & JORDIE BELLAIRE
cover art

HEATHER ANTOS
assistant editor

JORDAN D. WHITE
editor

DEADPOOL created by
ROB LIEFELD & FABIAN NICIEZA

collection editor JENNIFER GRÜNWALD
assistant editor CAITLIN O'CONNELL
associate managing editor KATERI WOODY
editor, special projects MARK D. BEAZLEY
vp production & special projects JEFF YOUNGQUIST
svp print, sales & marketing DAVID GABRIEL
book designer ADAM DEL RE

editor in chief AXEL ALONSO
chief creative officer JOE QUESADA
president DAN BUCKLEY
executive producer ALAN FINE

DEADPOOL: WORLD'S GREATEST VOL. 9 — DEADPOOL IN SPACE. Contains material originally published in magazine form as DEADPOOL #30. First printing 2017. ISBN# 978-1-302-90760-0. Published by MARVEL WORLDWIDE, INC., a subsidiary of MARVEL ENTERTAINMENT, LLC. OFFICE OF PUBLICATION: 135 West 50th Street, New York, NY 10020. Printed in Canada. DAN BUCKLEY, President, Marvel Entertainment; JOE QUESADA, Chief Creative Officer; TOM BREVOORT, SVP of Publishing; DAVID BOGART, SVP of Business Affairs & Operations, Publishing & Partnership; C.B. CEBULSKI, VP of Brand Management & Development, Asia; DAVID GABRIEL, SVP of Sales & Marketing, Publishing; JEFF YOUNGQUIST, VP of Production & Special Projects; DAN CARR, Executive Director of Publishing Technology; ALEX MORALES, Director of Publishing Operations; SUSAN CRESPI, Production Manager; STAN LEE, Chairman Emeritus. For information regarding advertising in Marvel Comics or on Marvel.com, please contact Vit DeBellis, Integrated Sales Manager, at vdebellis@marvel.com. For Marvel subscription inquiries, please call 888-511-5480. Manufactured between 7/21/2017 and 8/22/2017 by SOLISCO PRINTERS, SCOTT, QC, CANADA.

10 9 8 7 6 5 4 3 2 1

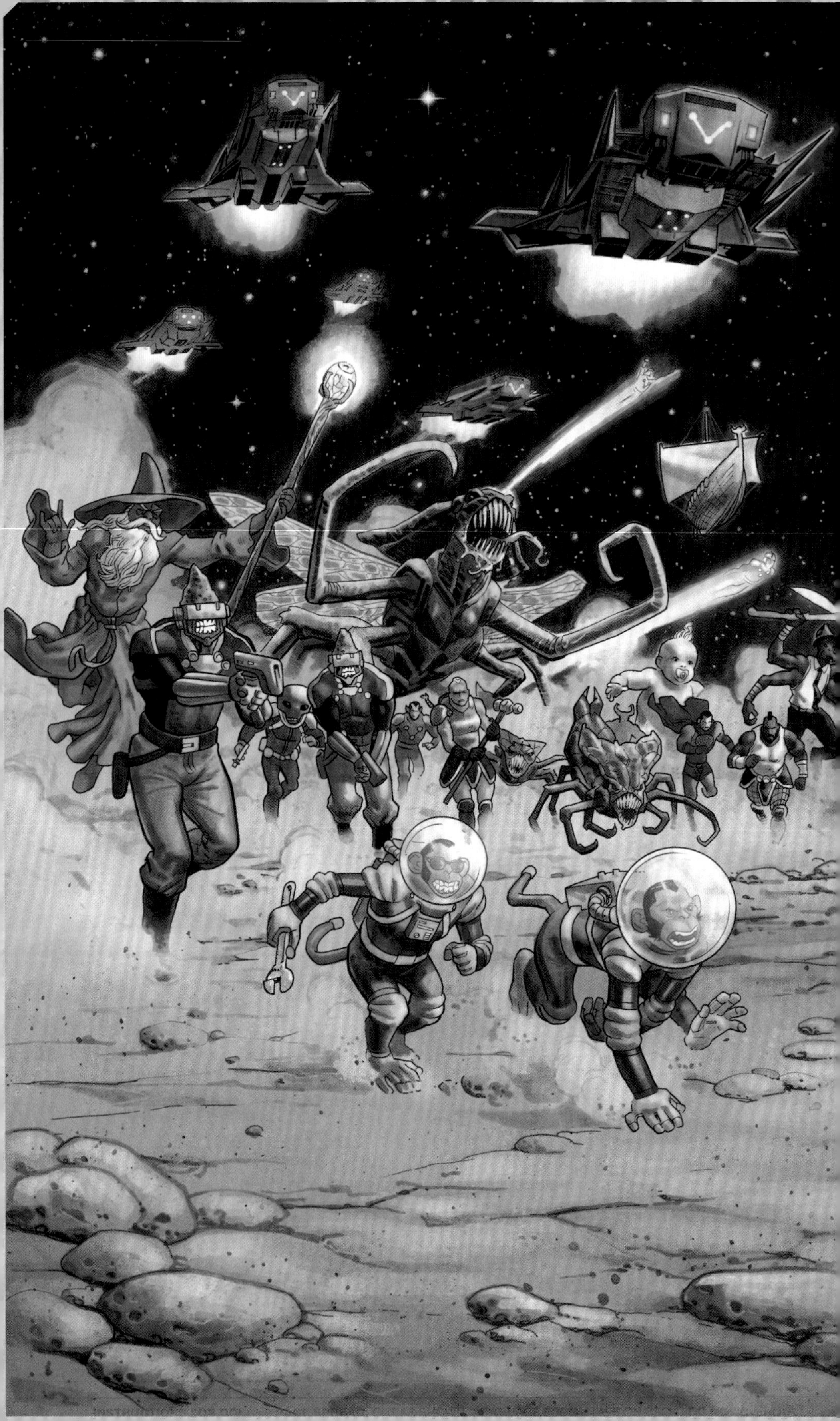

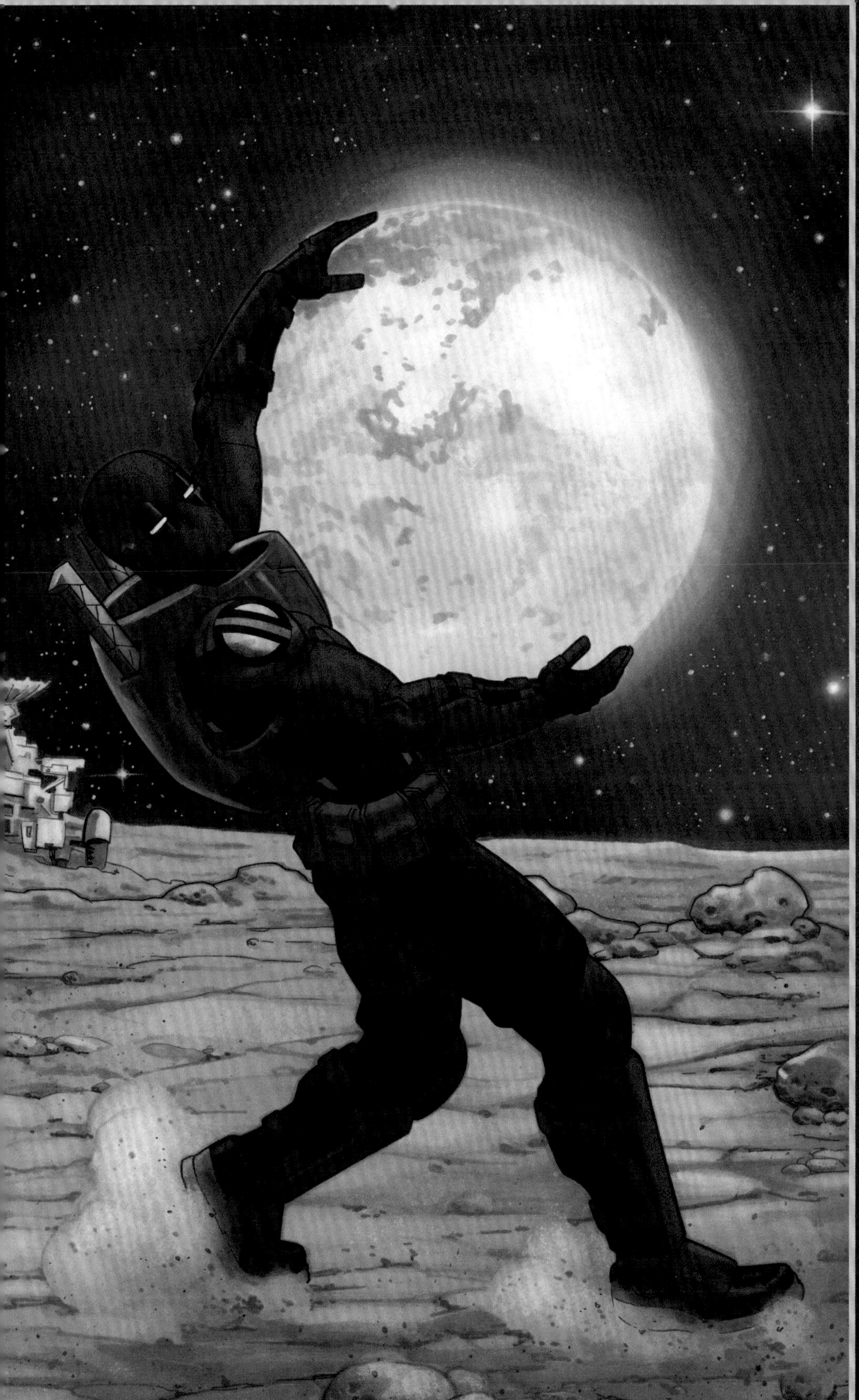

Avenger...Assassin...Superstar...Smelly person...Possibly the world's most skilled mercenary, definitely the world's most annoying, Wade Wilson was chosen for a to secret government program that gave him a healing factor allowing him to heal from wound. Somehow, despite making his money as a gun for hire, Wade has become on the most beloved "heroes" in the world. Call him the Merc with the Mouth...call him Regeneratin' Degenerate...call him...

DEADPOOL

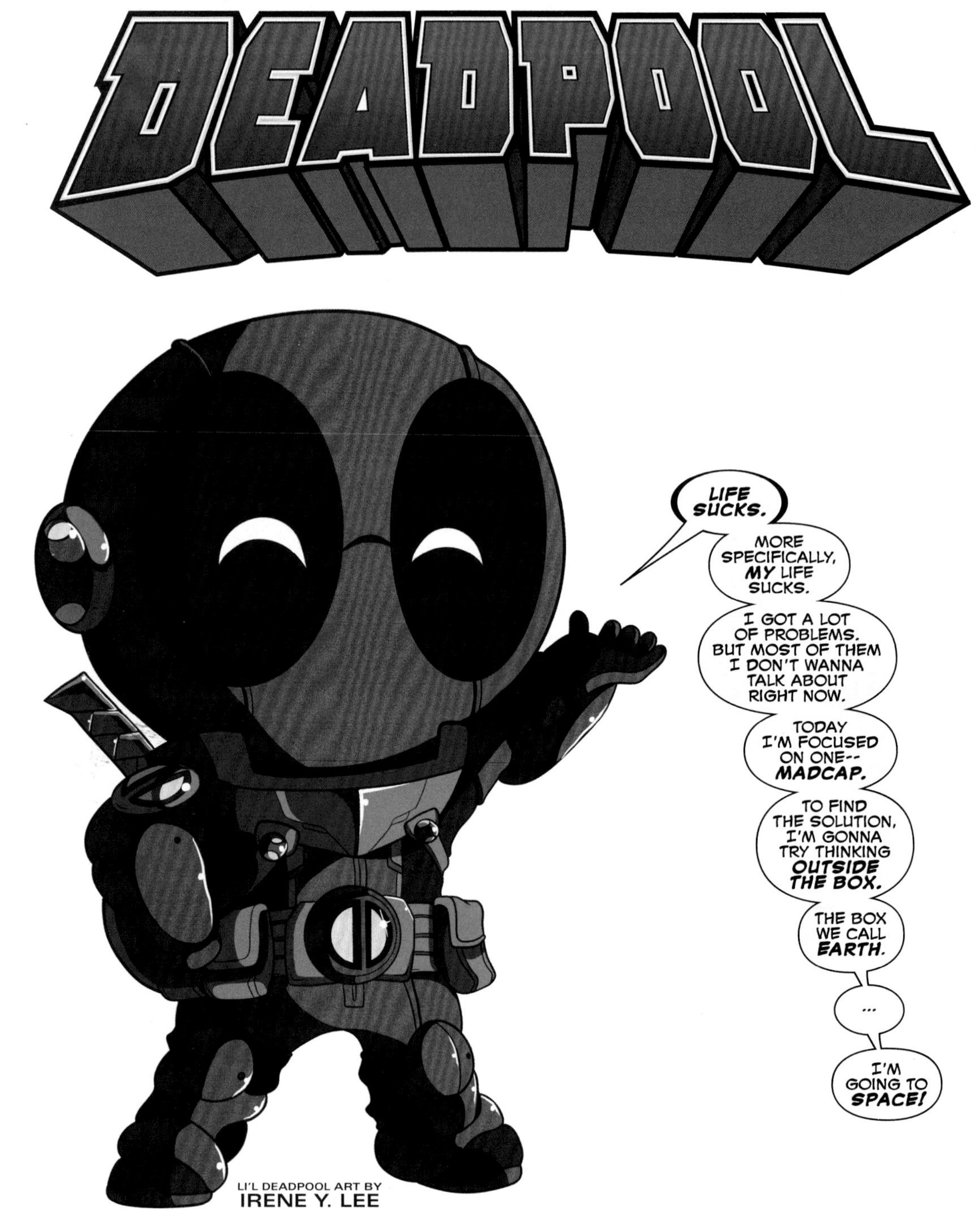

LIFE SUCKS.
MORE SPECIFICALLY, MY LIFE SUCKS.
I GOT A LOT OF PROBLEMS. BUT MOST OF THEM I DON'T WANNA TALK ABOUT RIGHT NOW.
TODAY I'M FOCUSED ON ONE-- MADCAP.
TO FIND THE SOLUTION, I'M GONNA TRY THINKING OUTSIDE THE BOX.
THE BOX WE CALL EARTH.
...
I'M GOING TO SPACE!

LI'L DEADPOOL ART BY
IRENE Y. LEE

A SPACE ODDITY

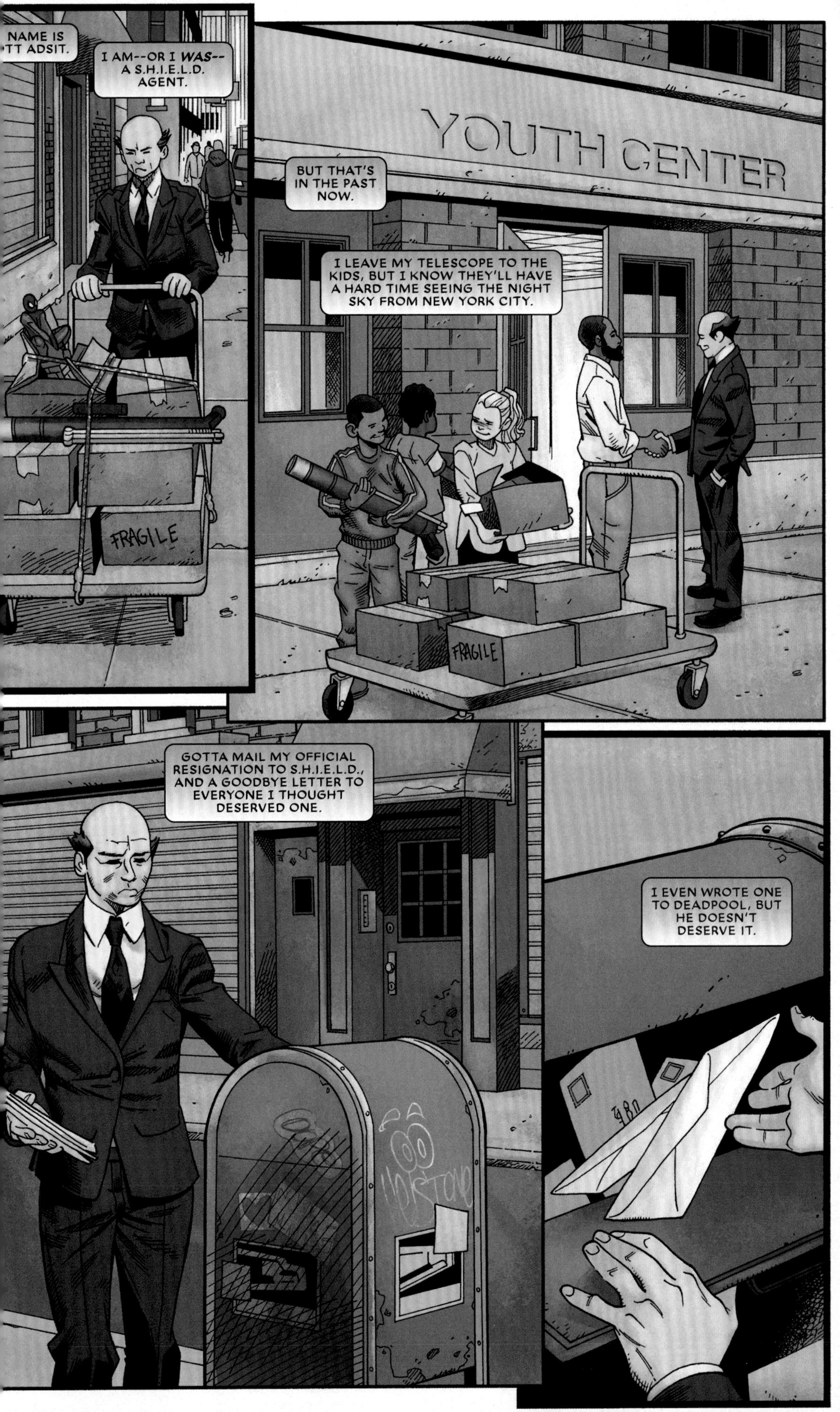

NAME IS
TT ADSIT.
I AM--OR I *WAS*--
A S.H.I.E.L.D.
AGENT.
FRAGILE
YOUTH CENTER
BUT THAT'S
IN THE PAST
NOW.
I LEAVE MY TELESCOPE TO THE
KIDS, BUT I KNOW THEY'LL HAVE
A HARD TIME SEEING THE NIGHT
SKY FROM NEW YORK CITY.
FRAGILE
GOTTA MAIL MY OFFICIAL
RESIGNATION TO S.H.I.E.L.D.,
AND A GOODBYE LETTER TO
EVERYONE I THOUGHT
DESERVED ONE.
I EVEN WROTE ONE
TO DEADPOOL, BUT
HE DOESN'T
DESERVE IT.

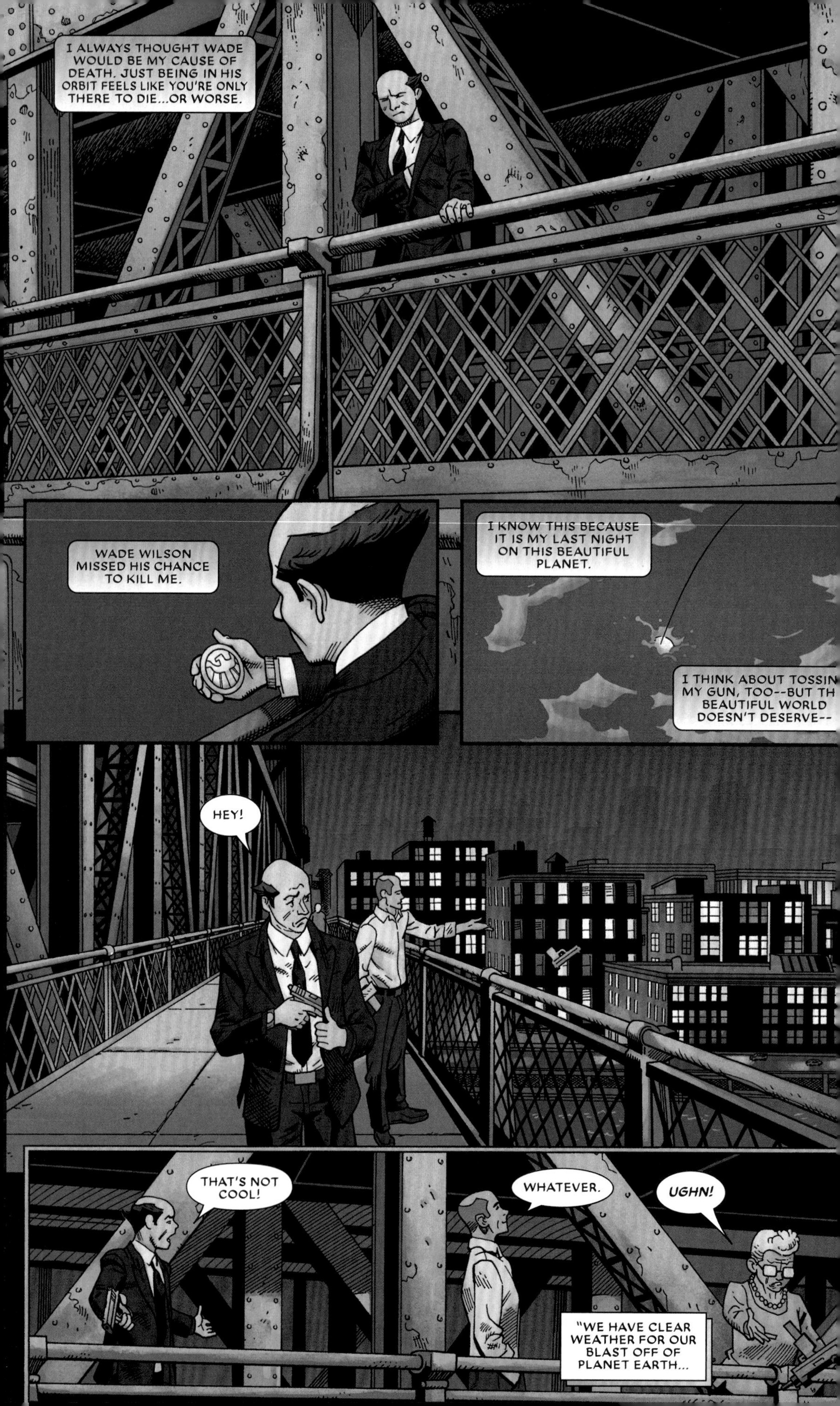
I ALWAYS THOUGHT WADE WOULD BE MY CAUSE OF DEATH. JUST BEING IN HIS ORBIT FEELS LIKE YOU'RE ONLY THERE TO DIE...OR WORSE.
WADE WILSON MISSED HIS CHANCE TO KILL ME.
I KNOW THIS BECAUSE IT IS MY LAST NIGHT ON THIS BEAUTIFUL PLANET.
I THINK ABOUT TOSSIN MY GUN, TOO--BUT TH BEAUTIFUL WORLD DOESN'T DESERVE--
HEY!
THAT'S NOT COOL!
WHATEVER.
UGHN!
"WE HAVE CLEAR WEATHER FOR OUR BLAST OFF OF PLANET EARTH...

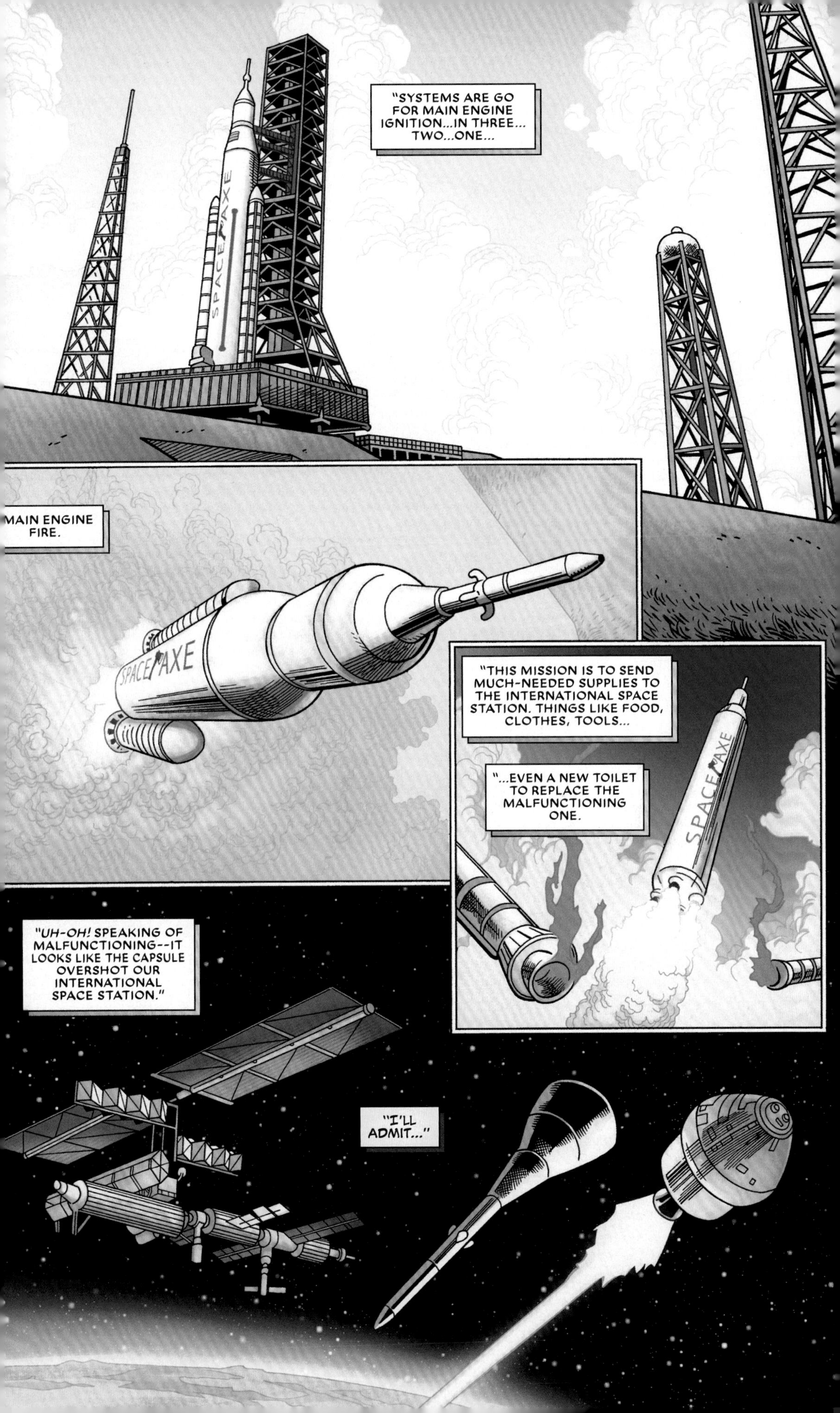
"SYSTEMS ARE GO FOR MAIN ENGINE IGNITION...IN THREE... TWO...ONE...
MAIN ENGINE FIRE.
SPACE AXE
"THIS MISSION IS TO SEND MUCH-NEEDED SUPPLIES TO THE INTERNATIONAL SPACE STATION. THINGS LIKE FOOD, CLOTHES, TOOLS...
"...EVEN A NEW TOILET TO REPLACE THE MALFUNCTIONING ONE.
"UH-OH! SPEAKING OF MALFUNCTIONING--IT LOOKS LIKE THE CAPSULE OVERSHOT OUR INTERNATIONAL SPACE STATION."
"I'LL ADMIT..."

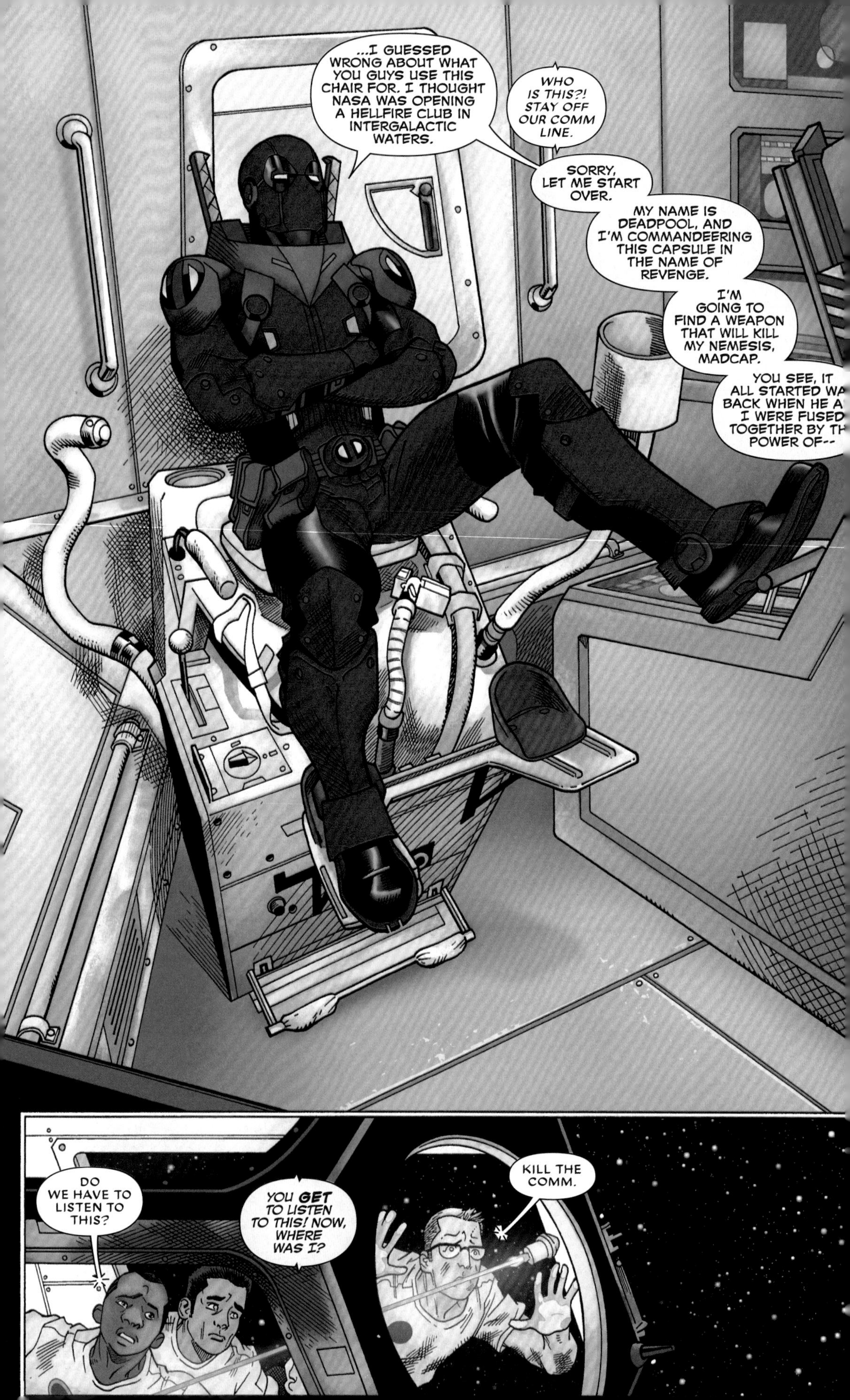
...I GUESSED WRONG ABOUT WHAT YOU GUYS USE THIS CHAIR FOR. I THOUGHT NASA WAS OPENING A HELLFIRE CLUB IN INTERGALACTIC WATERS.
WHO IS THIS?! STAY OFF OUR COMM LINE.
SORRY, LET ME START OVER.
MY NAME IS DEADPOOL, AND I'M COMMANDEERING THIS CAPSULE IN THE NAME OF REVENGE.
I'M GOING TO FIND A WEAPON THAT WILL KILL MY NEMESIS, MADCAP.
YOU SEE, IT ALL STARTED WA BACK WHEN HE A I WERE FUSED TOGETHER BY TH POWER OF--
DO WE HAVE TO LISTEN TO THIS?
YOU **GET** TO LISTEN TO THIS! NOW, WHERE WAS I?
KILL THE COMM.

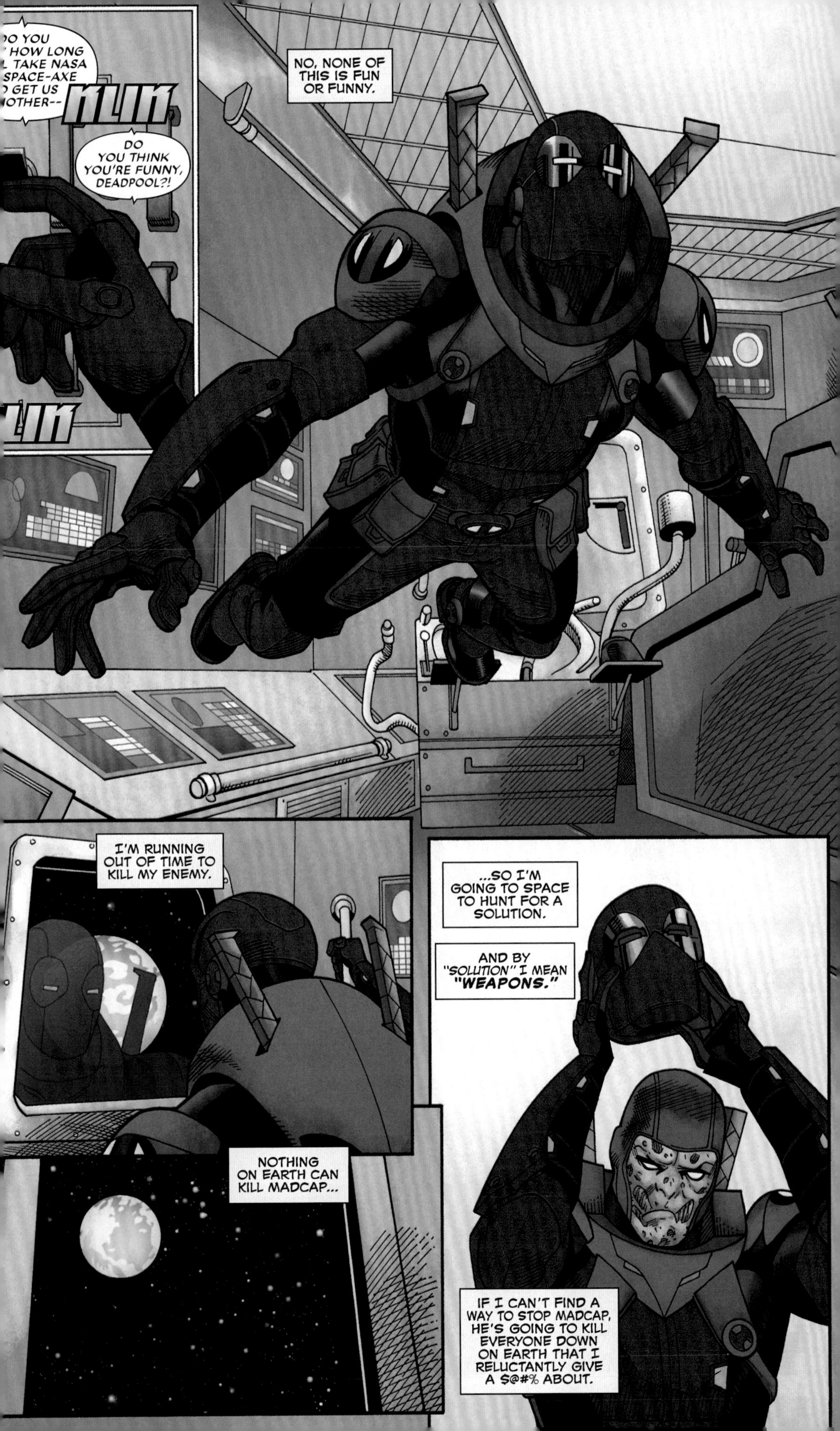
...DO YOU ...HOW LONG ...L TAKE NASA SPACE-AXE ...GET US ...OTHER--
KLIK
DO YOU THINK YOU'RE FUNNY, DEADPOOL?!
NO, NONE OF THIS IS FUN OR FUNNY.
KLIK
I'M RUNNING OUT OF TIME TO KILL MY ENEMY.
NOTHING ON EARTH CAN KILL MADCAP...
...SO I'M GOING TO SPACE TO HUNT FOR A SOLUTION.
AND BY "SOLUTION" I MEAN "WEAPONS."
IF I CAN'T FIND A WAY TO STOP MADCAP, HE'S GOING TO KILL EVERYONE DOWN ON EARTH THAT I RELUCTANTLY GIVE A $@#% ABOUT.

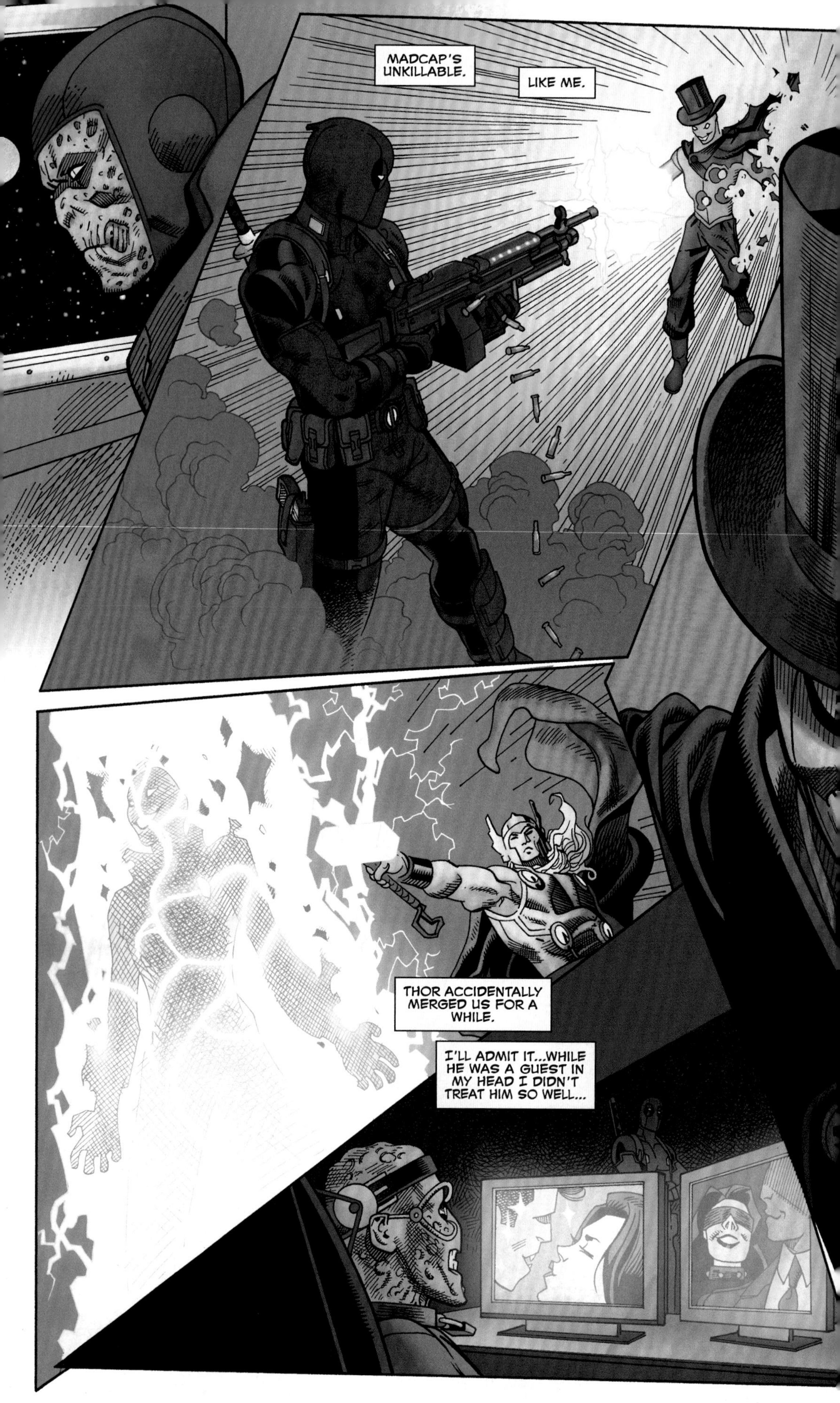
MADCAP'S UNKILLABLE.
LIKE ME.
THOR ACCIDENTALLY MERGED US FOR A WHILE.
I'LL ADMIT IT...WHILE HE WAS A GUEST IN MY HEAD I DIDN'T TREAT HIM SO WELL...

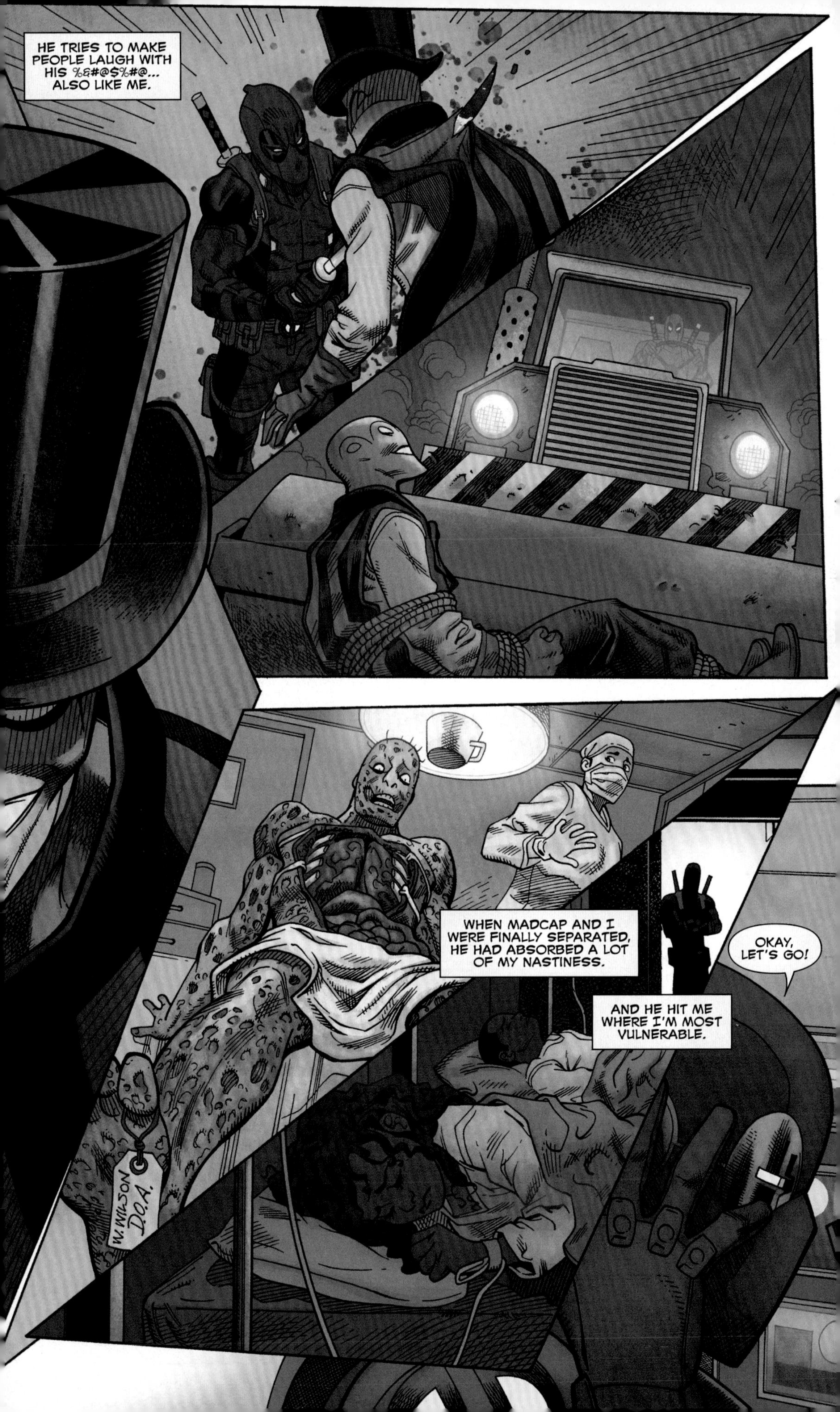
HE TRIES TO MAKE PEOPLE LAUGH WITH HIS %&#@$%#@... ALSO LIKE ME.
WHEN MADCAP AND I WERE FINALLY SEPARATED, HE HAD ABSORBED A LOT OF MY NASTINESS.
W. WILSON D.O.A.
OKAY, LET'S GO!
AND HE HIT ME WHERE I'M MOST VULNERABLE.

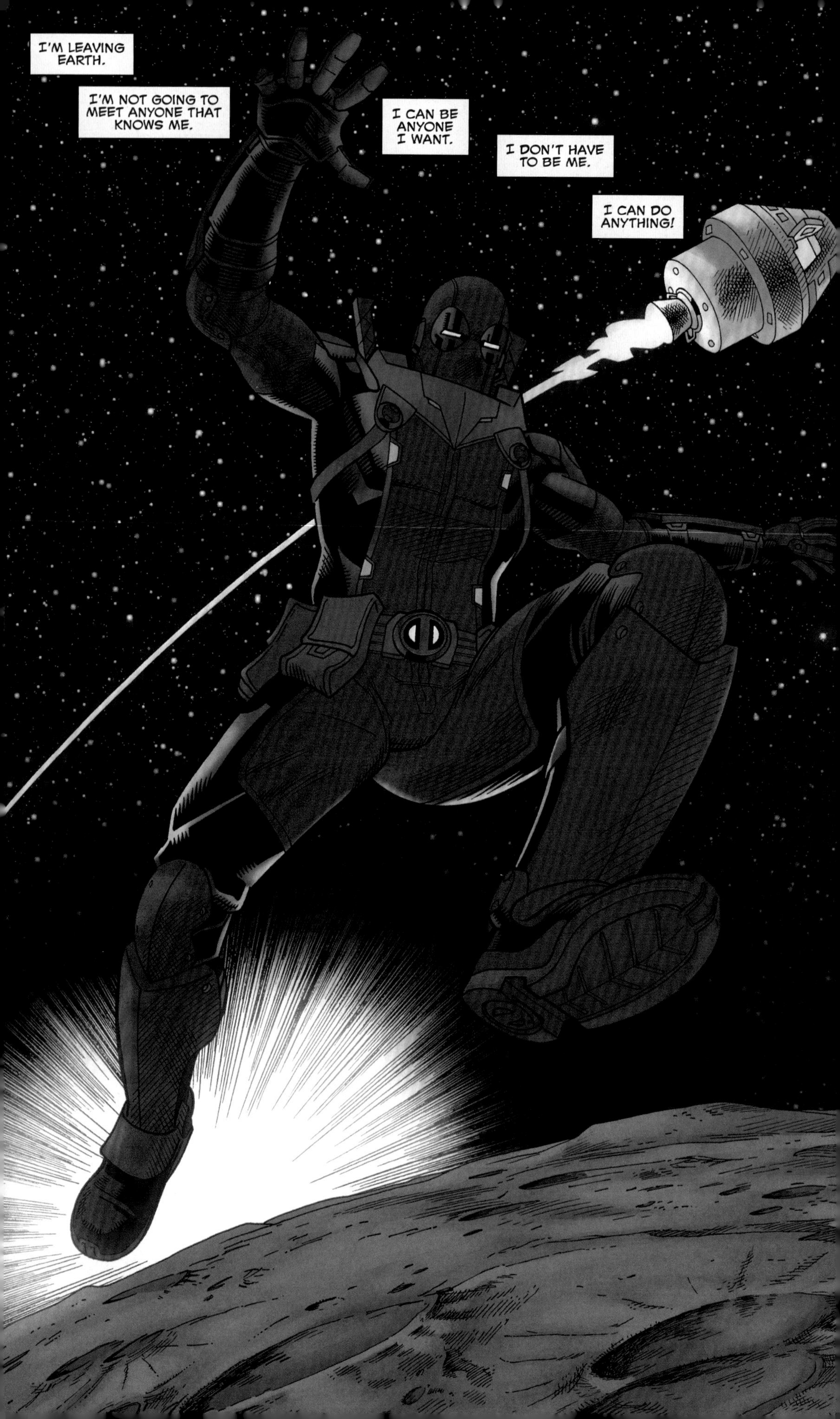
I'M LEAVING EARTH.
I'M NOT GOING TO MEET ANYONE THAT KNOWS ME.
I CAN BE ANYONE I WANT.
I DON'T HAVE TO BE ME.
I CAN DO ANYTHING!

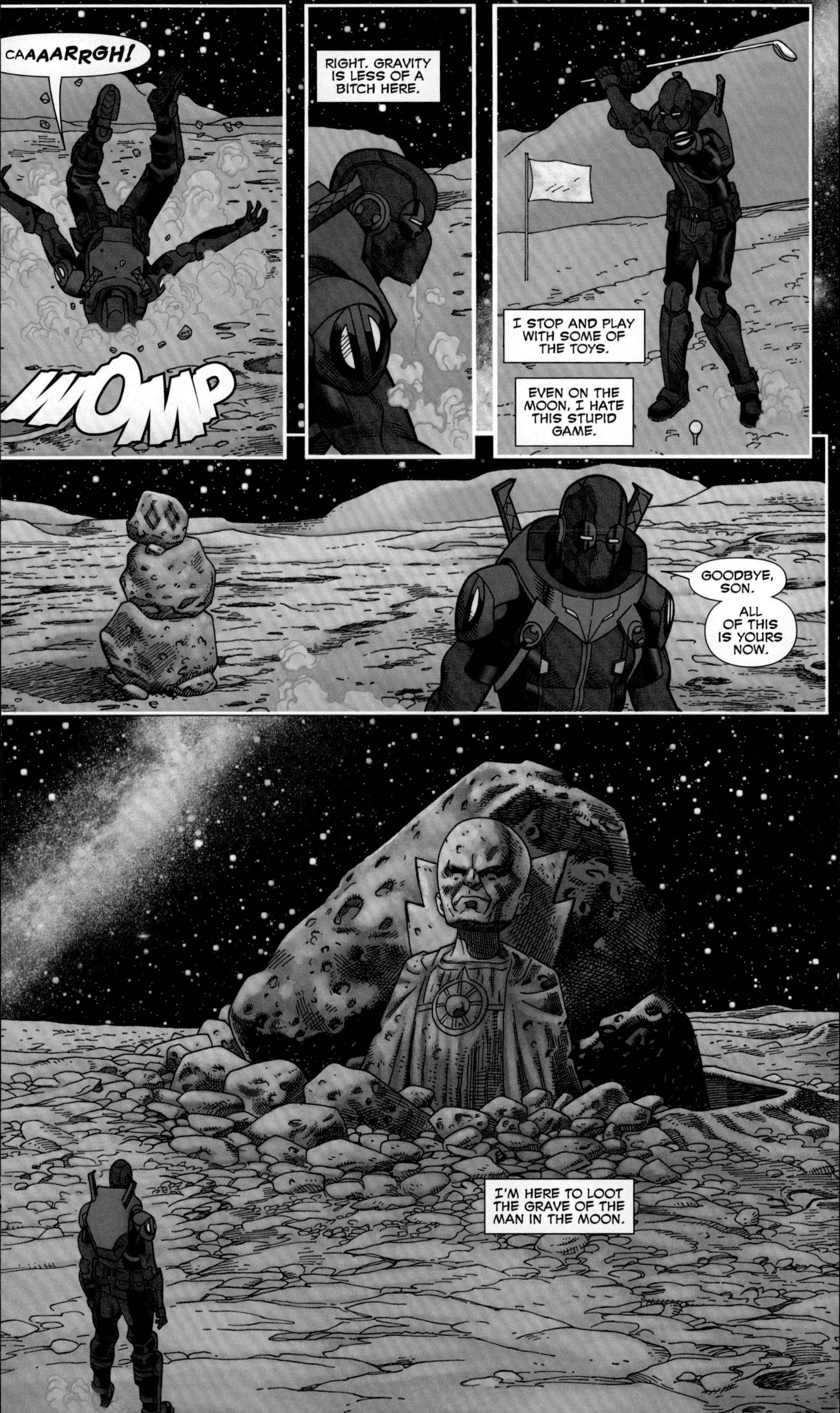
CAAAARRGH!
WOMP
RIGHT. GRAVITY IS LESS OF A BITCH HERE.
I STOP AND PLAY WITH SOME OF THE TOYS.
EVEN ON THE MOON, I HATE THIS STUPID GAME.
GOODBYE, SON.
ALL OF THIS IS YOURS NOW.
I'M HERE TO LOOT THE GRAVE OF THE MAN IN THE MOON.

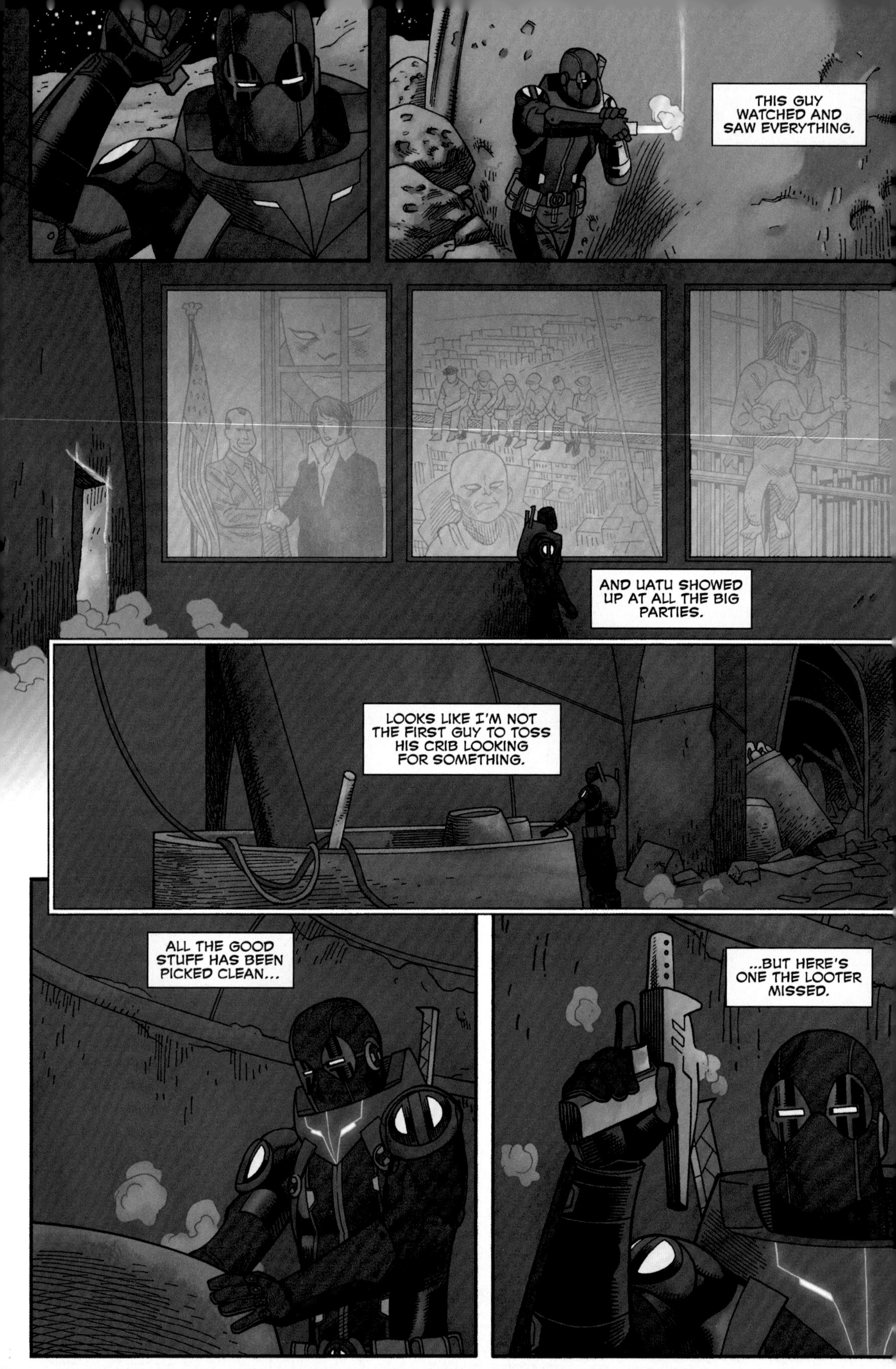
THIS GUY WATCHED AND SAW EVERYTHING.
AND UATU SHOWED UP AT ALL THE BIG PARTIES.
LOOKS LIKE I'M NOT THE FIRST GUY TO TOSS HIS CRIB LOOKING FOR SOMETHING.
ALL THE GOOD STUFF HAS BEEN PICKED CLEAN...
...BUT HERE'S ONE THE LOOTER MISSED.

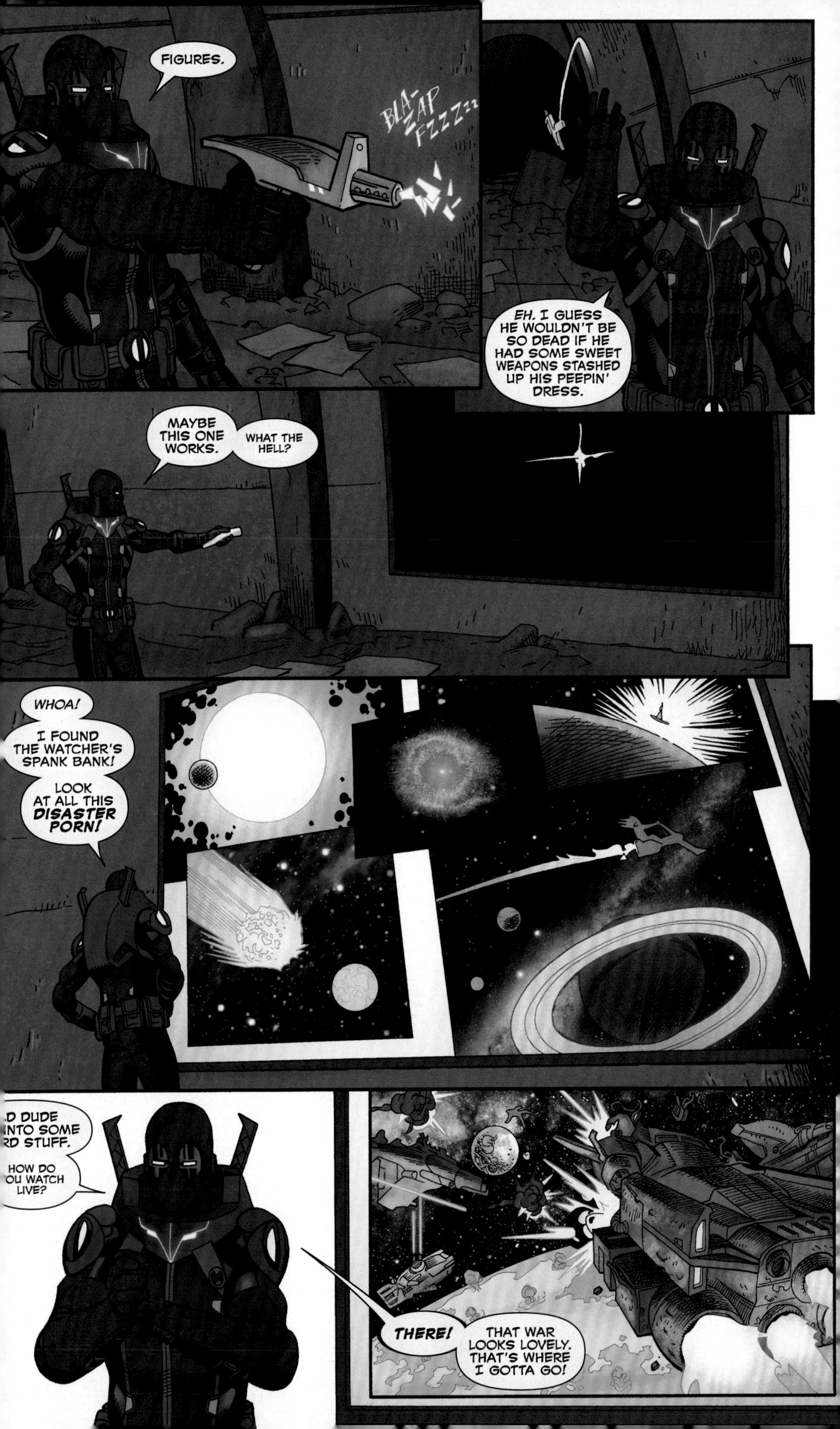
FIGURES.
BLA-ZAP FZZZzz
EH. I GUESS HE WOULDN'T BE SO DEAD IF HE HAD SOME SWEET WEAPONS STASHED UP HIS PEEPIN' DRESS.
MAYBE THIS ONE WORKS.
WHAT THE HELL?
WHOA!
I FOUND THE WATCHER'S SPANK BANK!
LOOK AT ALL THIS DISASTER PORN!
HOW DO
THERE!
THAT WAR LOOKS LOVELY. THAT'S WHERE I GOTTA GO!

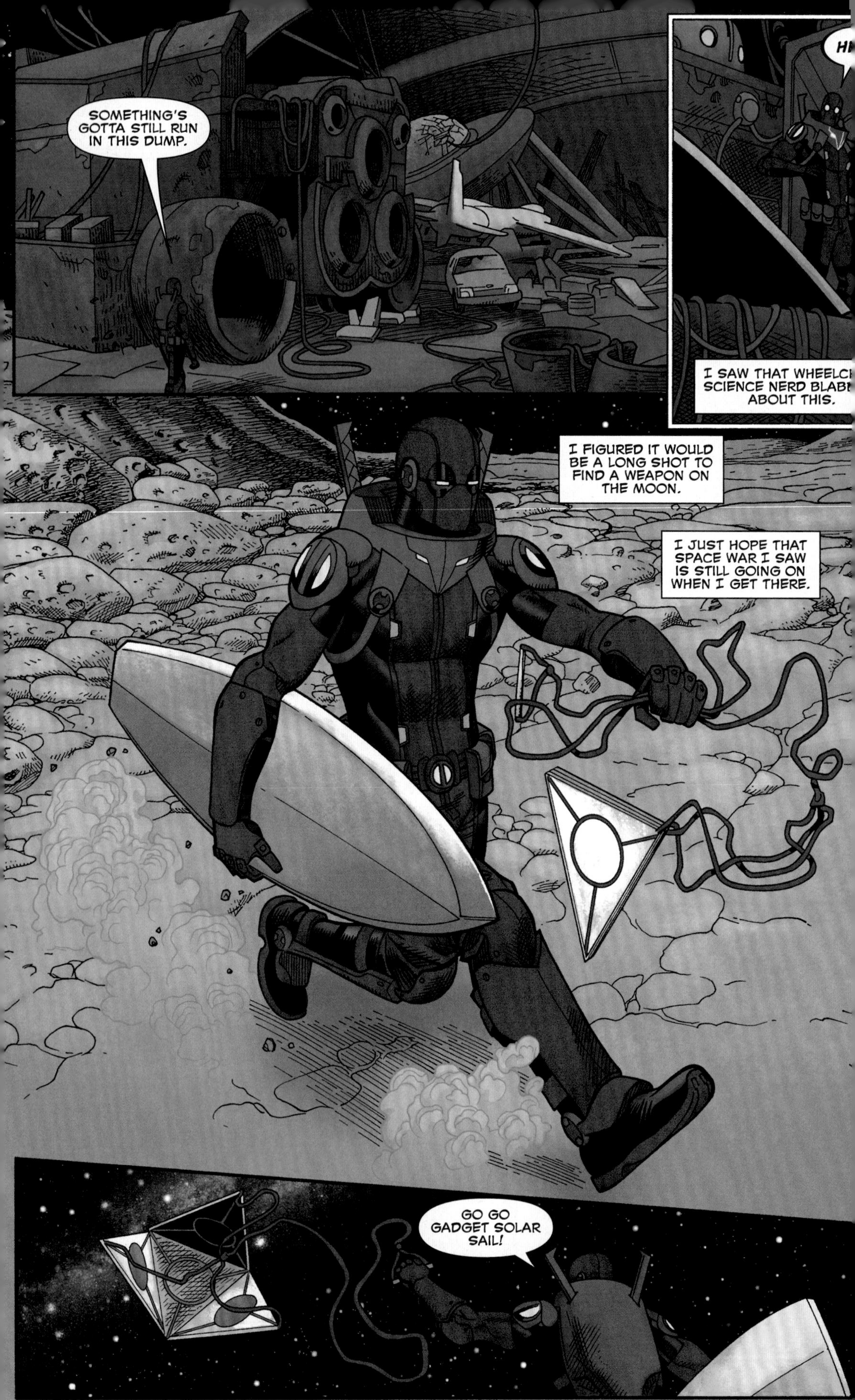
SOMETHING'S GOTTA STILL RUN IN THIS DUMP.
I SAW THAT WHEELC SCIENCE NERD BLAB ABOUT THIS.
I FIGURED IT WOULD BE A LONG SHOT TO FIND A WEAPON ON THE MOON.
I JUST HOPE THAT SPACE WAR I SAW IS STILL GOING ON WHEN I GET THERE.
GO GO GADGET SOLAR SAIL!

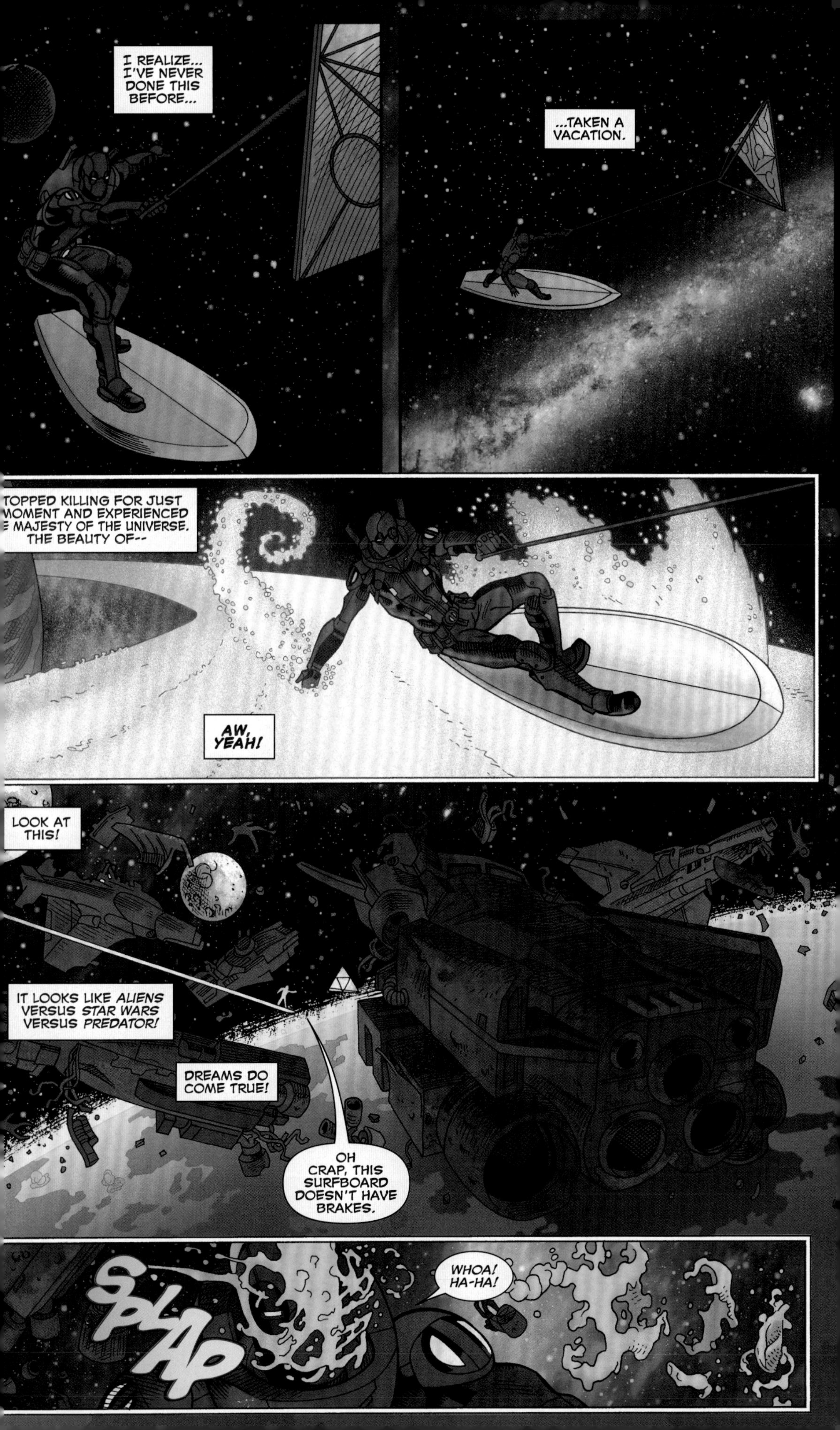
I REALIZE... I'VE NEVER DONE THIS BEFORE...
...TAKEN A VACATION.
TOPPED KILLING FOR JUST
MOMENT AND EXPERIENCED
E MAJESTY OF THE UNIVERSE.
THE BEAUTY OF--
AW, YEAH!
LOOK AT THIS!
IT LOOKS LIKE ALIENS VERSUS STAR WARS VERSUS PREDATOR!
DREAMS DO COME TRUE!
OH CRAP, THIS SURFBOARD DOESN'T HAVE BRAKES.
SPLAP
WHOA! HA-HA!

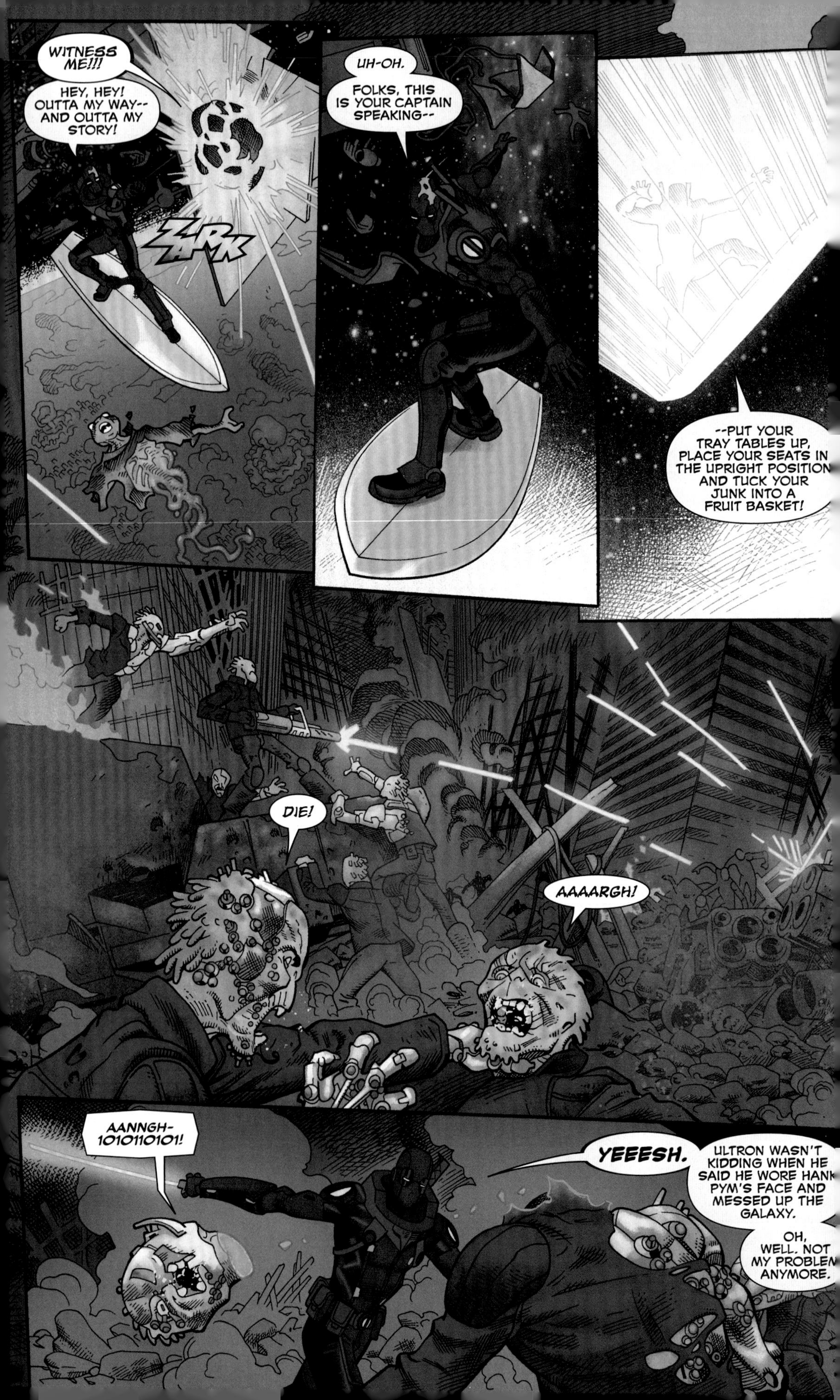
WITNESS ME!!!
HEY, HEY! OUTTA MY WAY-- AND OUTTA MY STORY!
ZARK
UH-OH.
FOLKS, THIS IS YOUR CAPTAIN SPEAKING--
--PUT YOUR TRAY TABLES UP, PLACE YOUR SEATS IN THE UPRIGHT POSITION AND TUCK YOUR JUNK INTO A FRUIT BASKET!
DIE!
AAAARGH!
AANNGH-1010110101!
YEEESH.
ULTRON WASN'T KIDDING WHEN HE SAID HE WORE HANK PYM'S FACE AND MESSED UP THE GALAXY.
OH, WELL. NOT MY PROBLEM ANYMORE.

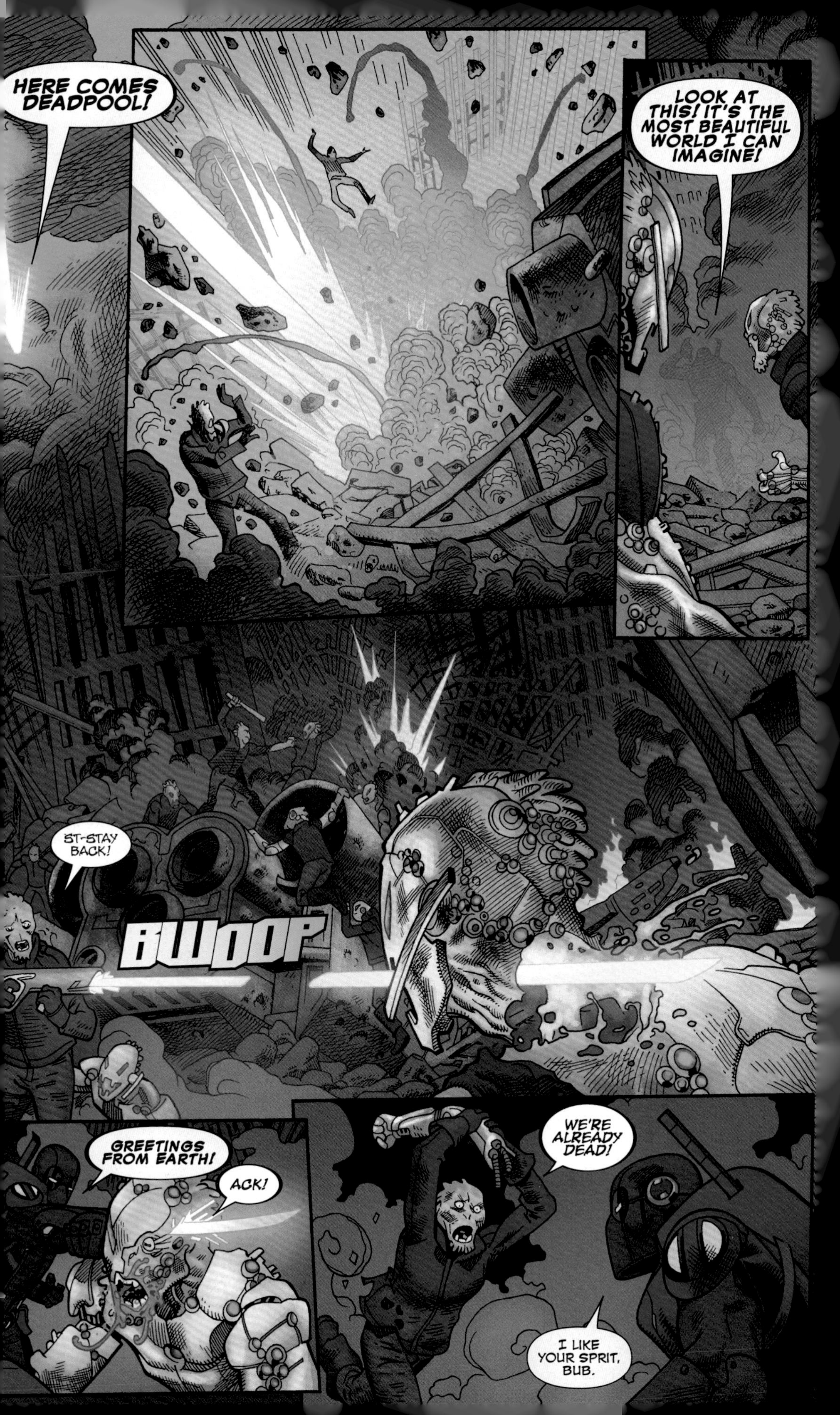
HERE COMES DEADPOOL!
LOOK AT THIS! IT'S THE MOST BEAUTIFUL WORLD I CAN IMAGINE!
ST-STAY BACK!
BWOOP
GREETINGS FROM EARTH!
ACK!
WE'RE ALREADY DEAD!
I LIKE YOUR SPRIT, BUB.

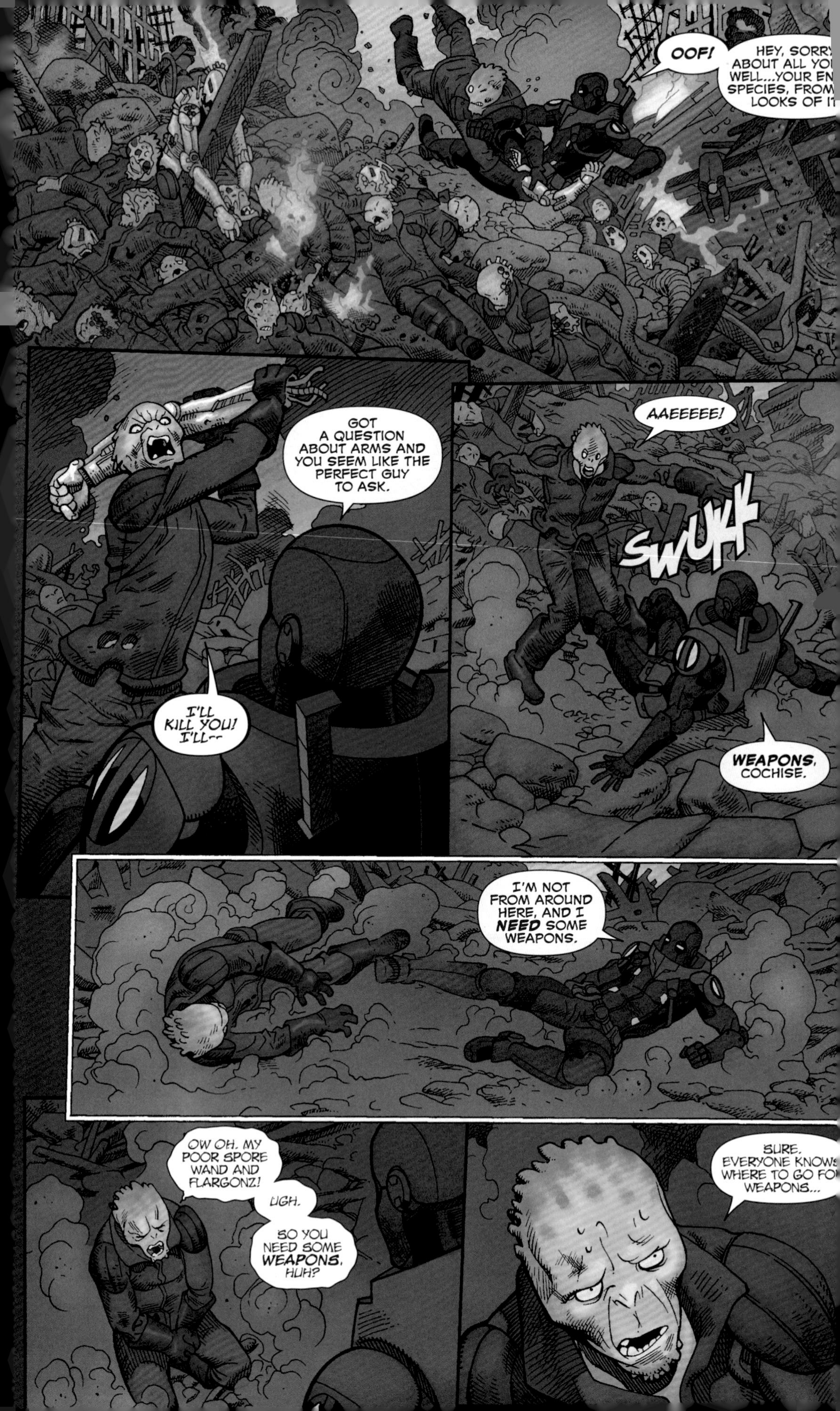
OOF!
HEY, SORRY ABOUT ALL YO WELL...YOUR EN SPECIES, FROM LOOKS OF IT
GOT A QUESTION ABOUT ARMS AND YOU SEEM LIKE THE PERFECT GUY TO ASK.
I'LL KILL YOU! I'LL--
AAEEEEE!
SWUKK
WEAPONS, COCHISE.
I'M NOT FROM AROUND HERE, AND I NEED SOME WEAPONS.
OW OH. MY POOR SPORE WAND AND FLARGONZ!
UGH.
SO YOU NEED SOME WEAPONS, HUH?
SURE. EVERYONE KNOWS WHERE TO GO FO WEAPONS...

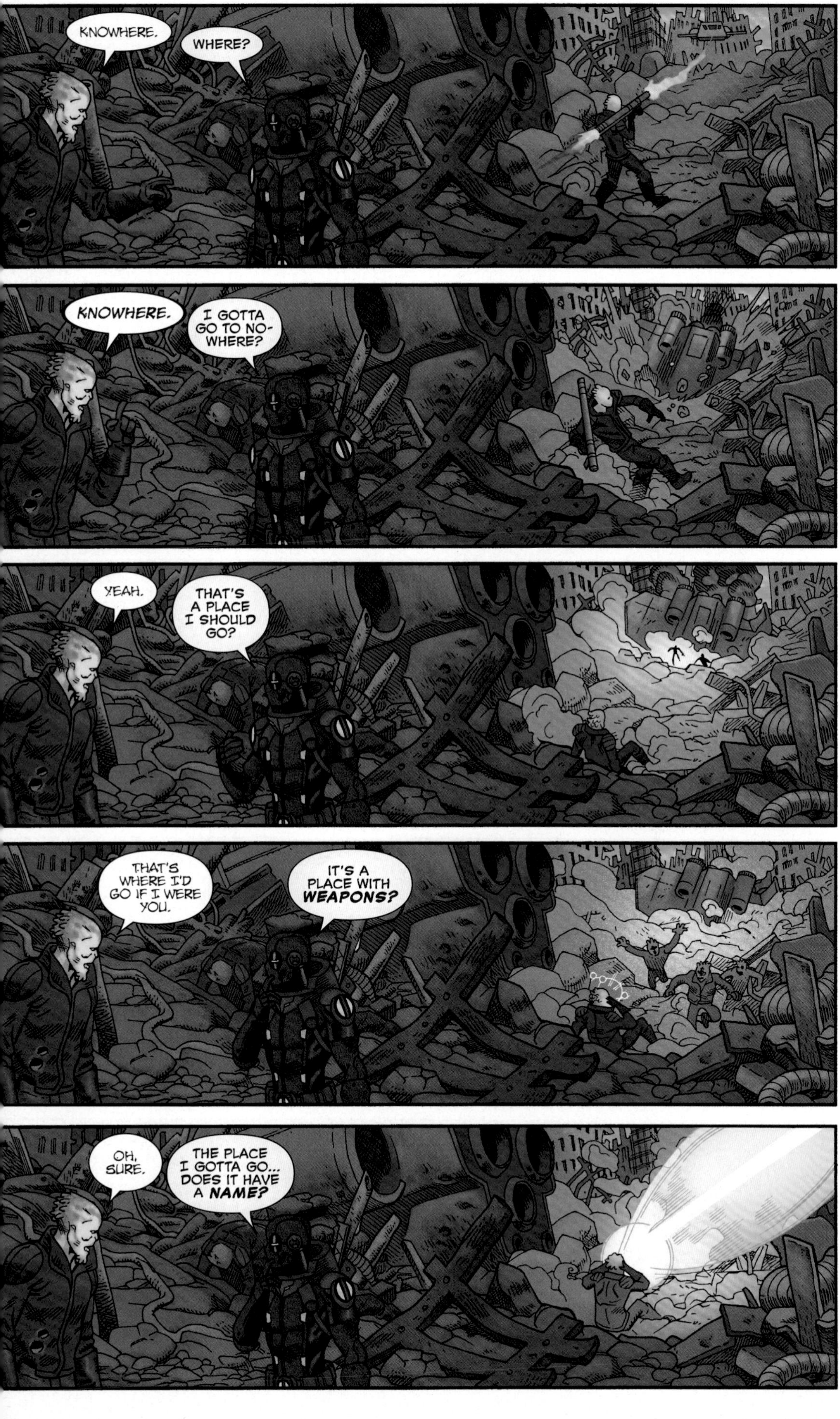
KNOWHERE.
WHERE?
KNOWHERE.
I GOTTA GO TO NO-WHERE?
YEAH.
THAT'S A PLACE I SHOULD GO?
THAT'S WHERE I'D GO IF I WERE YOU.
IT'S A PLACE WITH WEAPONS?
OH, SURE.
THE PLACE I GOTTA GO... DOES IT HAVE A NAME?

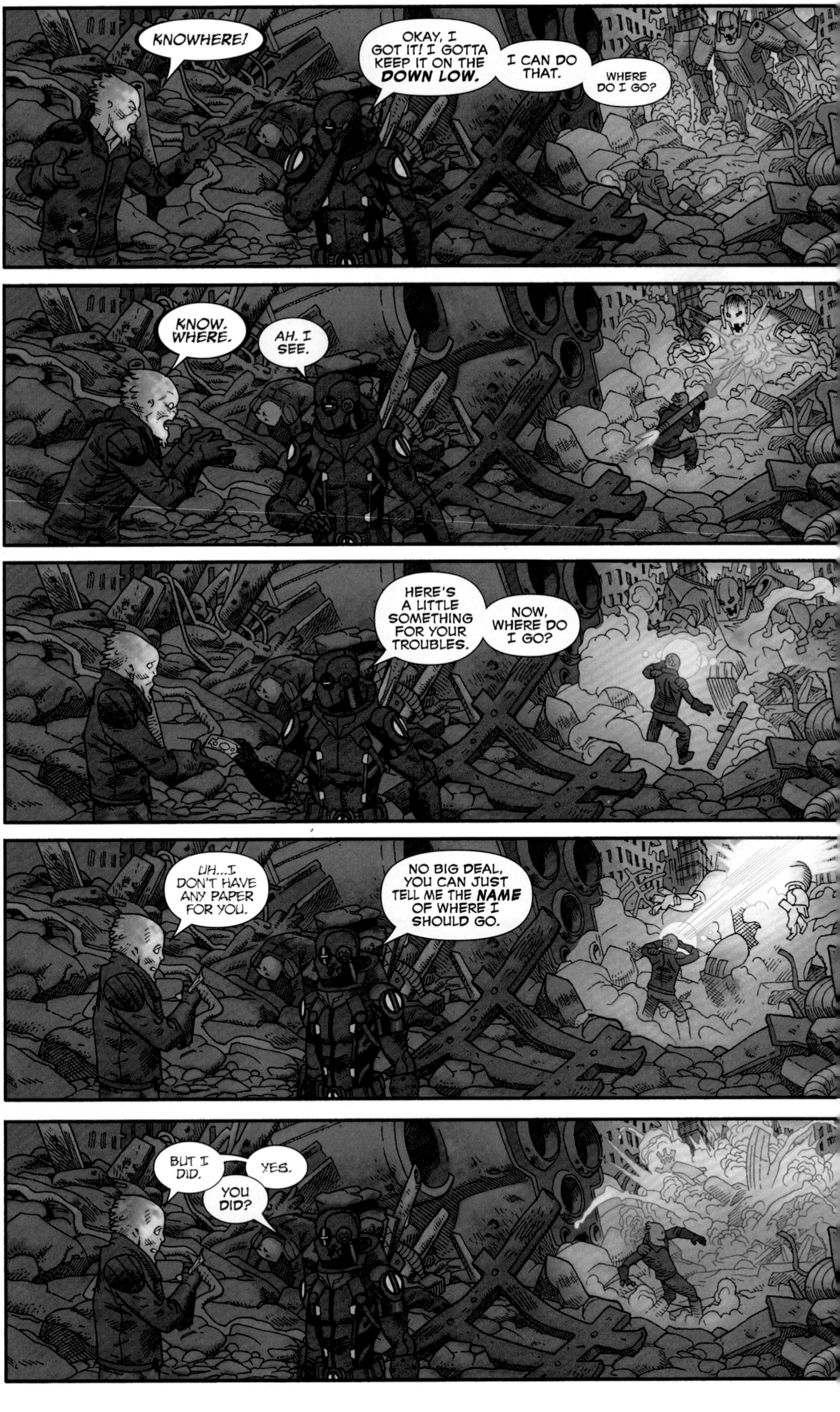
KNOWHERE!
OKAY, I GOT IT! I GOTTA KEEP IT ON THE DOWN LOW.
I CAN DO THAT.
WHERE DO I GO?
KNOW. WHERE.
AH. I SEE.
HERE'S A LITTLE SOMETHING FOR YOUR TROUBLES.
NOW, WHERE DO I GO?
UH...I DON'T HAVE ANY PAPER FOR YOU.
NO BIG DEAL, YOU CAN JUST TELL ME THE NAME OF WHERE I SHOULD GO.
BUT I DID.
YOU DID?
YES.

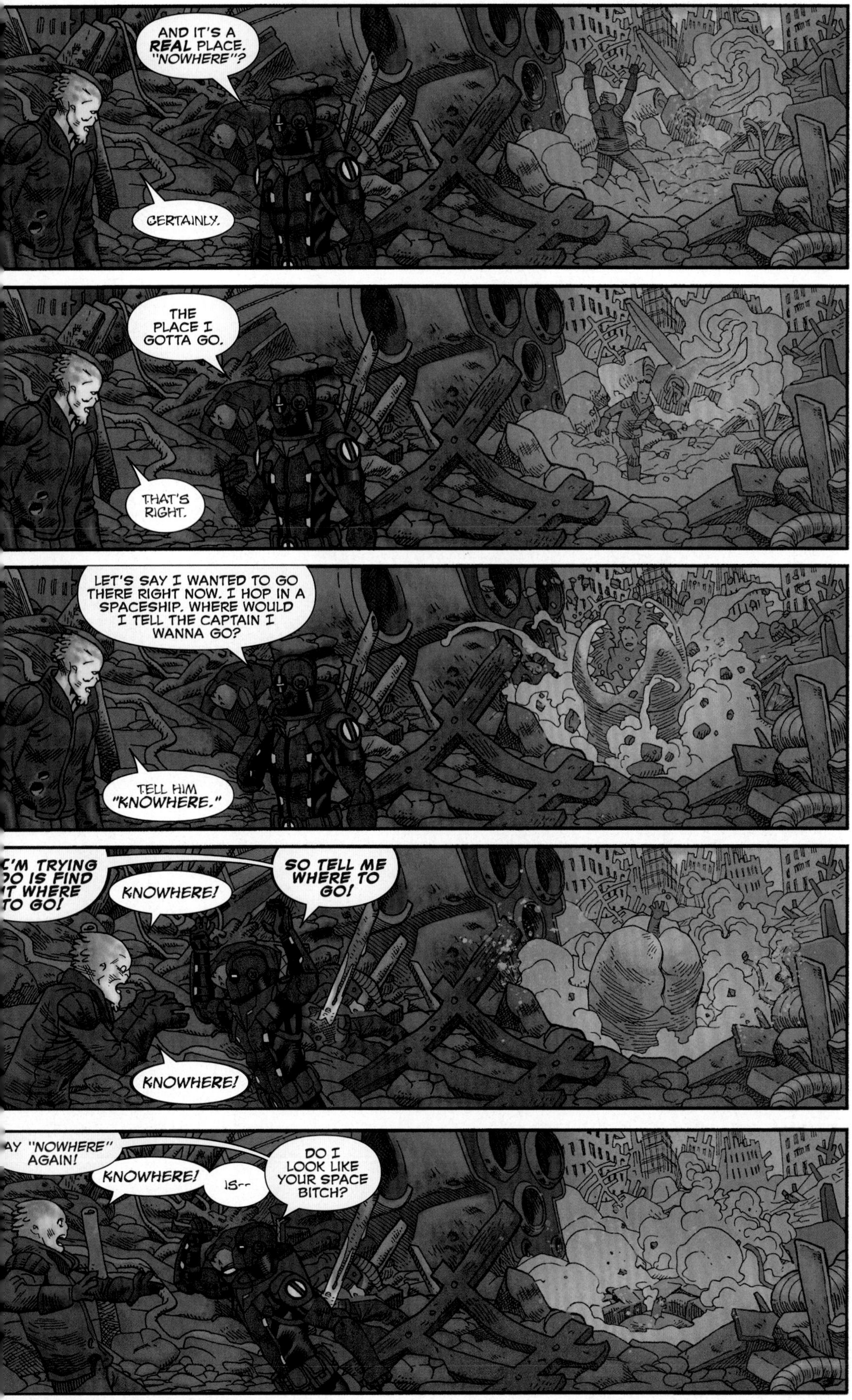
AND IT'S A *REAL* PLACE. "NOWHERE"?
CERTAINLY.
THE PLACE I GOTTA GO.
THAT'S RIGHT.
LET'S SAY I WANTED TO GO THERE RIGHT NOW. I HOP IN A SPACESHIP. WHERE WOULD I TELL THE CAPTAIN I WANNA GO?
TELL HIM "KNOWHERE."
'M TRYING DO IS FIND T WHERE TO GO!
KNOWHERE!
SO TELL ME WHERE TO GO!
KNOWHERE!
AY "NOWHERE" AGAIN!
KNOWHERE!
IS--
DO I LOOK LIKE YOUR SPACE BITCH?

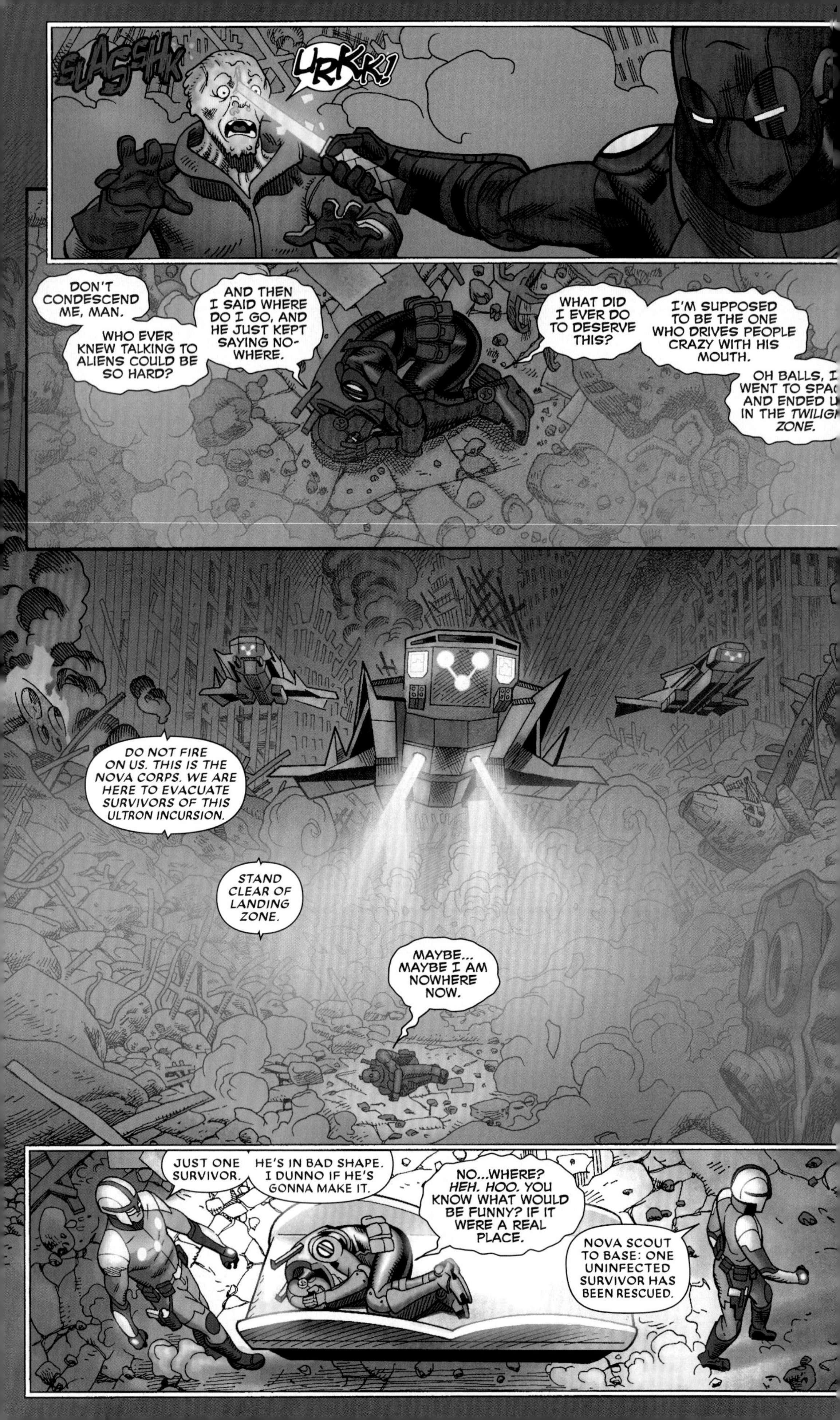
SLASSHK
URKKK!
DON'T CONDESCEND ME, MAN.
WHO EVER KNEW TALKING TO ALIENS COULD BE SO HARD?
AND THEN I SAID WHERE DO I GO, AND HE JUST KEPT SAYING NO-WHERE.
WHAT DID I EVER DO TO DESERVE THIS?
I'M SUPPOSED TO BE THE ONE WHO DRIVES PEOPLE CRAZY WITH HIS MOUTH.
DO NOT FIRE ON US. THIS IS THE NOVA CORPS. WE ARE HERE TO EVACUATE SURVIVORS OF THIS ULTRON INCURSION.
STAND CLEAR OF LANDING ZONE.
MAYBE... MAYBE I AM NOWHERE NOW.
JUST ONE SURVIVOR.
HE'S IN BAD SHAPE. I DUNNO IF HE'S GONNA MAKE IT.
NO...WHERE? *HEH. HOO.* YOU KNOW WHAT WOULD BE FUNNY? IF IT WERE A REAL PLACE.
NOVA SCOUT TO BASE: ONE UNINFECTED SURVIVOR HAS BEEN RESCUED.

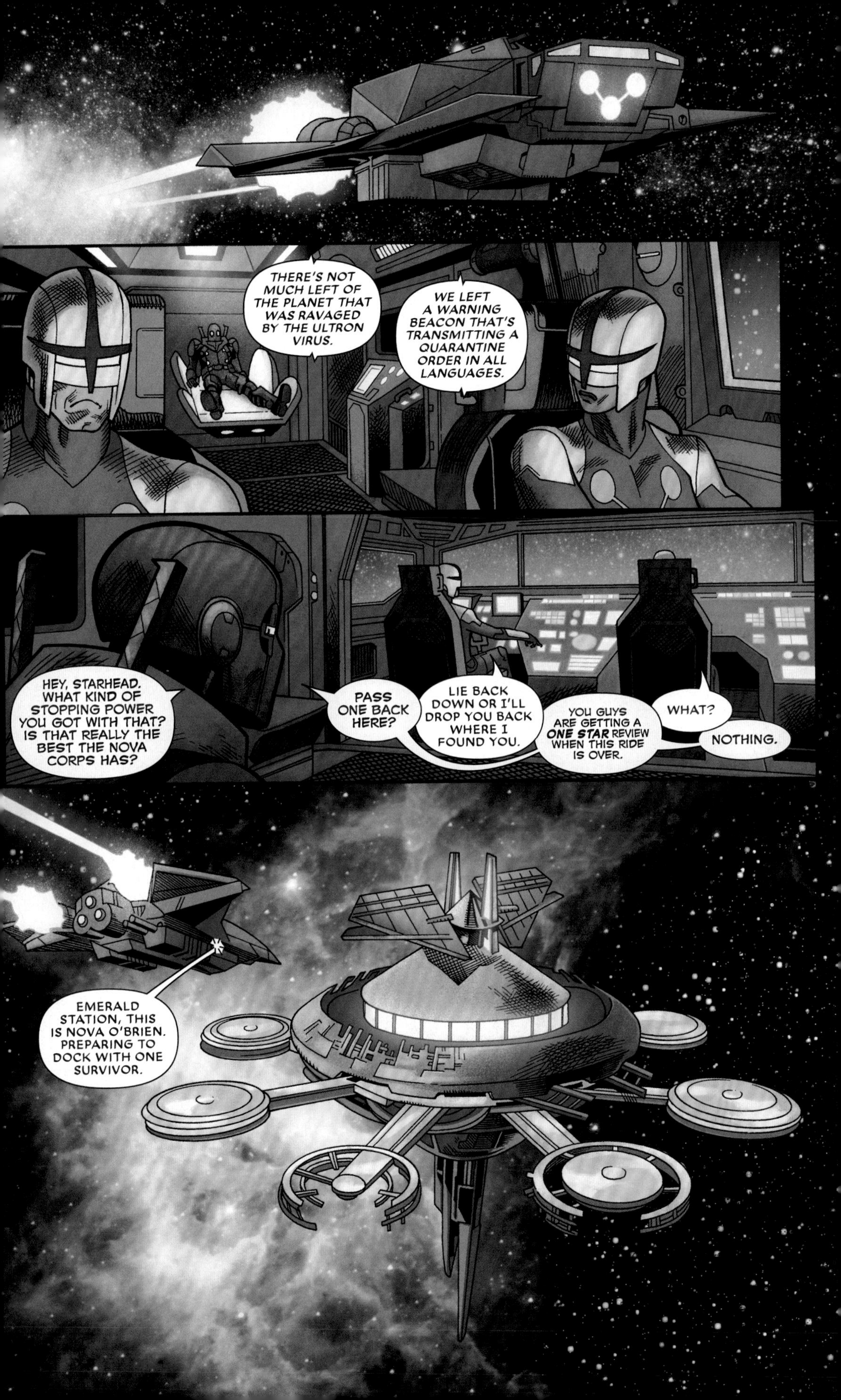

THERE'S NOT MUCH LEFT OF THE PLANET THAT WAS RAVAGED BY THE ULTRON VIRUS.
WE LEFT A WARNING BEACON THAT'S TRANSMITTING A QUARANTINE ORDER IN ALL LANGUAGES.
HEY, STARHEAD. WHAT KIND OF STOPPING POWER YOU GOT WITH THAT? IS THAT REALLY THE BEST THE NOVA CORPS HAS?
PASS ONE BACK HERE?
LIE BACK DOWN OR I'LL DROP YOU BACK WHERE I FOUND YOU.
YOU GUYS ARE GETTING A ONE STAR REVIEW WHEN THIS RIDE IS OVER.
WHAT?
NOTHING.
EMERALD STATION, THIS IS NOVA O'BRIEN. PREPARING TO DOCK WITH ONE SURVIVOR.

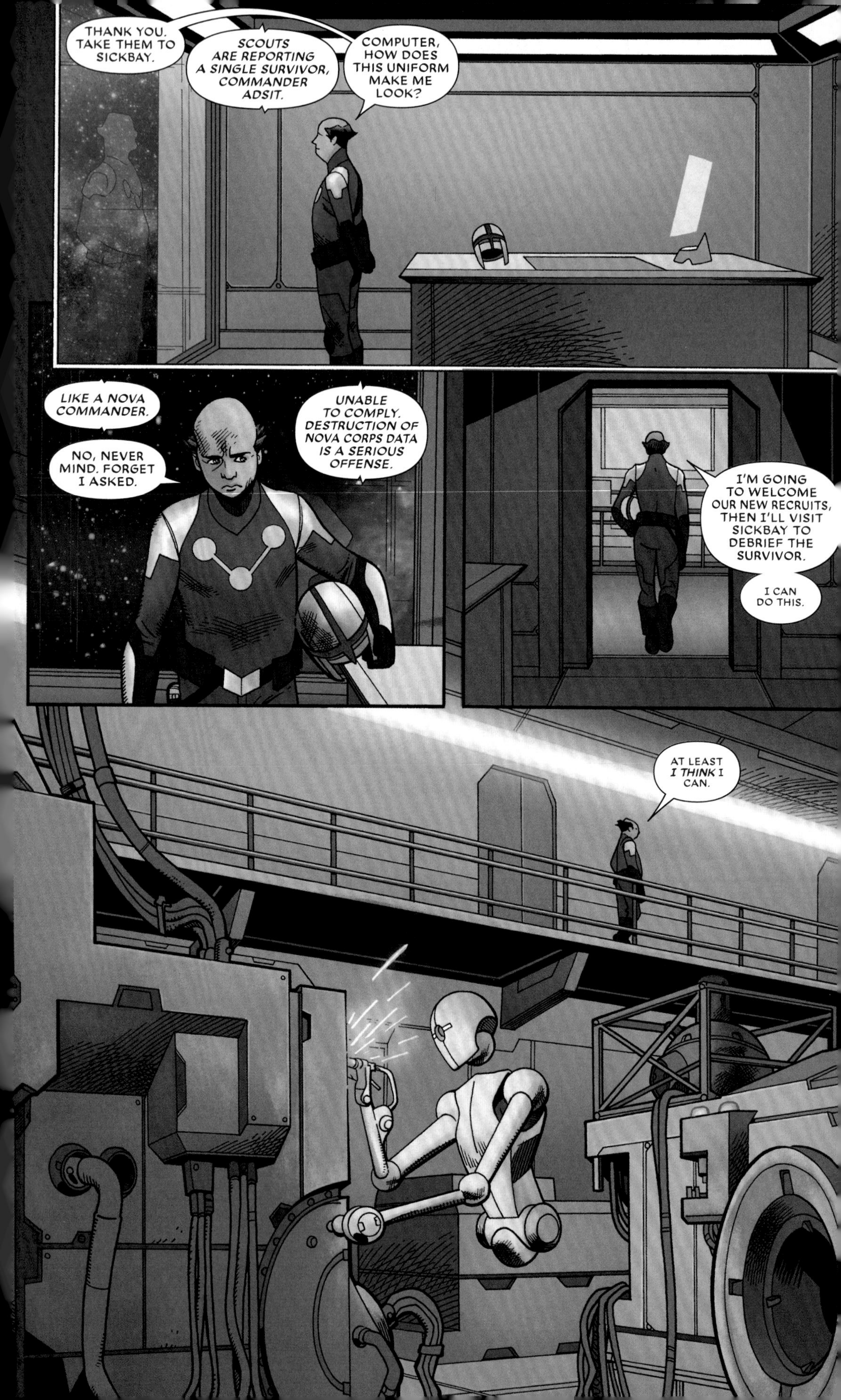

COMPUTER, HOW DOES THIS UNIFORM MAKE ME LOOK?
SCOUTS ARE REPORTING A SINGLE SURVIVOR, COMMANDER ADSIT.
THANK YOU. TAKE THEM TO SICKBAY.
LIKE A NOVA COMMANDER.
UNABLE TO COMPLY. DESTRUCTION OF NOVA CORPS DATA IS A SERIOUS OFFENSE.
NO, NEVER MIND. FORGET I ASKED.
I'M GOING TO WELCOME OUR NEW RECRUITS, THEN I'LL VISIT SICKBAY TO DEBRIEF THE SURVIVOR.
I CAN DO THIS.
AT LEAST I THINK I CAN.

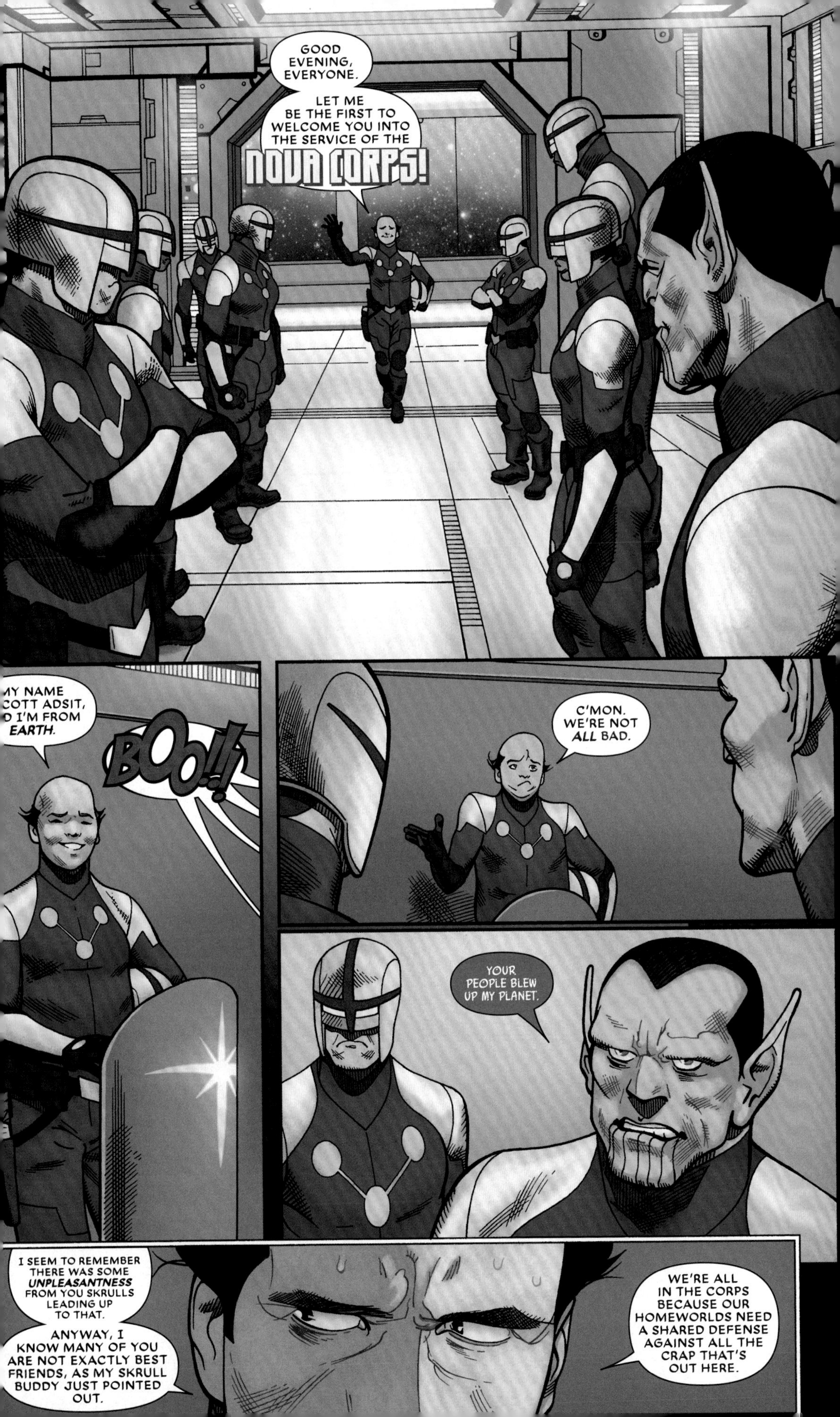

GOOD EVENING, EVERYONE.
LET ME BE THE FIRST TO WELCOME YOU INTO THE SERVICE OF THE NOVA CORPS!
MY NAME COTT ADSIT, D I'M FROM *EARTH*.
BOO!!
C'MON. WE'RE NOT *ALL* BAD.
YOUR PEOPLE BLEW UP MY PLANET.
I SEEM TO REMEMBER THERE WAS SOME *UNPLEASANTNESS* FROM YOU SKRULLS LEADING UP TO THAT.
ANYWAY, I KNOW MANY OF YOU ARE NOT EXACTLY BEST FRIENDS, AS MY SKRULL BUDDY JUST POINTED OUT.
WE'RE ALL IN THE CORPS BECAUSE OUR HOMEWORLDS NEED A SHARED DEFENSE AGAINST ALL THE CRAP THAT'S OUT HERE.

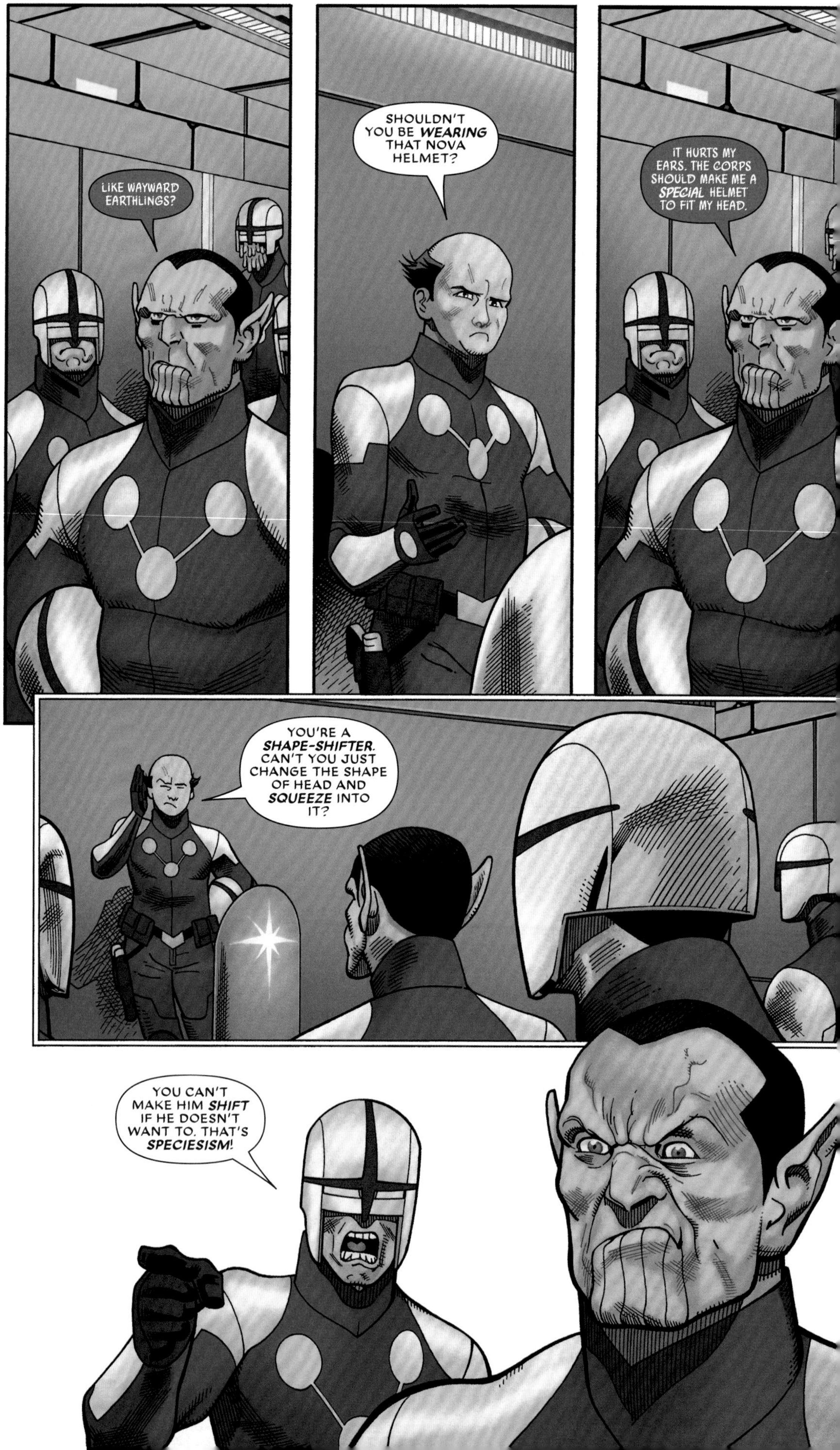
LIKE WAYWARD EARTHLINGS?
SHOULDN'T YOU BE WEARING THAT NOVA HELMET?
IT HURTS MY EARS. THE CORPS SHOULD MAKE ME A SPECIAL HELMET TO FIT MY HEAD.
YOU'RE A SHAPE-SHIFTER. CAN'T YOU JUST CHANGE THE SHAPE OF HEAD AND SQUEEZE INTO IT?
YOU CAN'T MAKE HIM SHIFT IF HE DOESN'T WANT TO. THAT'S SPECIESISM!

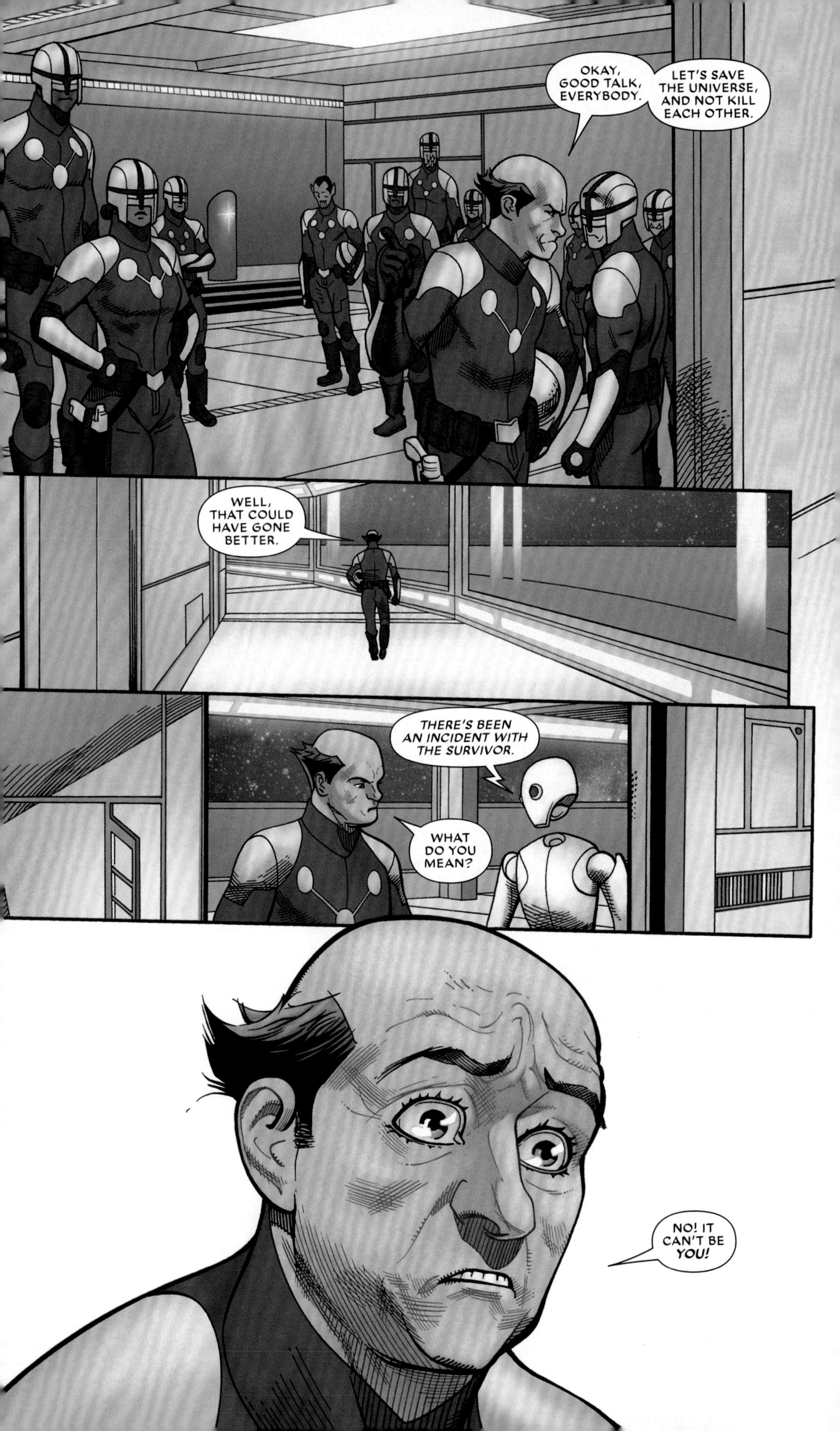

OKAY, GOOD TALK, EVERYBODY.
LET'S SAVE THE UNIVERSE, AND NOT KILL EACH OTHER.
WELL, THAT COULD HAVE GONE BETTER.
THERE'S BEEN AN INCIDENT WITH THE SURVIVOR.
WHAT DO YOU MEAN?
NO! IT CAN'T BE YOU!

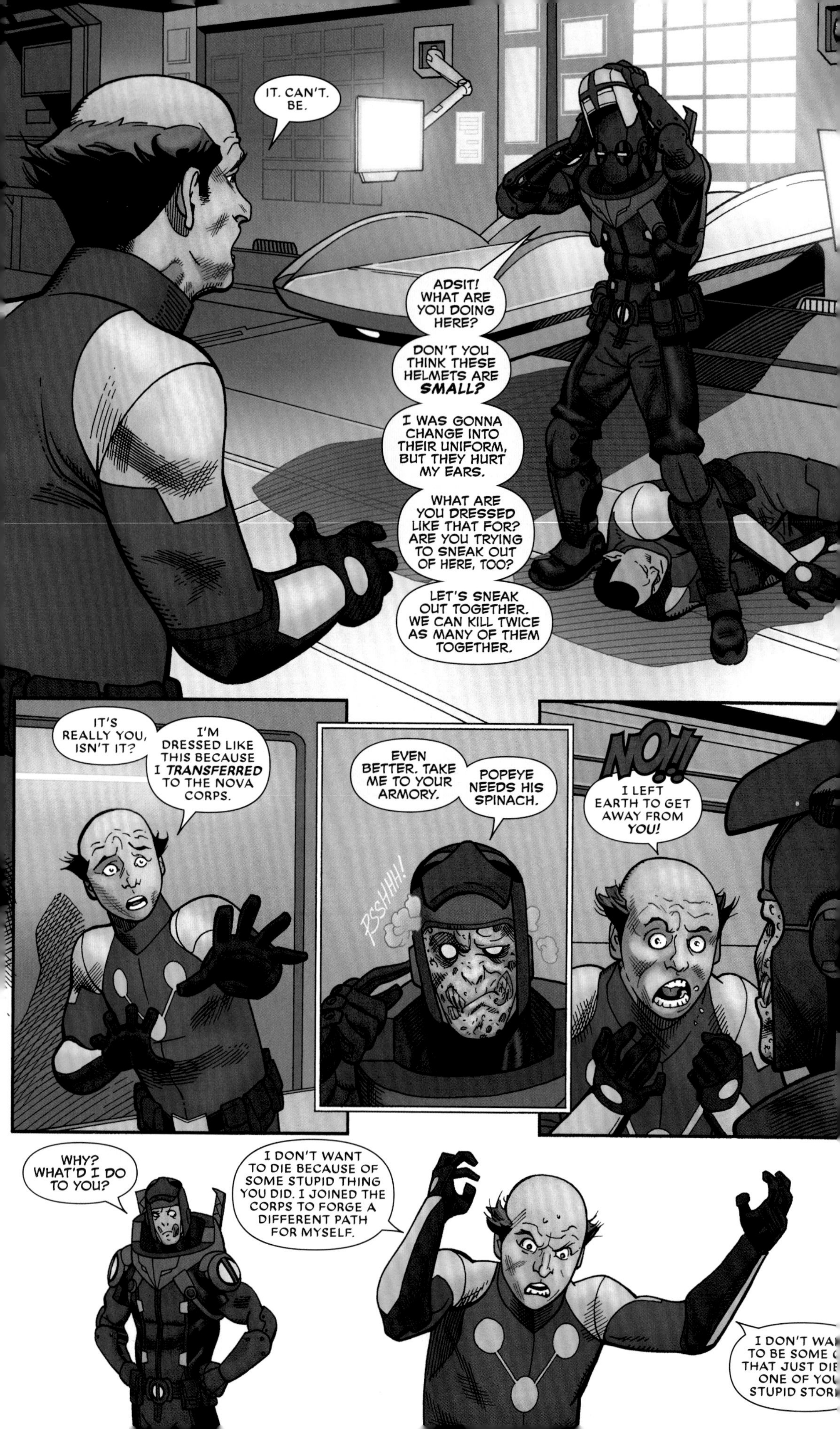
IT. CAN'T. BE.
ADSIT! WHAT ARE YOU DOING HERE?
DON'T YOU THINK THESE HELMETS ARE SMALL?
I WAS GONNA CHANGE INTO THEIR UNIFORM, BUT THEY HURT MY EARS.
WHAT ARE YOU DRESSED LIKE THAT FOR? ARE YOU TRYING TO SNEAK OUT OF HERE, TOO?
LET'S SNEAK OUT TOGETHER. WE CAN KILL TWICE AS MANY OF THEM TOGETHER.
IT'S REALLY YOU, ISN'T IT?
I'M DRESSED LIKE THIS BECAUSE I TRANSFERRED TO THE NOVA CORPS.
EVEN BETTER. TAKE ME TO YOUR ARMORY.
POPEYE NEEDS HIS SPINACH.
PSSHHH!
NO!!!
I LEFT EARTH TO GET AWAY FROM YOU!
WHY? WHAT'D I DO TO YOU?
I DON'T WANT TO DIE BECAUSE OF SOME STUPID THING YOU DID. I JOINED THE CORPS TO FORGE A DIFFERENT PATH FOR MYSELF.
I DON'T WA
TO BE SOME
THAT JUST DI
ONE OF YO
STUPID STOR

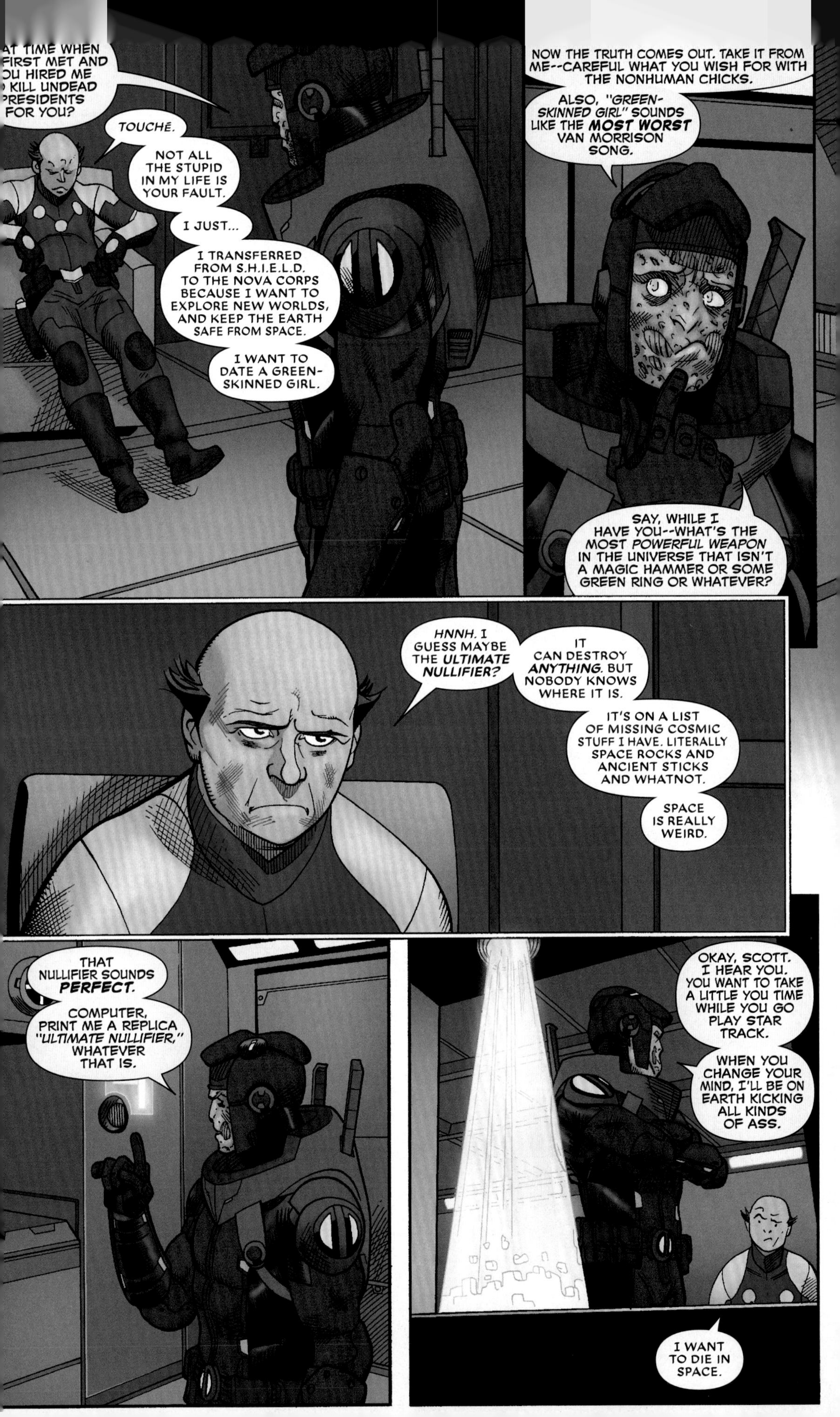
AT TIME WHEN FIRST MET AND OU HIRED ME KILL UNDEAD PRESIDENTS FOR YOU?
TOUCHÉ.
NOT ALL THE STUPID IN MY LIFE IS YOUR FAULT.
I JUST...
I TRANSFERRED FROM S.H.I.E.L.D. TO THE NOVA CORPS BECAUSE I WANT TO EXPLORE NEW WORLDS, AND KEEP THE EARTH SAFE FROM SPACE.
I WANT TO DATE A GREEN-SKINNED GIRL.
NOW THE TRUTH COMES OUT. TAKE IT FROM ME--CAREFUL WHAT YOU WISH FOR WITH THE NONHUMAN CHICKS.
ALSO, "GREEN-SKINNED GIRL" SOUNDS LIKE THE MOST WORST VAN MORRISON SONG.
SAY, WHILE I HAVE YOU--WHAT'S THE MOST POWERFUL WEAPON IN THE UNIVERSE THAT ISN'T A MAGIC HAMMER OR SOME GREEN RING OR WHATEVER?
HNNH. I GUESS MAYBE THE ULTIMATE NULLIFIER?
IT CAN DESTROY ANYTHING. BUT NOBODY KNOWS WHERE IT IS.
IT'S ON A LIST OF MISSING COSMIC STUFF I HAVE. LITERALLY SPACE ROCKS AND ANCIENT STICKS AND WHATNOT.
SPACE IS REALLY WEIRD.
THAT NULLIFIER SOUNDS PERFECT.
COMPUTER, PRINT ME A REPLICA "ULTIMATE NULLIFIER," WHATEVER THAT IS.
OKAY, SCOTT. I HEAR YOU. YOU WANT TO TAKE A LITTLE YOU TIME WHILE YOU GO PLAY STAR TRACK.
WHEN YOU CHANGE YOUR MIND, I'LL BE ON EARTH KICKING ALL KINDS OF ASS.
I WANT TO DIE IN SPACE.

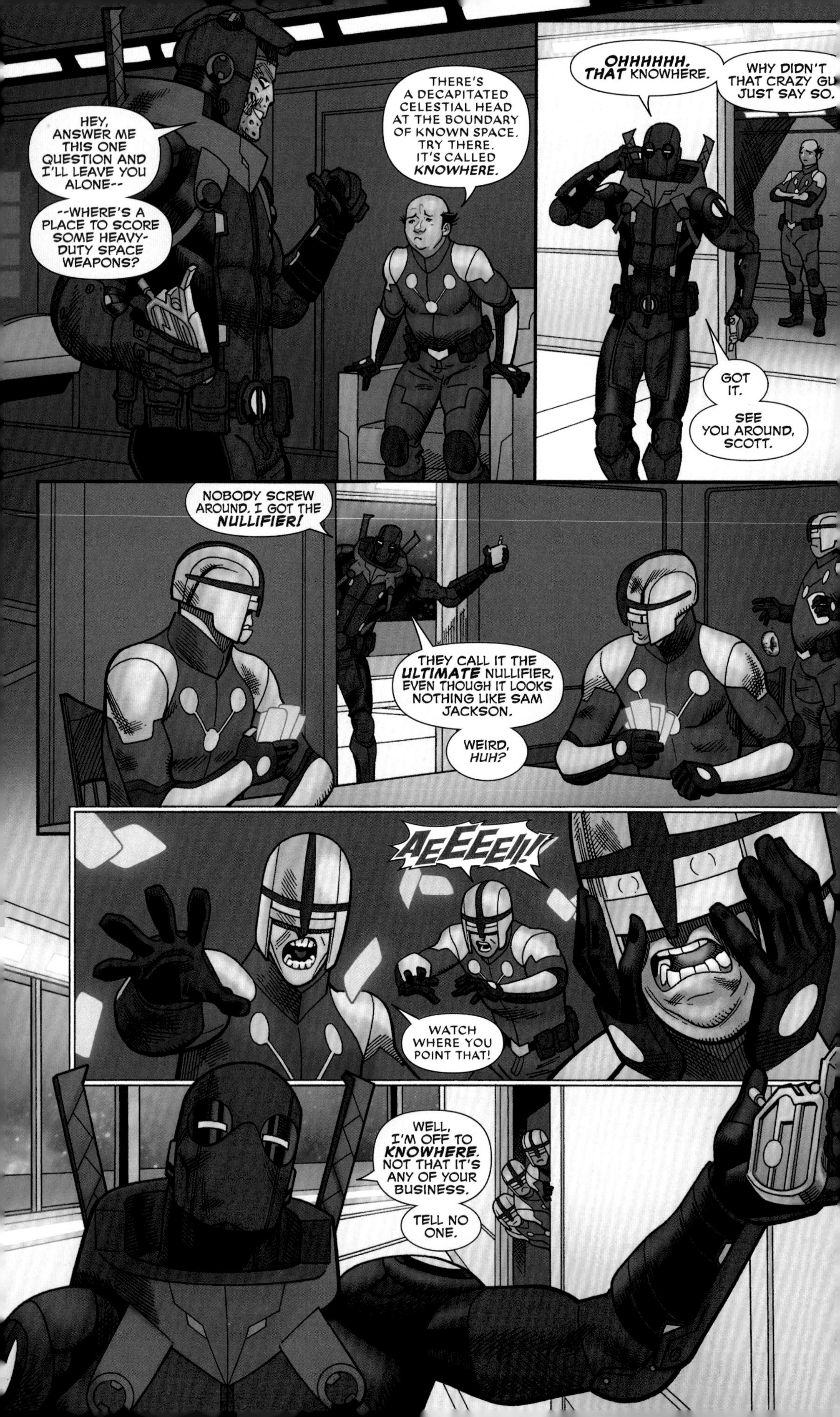
HEY, ANSWER ME THIS ONE QUESTION AND I'LL LEAVE YOU ALONE--
--WHERE'S A PLACE TO SCORE SOME HEAVY-DUTY SPACE WEAPONS?
THERE'S A DECAPITATED CELESTIAL HEAD AT THE BOUNDARY OF KNOWN SPACE. TRY THERE. IT'S CALLED KNOWHERE.
OHHHHHH. THAT KNOWHERE.
WHY DIDN'T THAT CRAZY GU JUST SAY SO.
GOT IT.
SEE YOU AROUND, SCOTT.
NOBODY SCREW AROUND. I GOT THE NULLIFIER!
THEY CALL IT THE ULTIMATE NULLIFIER, EVEN THOUGH IT LOOKS NOTHING LIKE SAM JACKSON.
WEIRD, HUH?
AEEEEII!
WATCH WHERE YOU POINT THAT!
WELL, I'M OFF TO KNOWHERE. NOT THAT IT'S ANY OF YOUR BUSINESS.
TELL NO ONE.

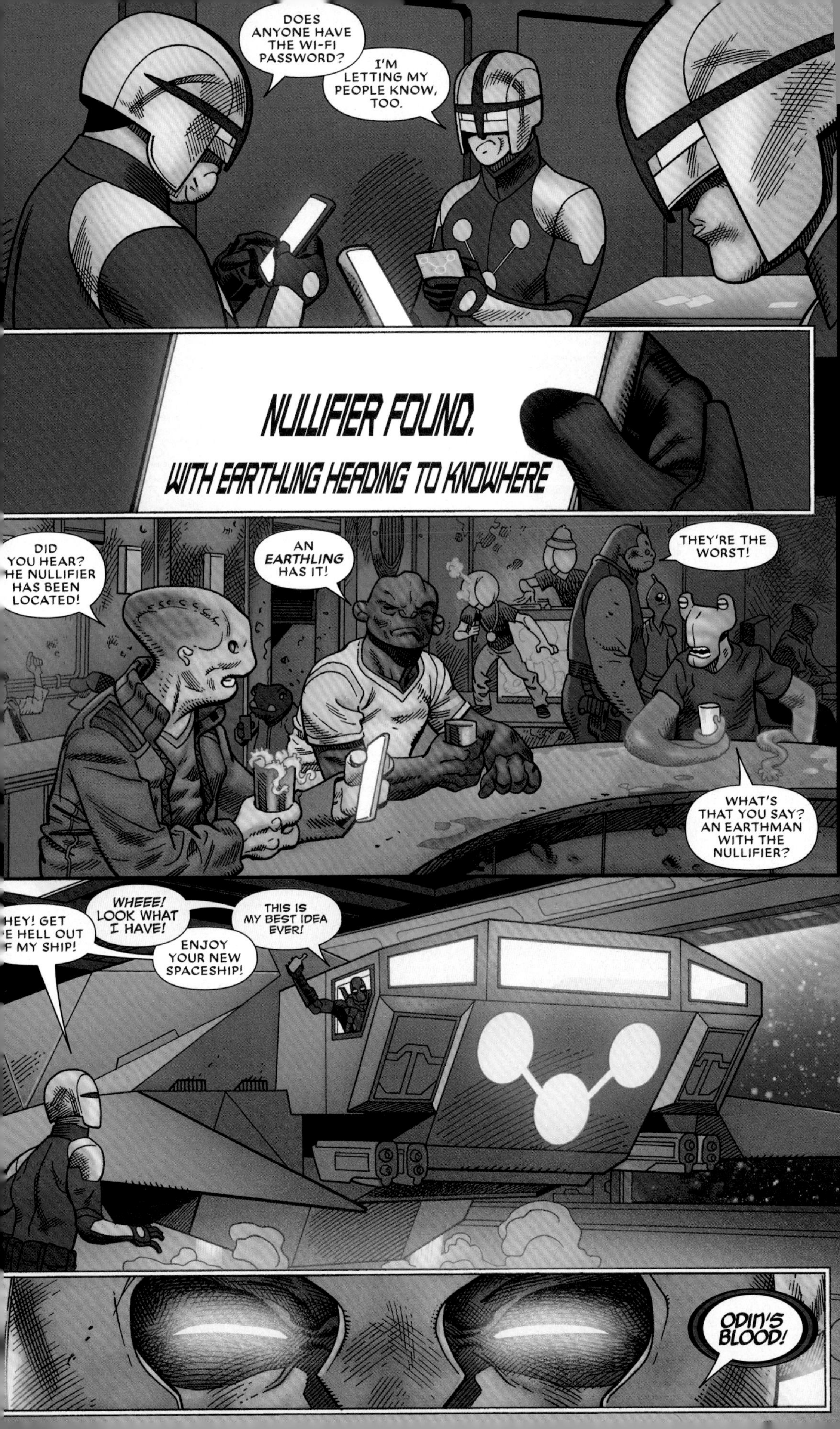
DOES ANYONE HAVE THE WI-FI PASSWORD?
I'M LETTING MY PEOPLE KNOW, TOO.
NULLIFIER FOUND.
WITH EARTHLING HEADING TO KNOWHERE
DID YOU HEAR? HE NULLIFIER HAS BEEN LOCATED!
AN EARTHLING HAS IT!
THEY'RE THE WORST!
WHAT'S THAT YOU SAY? AN EARTHMAN WITH THE NULLIFIER?
HEY! GET E HELL OUT F MY SHIP!
WHEEE! LOOK WHAT I HAVE!
THIS IS MY BEST IDEA EVER!
ENJOY YOUR NEW SPACESHIP!
ODIN'S BLOOD!

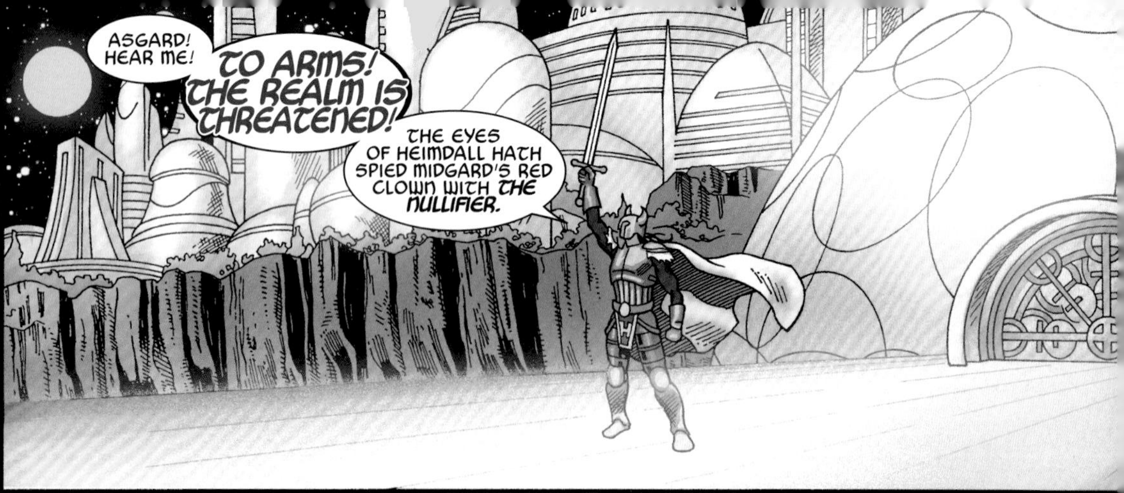
ASGARD! HEAR ME!
TO ARMS! THE REALM IS THREATENED!
THE EYES OF HEIMDALL HATH SPIED MIDGARD'S RED CLOWN WITH THE NULLIFIER.

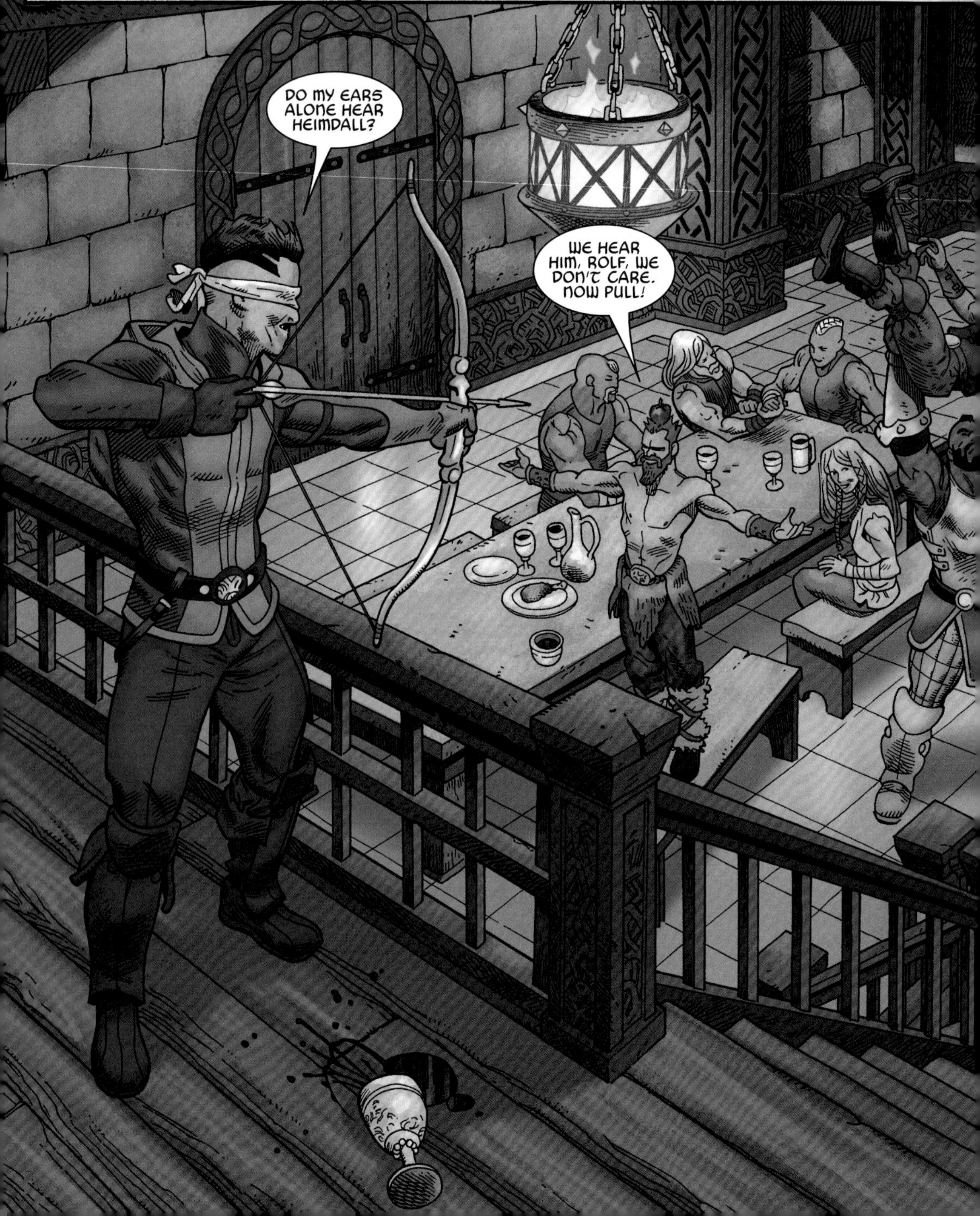
DO MY EARS ALONE HEAR HEIMDALL?
WE HEAR HIM, ROLF, WE DON'T CARE. NOW PULL!

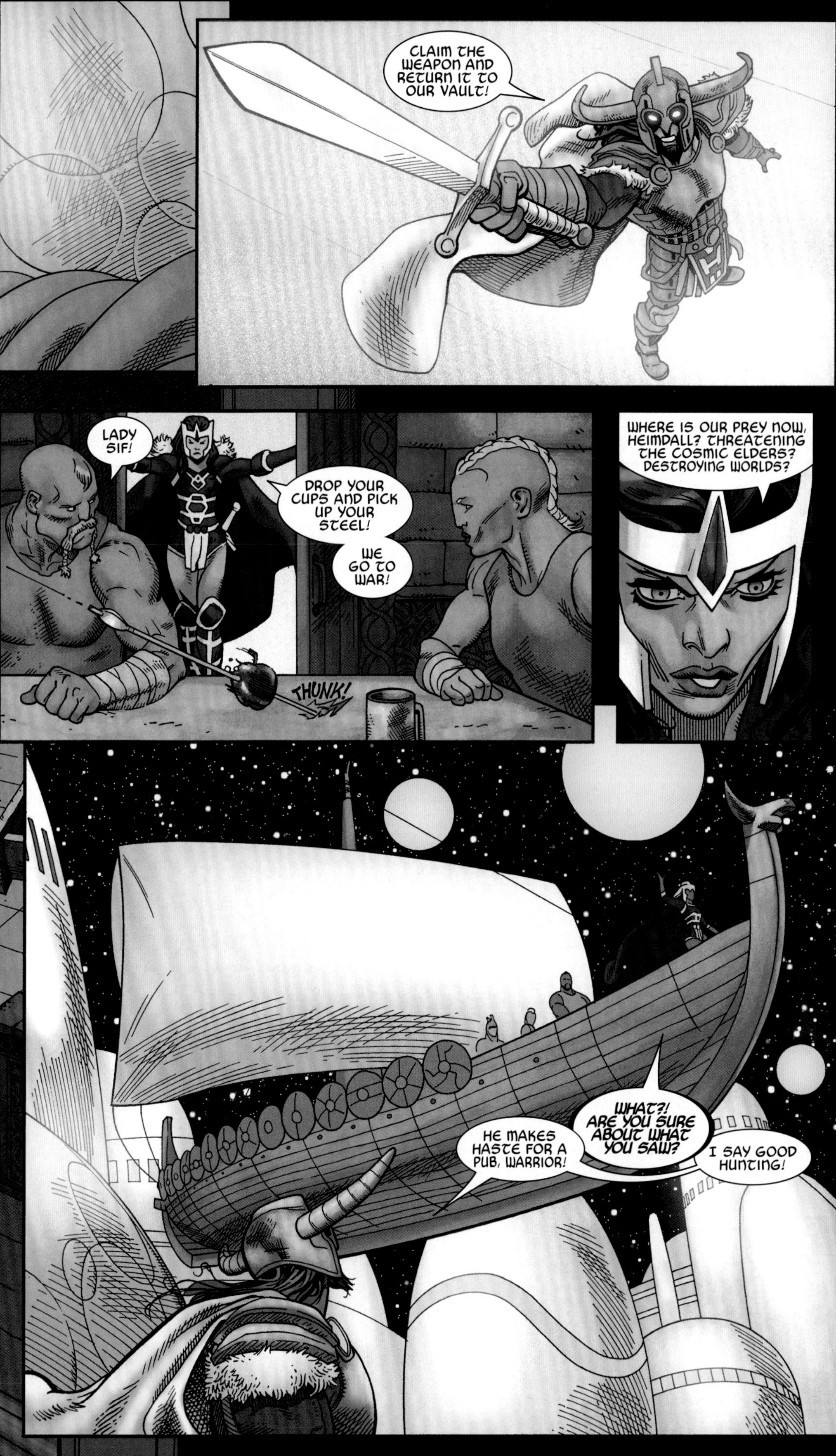
CLAIM THE WEAPON AND RETURN IT TO OUR VAULT!
LADY SIF!
DROP YOUR CUPS AND PICK UP YOUR STEEL!
WE GO TO WAR!
THUNK!
WHERE IS OUR PREY NOW, HEIMDALL? THREATENING THE COSMIC ELDERS? DESTROYING WORLDS?
HE MAKES HASTE FOR A PUB, WARRIOR!
WHAT?! ARE YOU SURE ABOUT WHAT YOU SAW?
I SAY GOOD HUNTING!

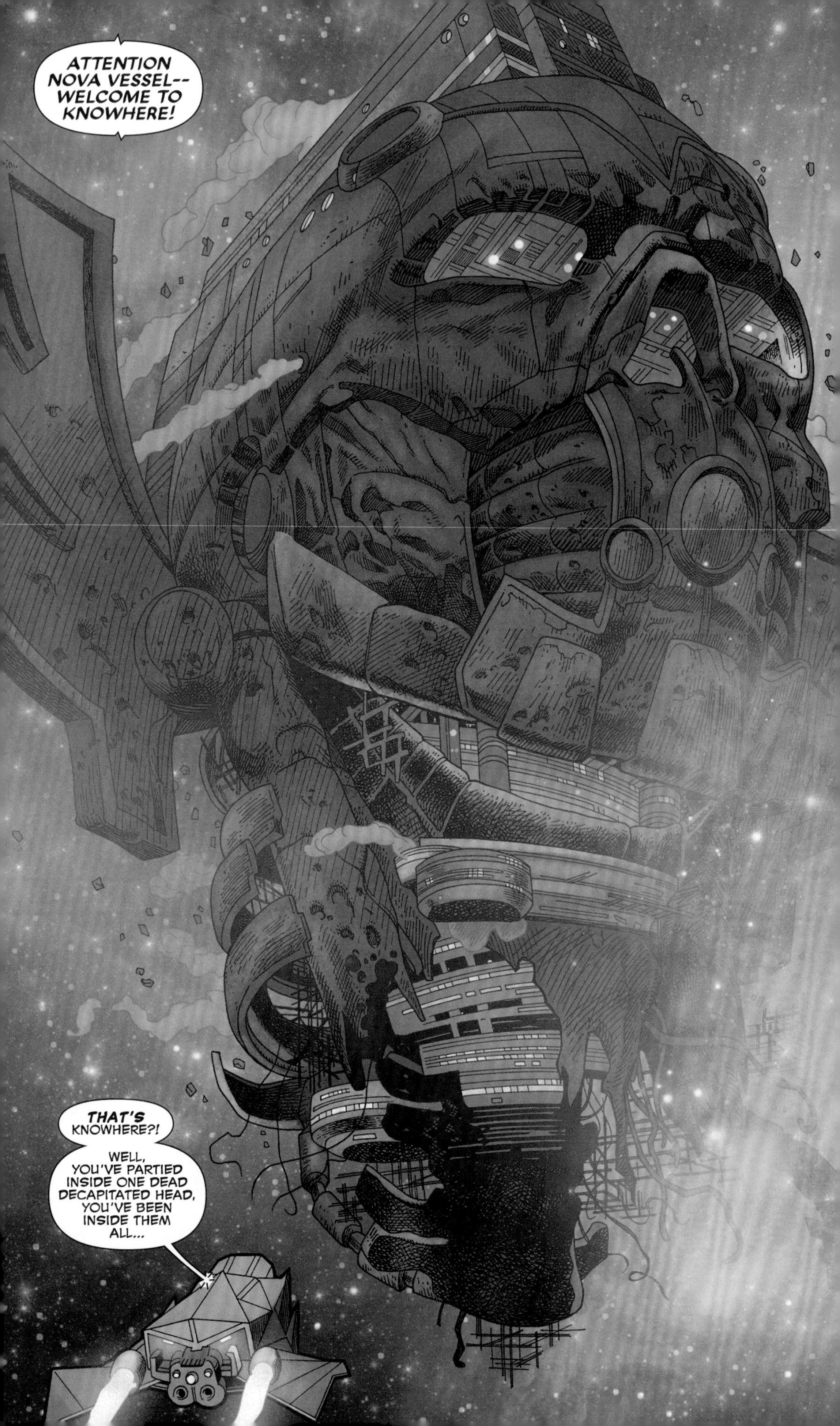
ATTENTION NOVA VESSEL-- WELCOME TO KNOWHERE!
THAT'S KNOWHERE?!
WELL, YOU'VE PARTIED INSIDE ONE DEAD DECAPITATED HEAD, YOU'VE BEEN INSIDE THEM ALL...

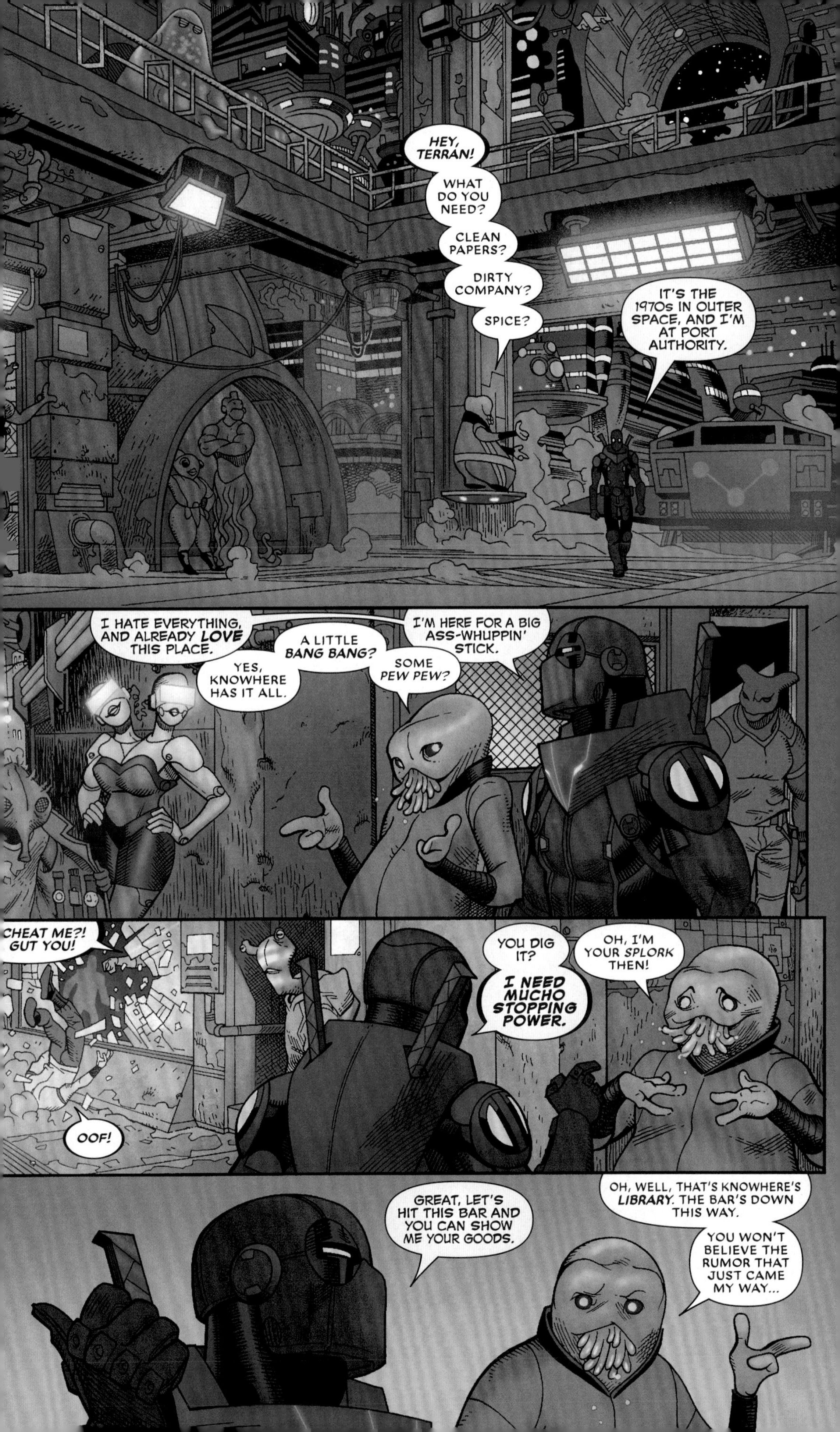
HEY, TERRAN!
WHAT DO YOU NEED?
CLEAN PAPERS?
DIRTY COMPANY?
SPICE?
IT'S THE 1970s IN OUTER SPACE, AND I'M AT PORT AUTHORITY.
I HATE EVERYTHING, AND ALREADY LOVE THIS PLACE.
YES, KNOWHERE HAS IT ALL.
A LITTLE BANG BANG?
SOME PEW PEW?
I'M HERE FOR A BIG ASS-WHUPPIN' STICK.
CHEAT ME?! GUT YOU!
OOF!
YOU DIG IT?
I NEED MUCHO STOPPING POWER.
OH, I'M YOUR SPLORK THEN!
GREAT, LET'S HIT THIS BAR AND YOU CAN SHOW ME YOUR GOODS.
OH, WELL, THAT'S KNOWHERE'S LIBRARY. THE BAR'S DOWN THIS WAY.
YOU WON'T BELIEVE THE RUMOR THAT JUST CAME MY WAY...

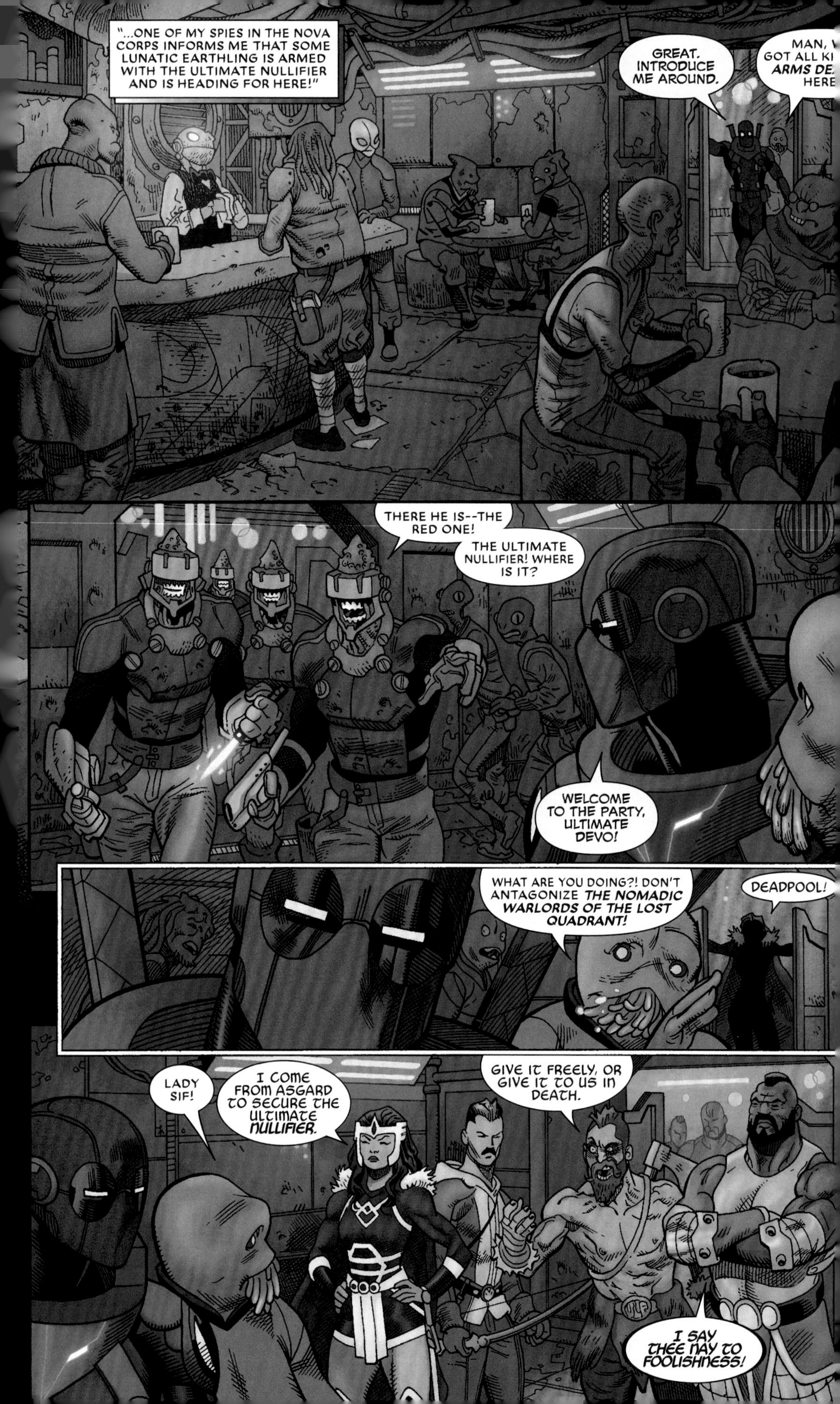
"...ONE OF MY SPIES IN THE NOVA CORPS INFORMS ME THAT SOME LUNATIC EARTHLING IS ARMED WITH THE ULTIMATE NULLIFIER AND IS HEADING FOR HERE!"
GREAT. INTRODUCE ME AROUND.
THERE HE IS--THE RED ONE!
THE ULTIMATE NULLIFIER! WHERE IS IT?
WELCOME TO THE PARTY, ULTIMATE DEVO!
WHAT ARE YOU DOING?! DON'T ANTAGONIZE *THE NOMADIC WARLORDS OF THE LOST QUADRANT!*
DEADPOOL!
LADY SIF!
I COME FROM ASGARD TO SECURE THE ULTIMATE *NULLIFIER.*
GIVE IT FREELY, OR GIVE IT TO US IN DEATH.
I SAY THEE NAY TO FOOLISHNESS!

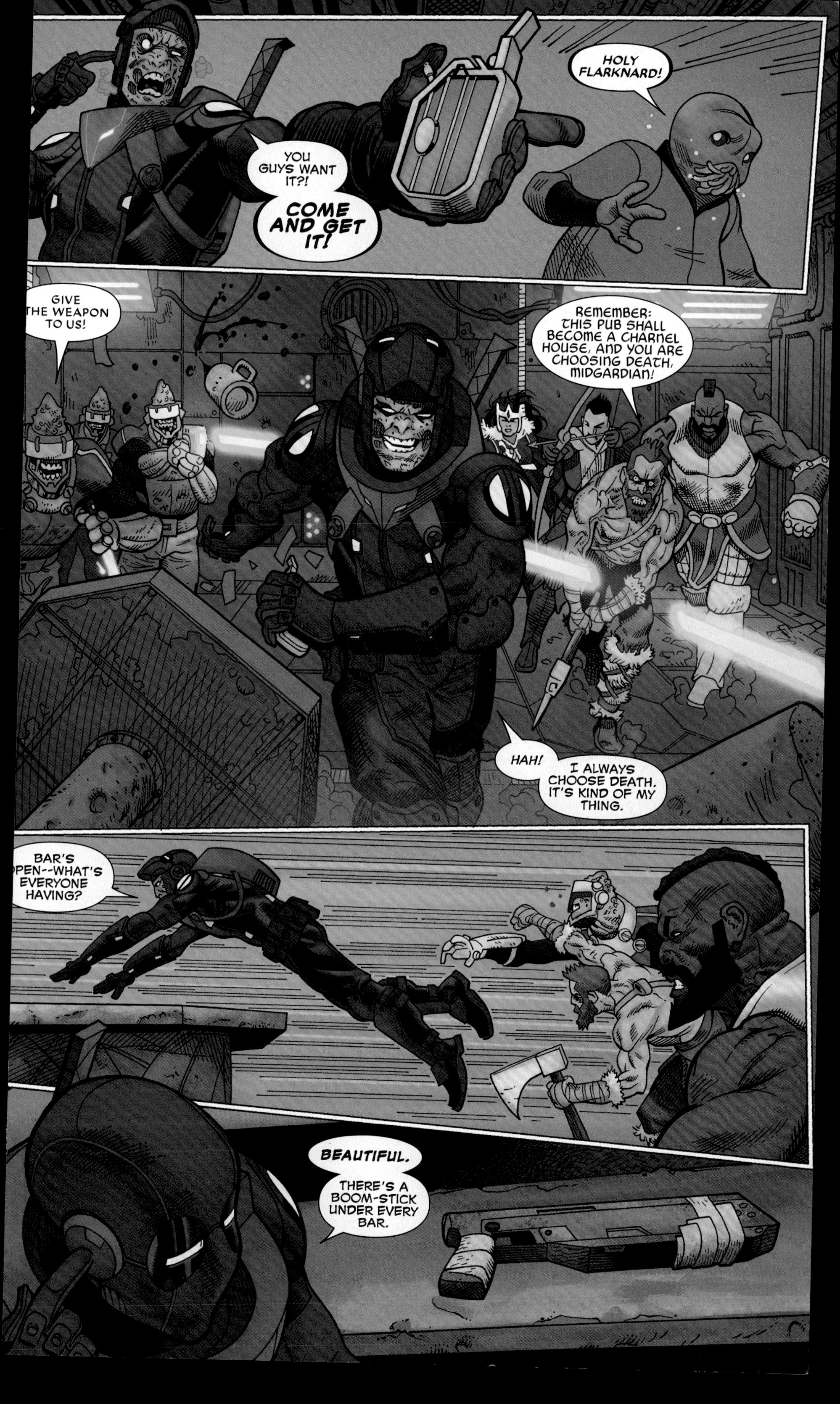

YOU GUYS WANT IT?!
COME AND GET IT!
HOLY FLARKNARD!
GIVE THE WEAPON TO US!
REMEMBER: THIS PUB SHALL BECOME A CHARNEL HOUSE, AND YOU ARE CHOOSING DEATH, MIDGARDIAN!
HAH!
I ALWAYS CHOOSE DEATH. IT'S KIND OF MY THING.
BAR'S OPEN--WHAT'S EVERYONE HAVING?
BEAUTIFUL.
THERE'S A BOOM-STICK UNDER EVERY BAR.

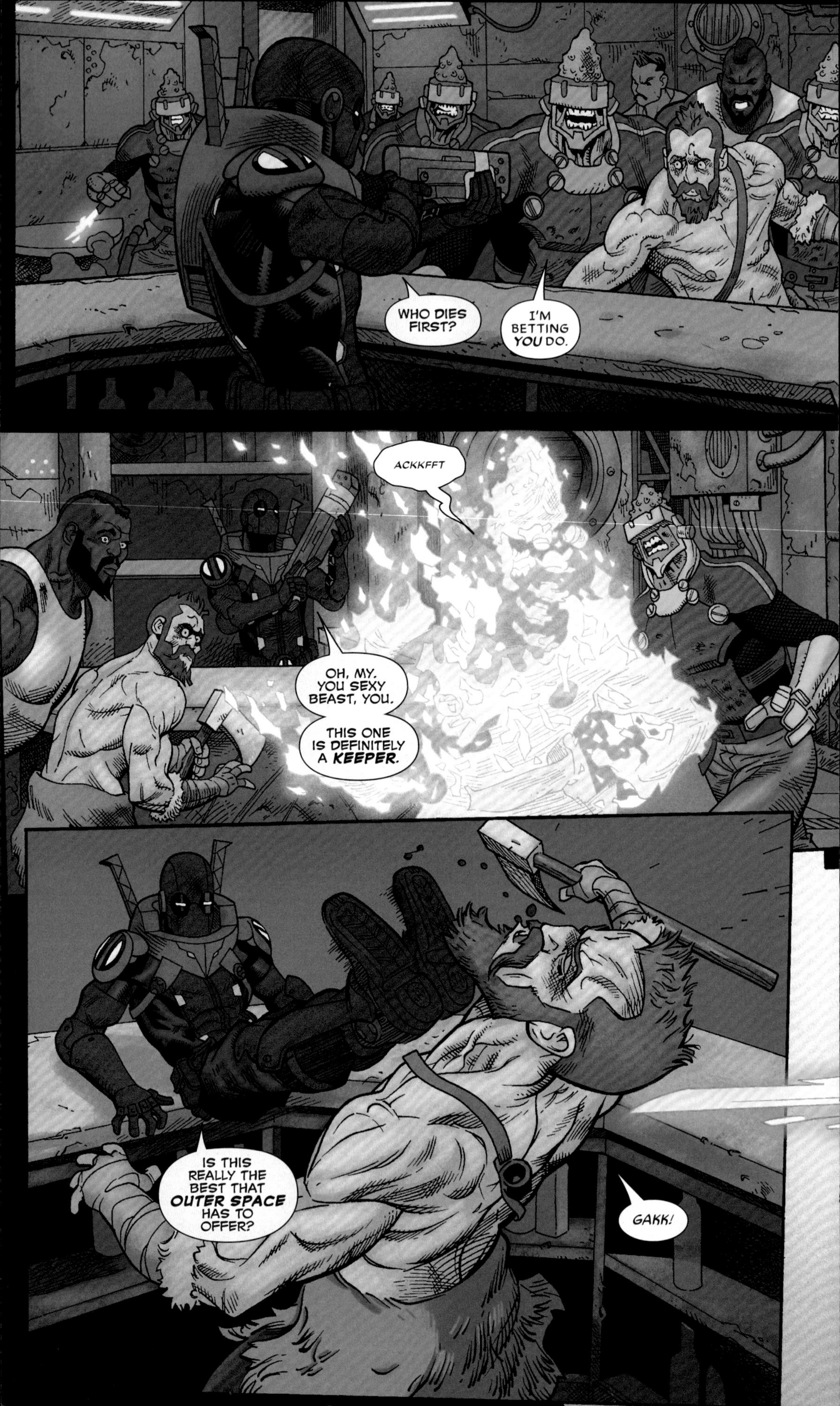
WHO DIES FIRST?
I'M BETTING YOU DO.
ACKKFFT
OH, MY. YOU SEXY BEAST, YOU.
THIS ONE IS DEFINITELY A KEEPER.
IS THIS REALLY THE BEST THAT OUTER SPACE HAS TO OFFER?
GAKK!

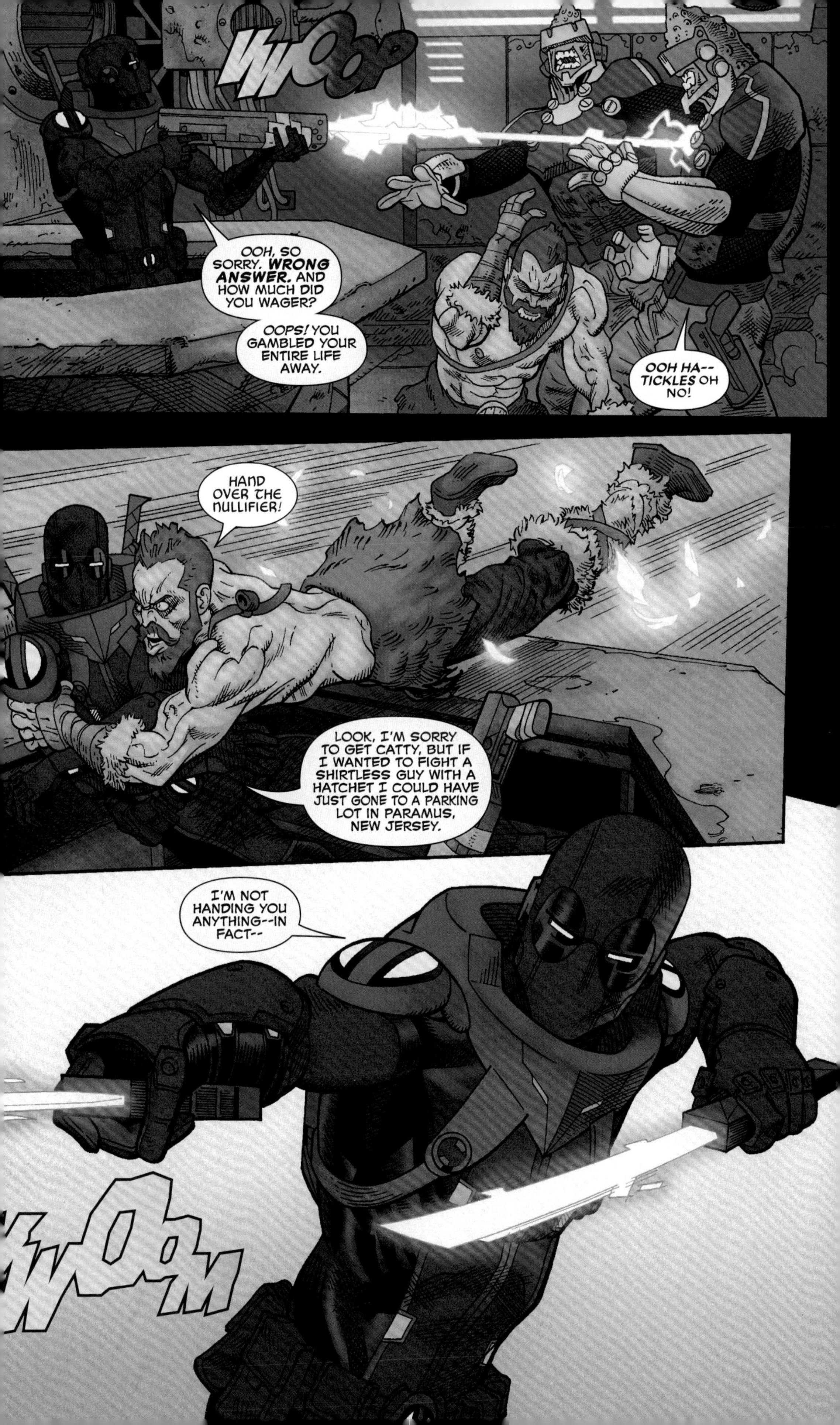
WOOP
OOH, SO SORRY. WRONG ANSWER. AND HOW MUCH DID YOU WAGER?
OOPS! YOU GAMBLED YOUR ENTIRE LIFE AWAY.
OOH HA-- TICKLES OH NO!
HAND OVER THE NULLIFIER!
LOOK, I'M SORRY TO GET CATTY, BUT IF I WANTED TO FIGHT A SHIRTLESS GUY WITH A HATCHET I COULD HAVE JUST GONE TO A PARKING LOT IN PARAMUS, NEW JERSEY.
I'M NOT HANDING YOU ANYTHING--IN FACT--
WOOM

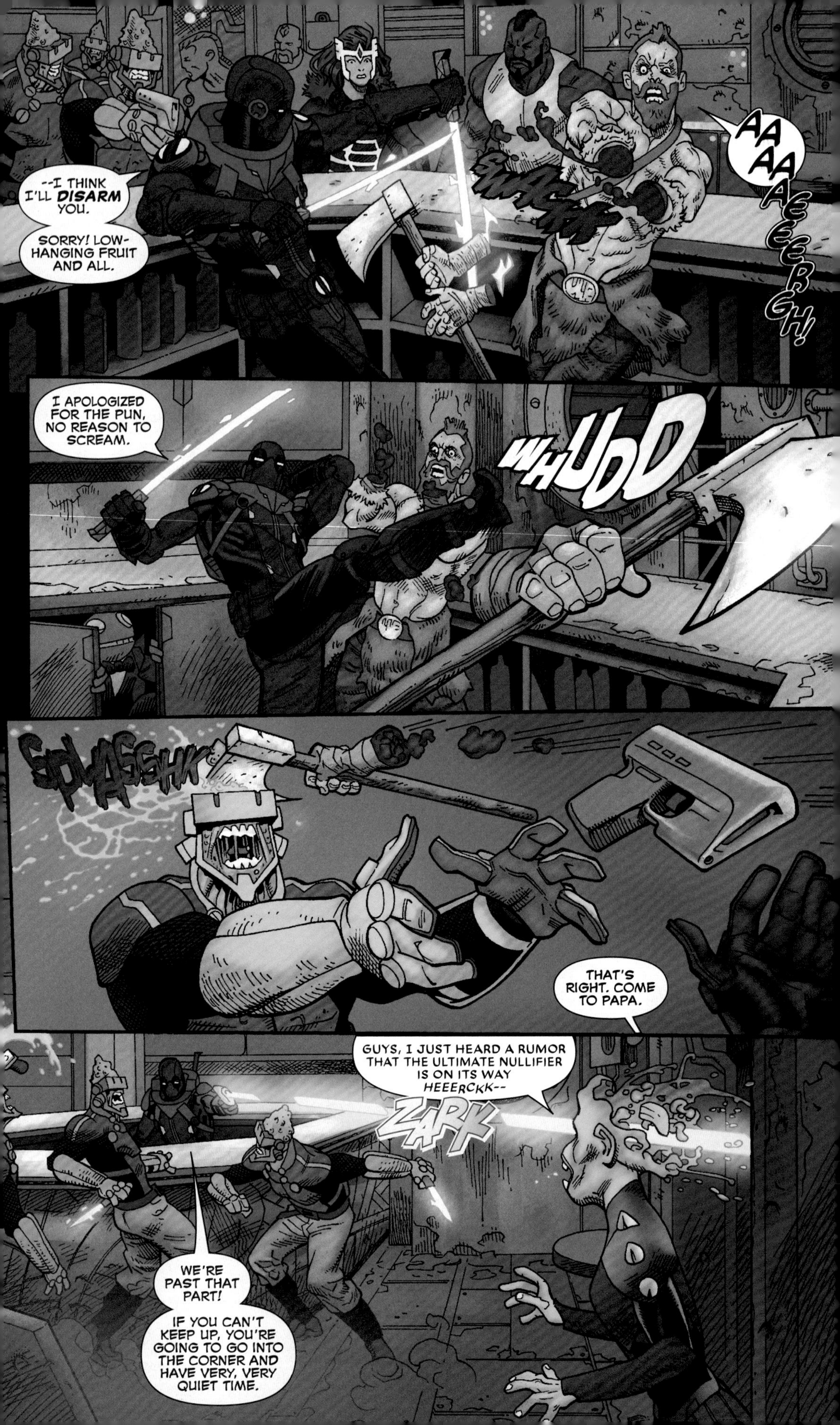
--I THINK I'LL DISARM YOU.
SORRY! LOW-HANGING FRUIT AND ALL.
SHHASHK
AAAAAEEERGH!
I APOLOGIZED FOR THE PUN, NO REASON TO SCREAM.
WHUDD
SPLASSHK
THAT'S RIGHT. COME TO PAPA.
GUYS, I JUST HEARD A RUMOR THAT THE ULTIMATE NULLIFIER IS ON ITS WAY HEEERCKK--
ZARK
WE'RE PAST THAT PART!
IF YOU CAN'T KEEP UP, YOU'RE GOING TO GO INTO THE CORNER AND HAVE VERY, VERY QUIET TIME.

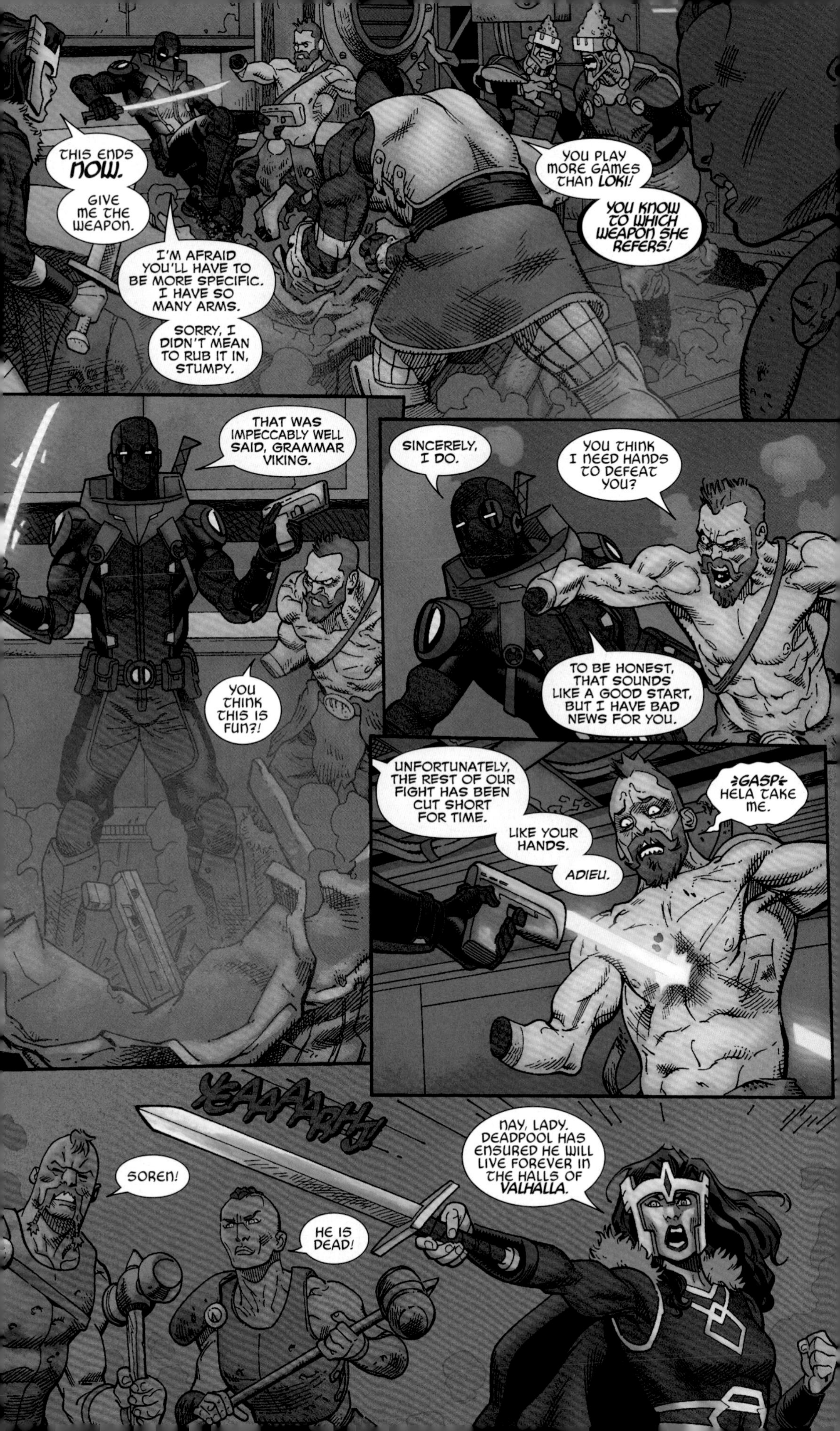
THIS ENDS NOW.
GIVE ME THE WEAPON.
I'M AFRAID YOU'LL HAVE TO BE MORE SPECIFIC. I HAVE SO MANY ARMS.
SORRY, I DIDN'T MEAN TO RUB IT IN, STUMPY.
YOU PLAY MORE GAMES THAN LOKI!
YOU KNOW TO WHICH WEAPON SHE REFERS!
THAT WAS IMPECCABLY WELL SAID, GRAMMAR VIKING.
YOU THINK THIS IS FUN?!
SINCERELY, I DO.
YOU THINK I NEED HANDS TO DEFEAT YOU?
TO BE HONEST, THAT SOUNDS LIKE A GOOD START, BUT I HAVE BAD NEWS FOR YOU.
UNFORTUNATELY, THE REST OF OUR FIGHT HAS BEEN CUT SHORT FOR TIME.
LIKE YOUR HANDS.
ADIEU.
GASP HELA TAKE ME.
YEAAAARH!
SOREN!
HE IS DEAD!
NAY, LADY. DEADPOOL HAS ENSURED HE WILL LIVE FOREVER IN THE HALLS OF VALHALLA.

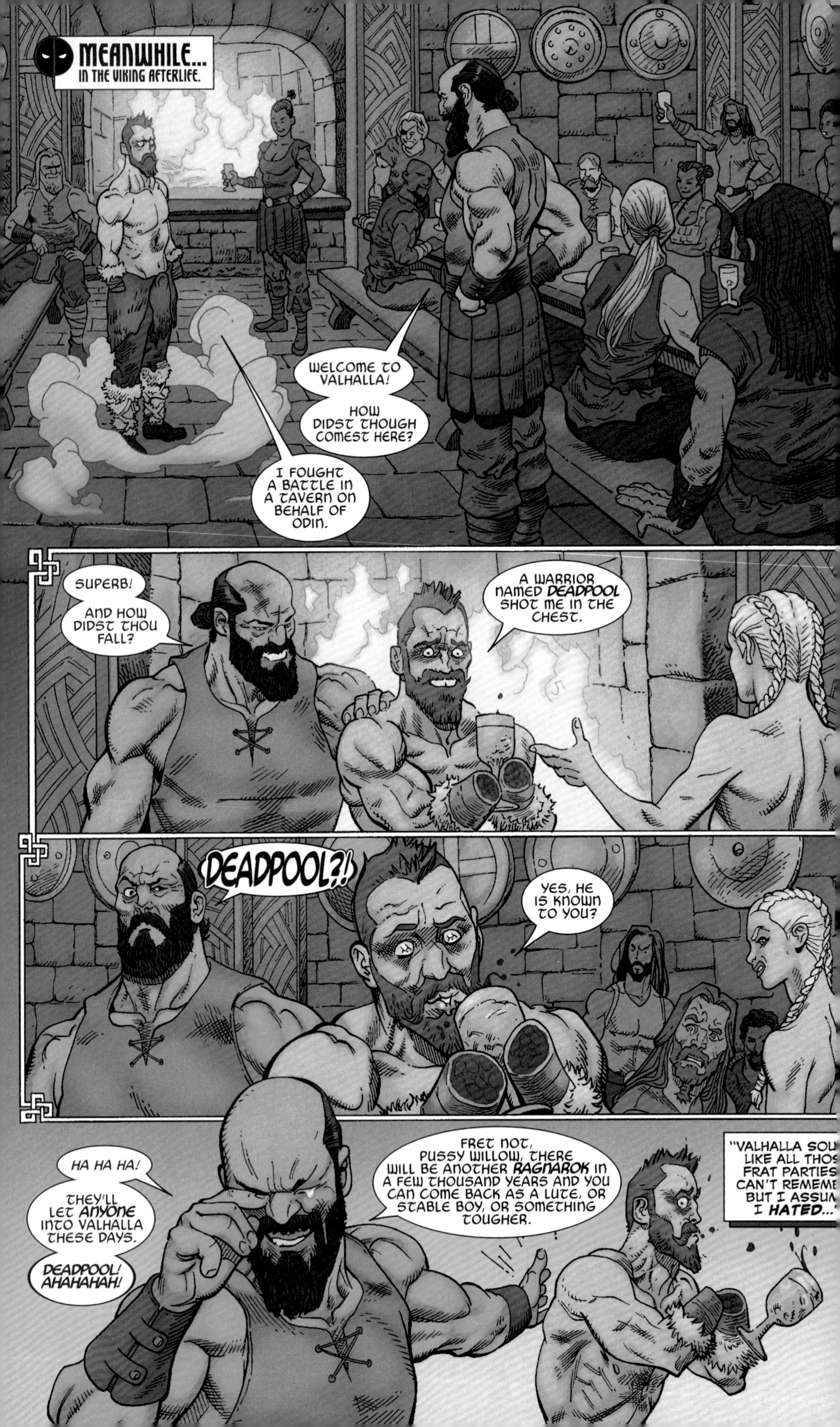
MEANWHILE... IN THE VIKING AFTERLIFE.
WELCOME TO VALHALLA!
HOW DIDST THOUGH COMEST HERE?
I FOUGHT A BATTLE IN A TAVERN ON BEHALF OF ODIN.
SUPERB!
AND HOW DIDST THOU FALL?
A WARRIOR NAMED DEADPOOL SHOT ME IN THE CHEST.
DEADPOOL?!
YES, HE IS KNOWN TO YOU?
HA HA HA!
THEY'LL LET ANYONE INTO VALHALLA THESE DAYS.
DEADPOOL! AHAHAHAH!
FRET NOT, PUSSY WILLOW, THERE WILL BE ANOTHER RAGNAROK IN A FEW THOUSAND YEARS AND YOU CAN COME BACK AS A LUTE, OR STABLE BOY, OR SOMETHING TOUGHER.

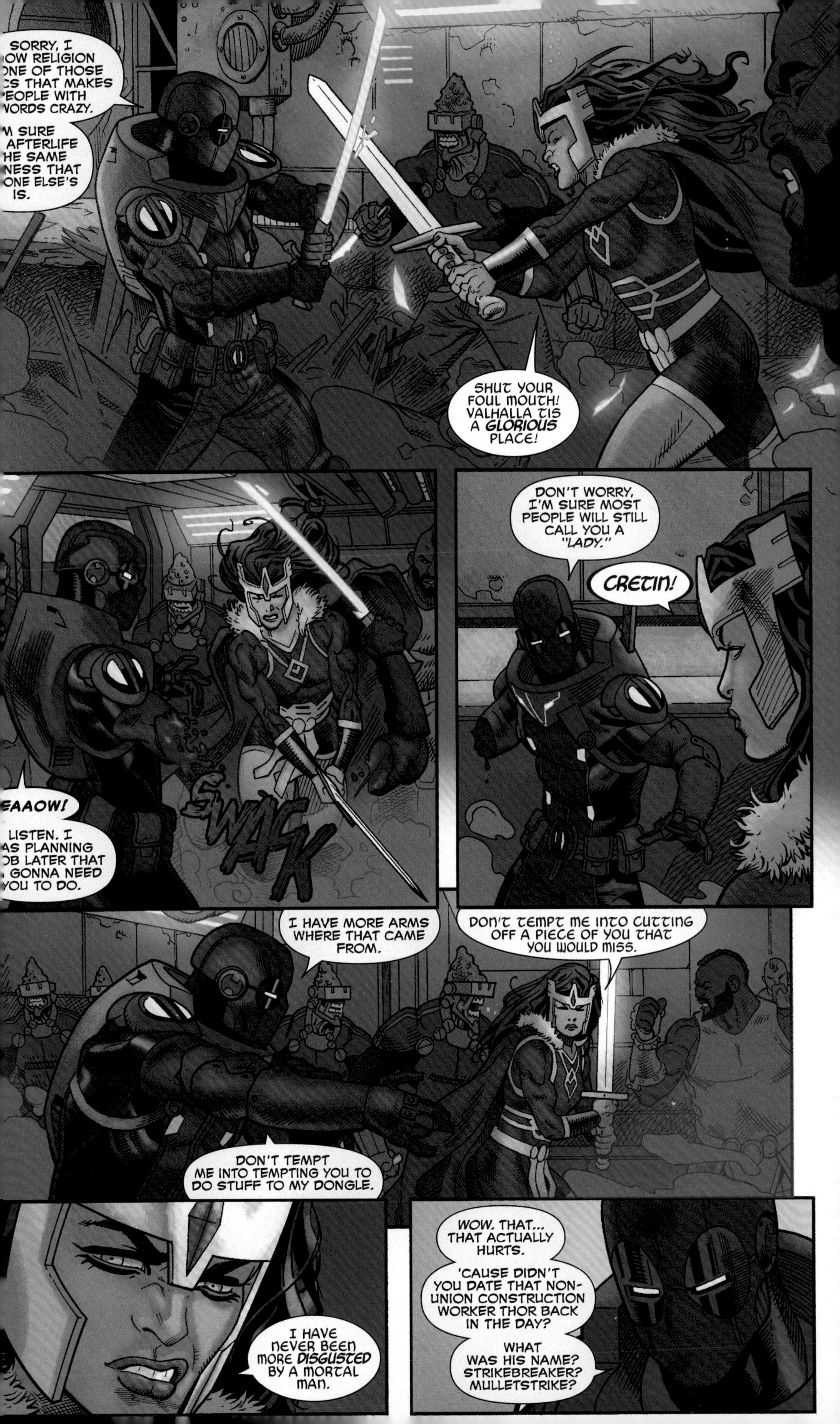

SORRY, I
OW RELIGION
ONE OF THOSE
CS THAT MAKES
EOPLE WITH
WORDS CRAZY.
M SURE
AFTERLIFE
HE SAME
NESS THAT
ONE ELSE'S
IS.
SHUT YOUR FOUL MOUTH! VALHALLA TIS A GLORIOUS PLACE!
EAAOW!
LISTEN. I
AS PLANNING
OB LATER THAT
GONNA NEED
YOU TO DO.
SWAK
DON'T WORRY, I'M SURE MOST PEOPLE WILL STILL CALL YOU A "LADY."
CRETIN!
I HAVE MORE ARMS WHERE THAT CAME FROM.
DON'T TEMPT ME INTO CUTTING OFF A PIECE OF YOU THAT YOU WOULD MISS.
DON'T TEMPT ME INTO TEMPTING YOU TO DO STUFF TO MY DONGLE.
I HAVE NEVER BEEN MORE DISGUSTED BY A MORTAL MAN.
WOW. THAT... THAT ACTUALLY HURTS.
'CAUSE DIDN'T YOU DATE THAT NON-UNION CONSTRUCTION WORKER THOR BACK IN THE DAY?
WHAT WAS HIS NAME? STRIKEBREAKER? MULLETSTRIKE?

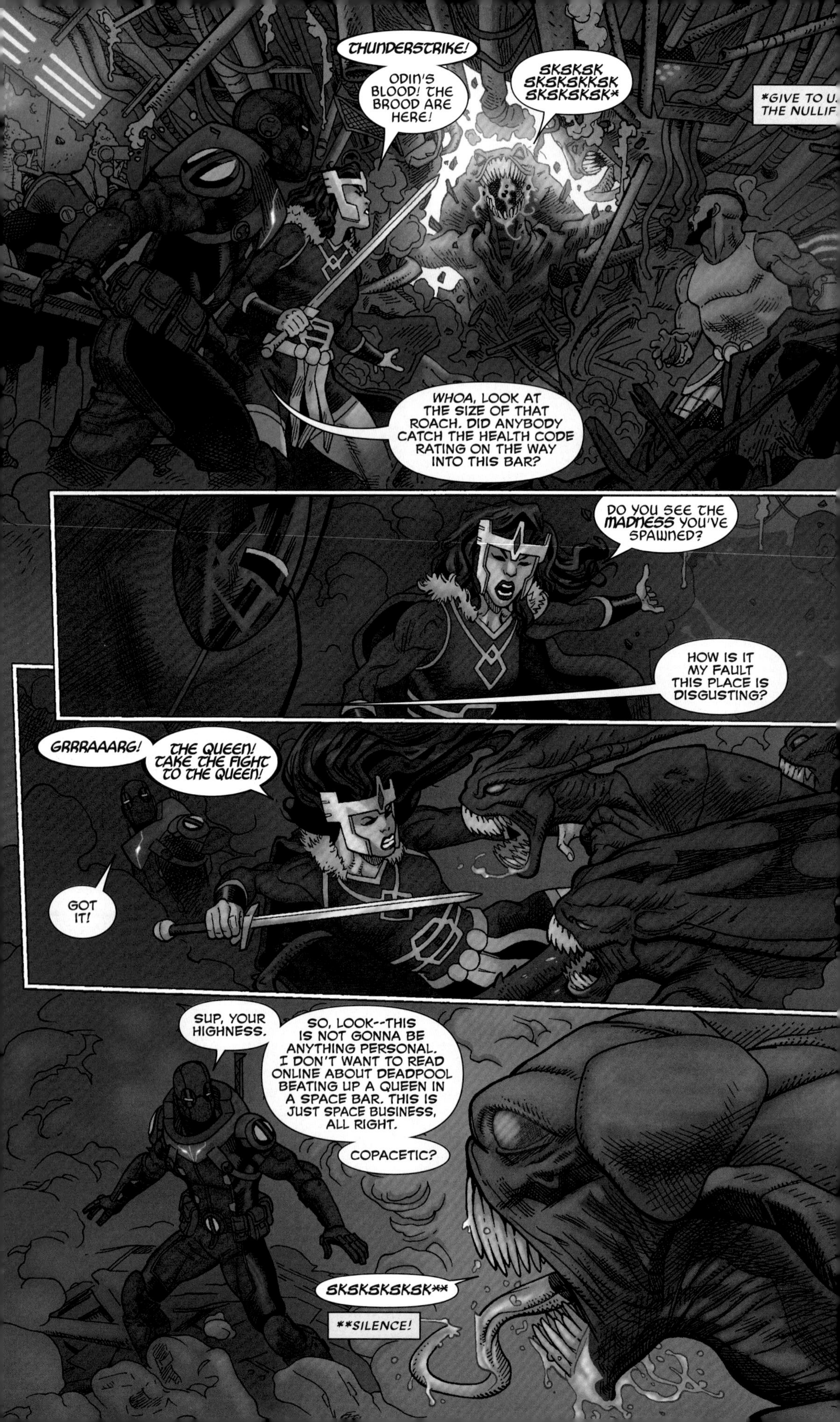
THUNDERSTRIKE!
ODIN'S BLOOD! THE BROOD ARE HERE!
SKSKSK SKSKSKKSK SKSKSKSK*
*GIVE TO U... THE NULLIF...
WHOA, LOOK AT THE SIZE OF THAT ROACH. DID ANYBODY CATCH THE HEALTH CODE RATING ON THE WAY INTO THIS BAR?
DO YOU SEE THE MADNESS YOU'VE SPAWNED?
HOW IS IT MY FAULT THIS PLACE IS DISGUSTING?
GRRRAAARG!
THE QUEEN! TAKE THE FIGHT TO THE QUEEN!
GOT IT!
SUP, YOUR HIGHNESS.
SO, LOOK--THIS IS NOT GONNA BE ANYTHING PERSONAL. I DON'T WANT TO READ ONLINE ABOUT DEADPOOL BEATING UP A QUEEN IN A SPACE BAR. THIS IS JUST SPACE BUSINESS, ALL RIGHT.
COPACETIC?
SKSKSKSKSK**
**SILENCE!

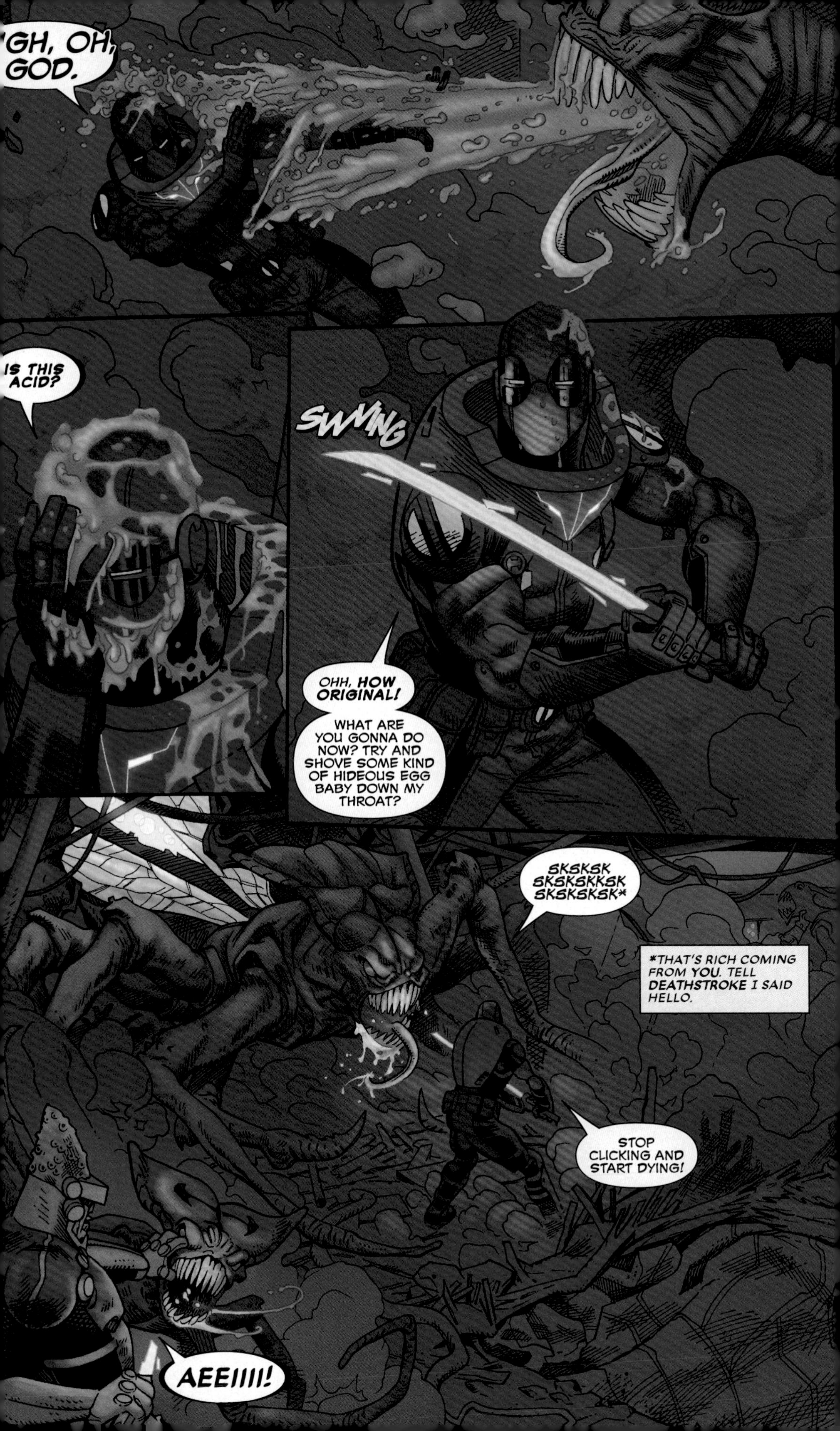
GH, OH, GOD.
IS THIS ACID?
SWING
OHH, HOW ORIGINAL!
WHAT ARE YOU GONNA DO NOW? TRY AND SHOVE SOME KIND OF HIDEOUS EGG BABY DOWN MY THROAT?
SKSKSK SKSKSKKSK SKSKSKSK*
*THAT'S RICH COMING FROM YOU. TELL DEATHSTROKE I SAID HELLO.
STOP CLICKING AND START DYING!
AEEIIII!

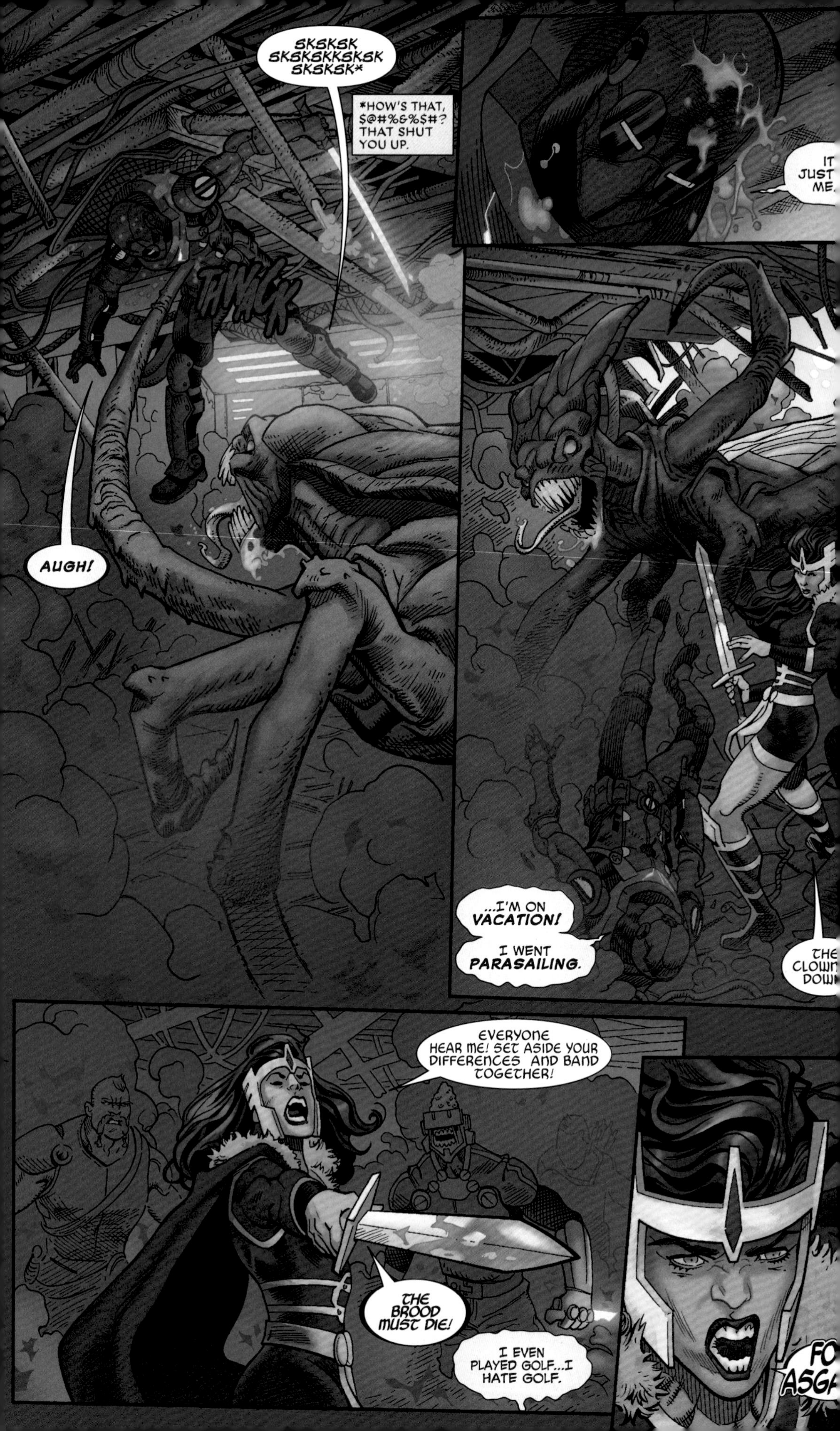
SKSKSK SKSKSKKSKSK SKSKSK*
*HOW'S THAT, $@#%&%$#? THAT SHUT YOU UP.
THWACK
AUGH!
IT JUST ME.
...I'M ON VACATION!
I WENT PARASAILING.
EVERYONE HEAR ME! SET ASIDE YOUR DIFFERENCES AND BAND TOGETHER!
THE BROOD MUST DIE!
I EVEN PLAYED GOLF...I HATE GOLF.

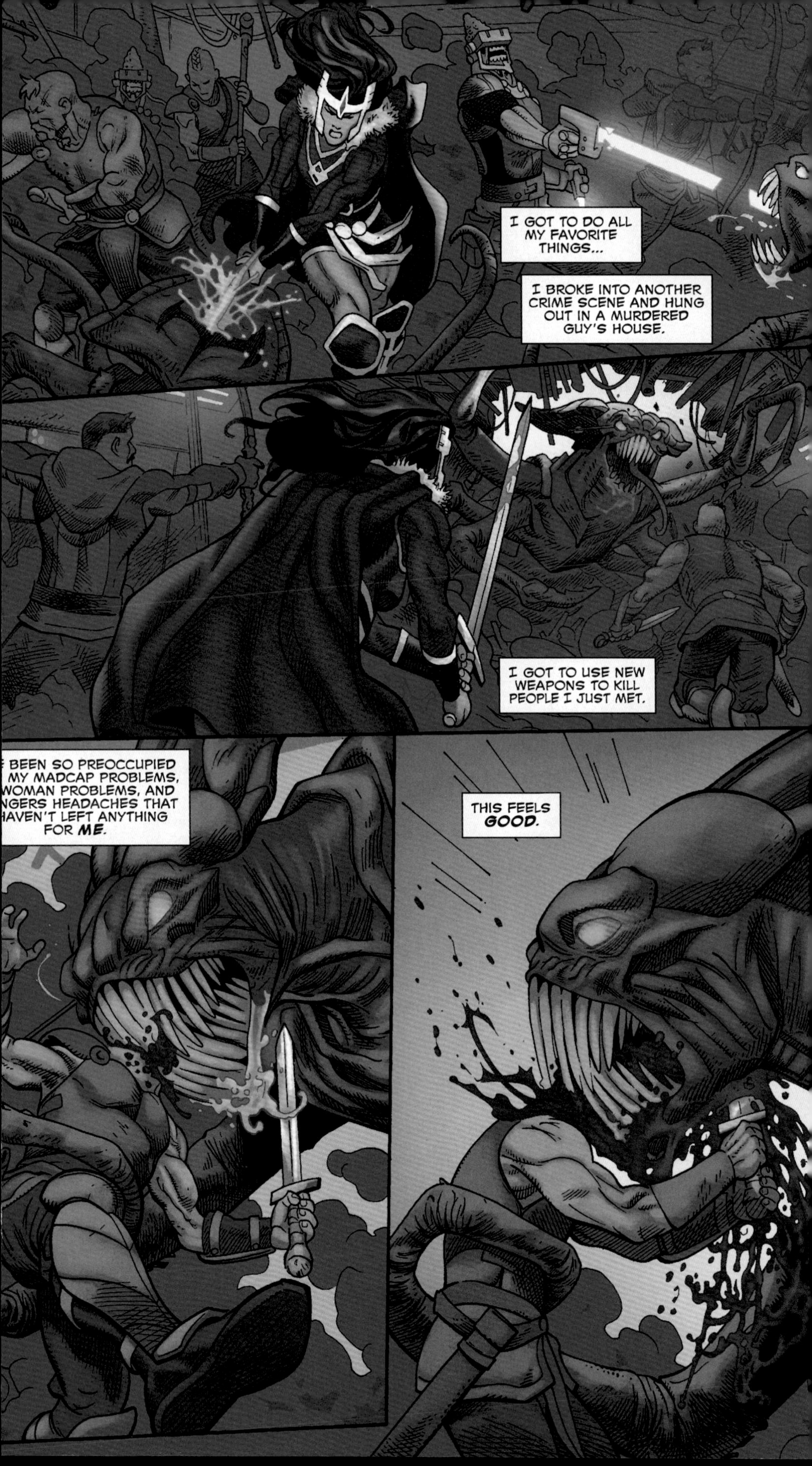

I GOT TO DO ALL MY FAVORITE THINGS...
I BROKE INTO ANOTHER CRIME SCENE AND HUNG OUT IN A MURDERED GUY'S HOUSE.
I GOT TO USE NEW WEAPONS TO KILL PEOPLE I JUST MET.
BEEN SO PREOCCUPIED MY MADCAP PROBLEMS, WOMAN PROBLEMS, AND NGERS HEADACHES THAT HAVEN'T LEFT ANYTHING FOR ***ME***.
THIS FEELS ***GOOD***.

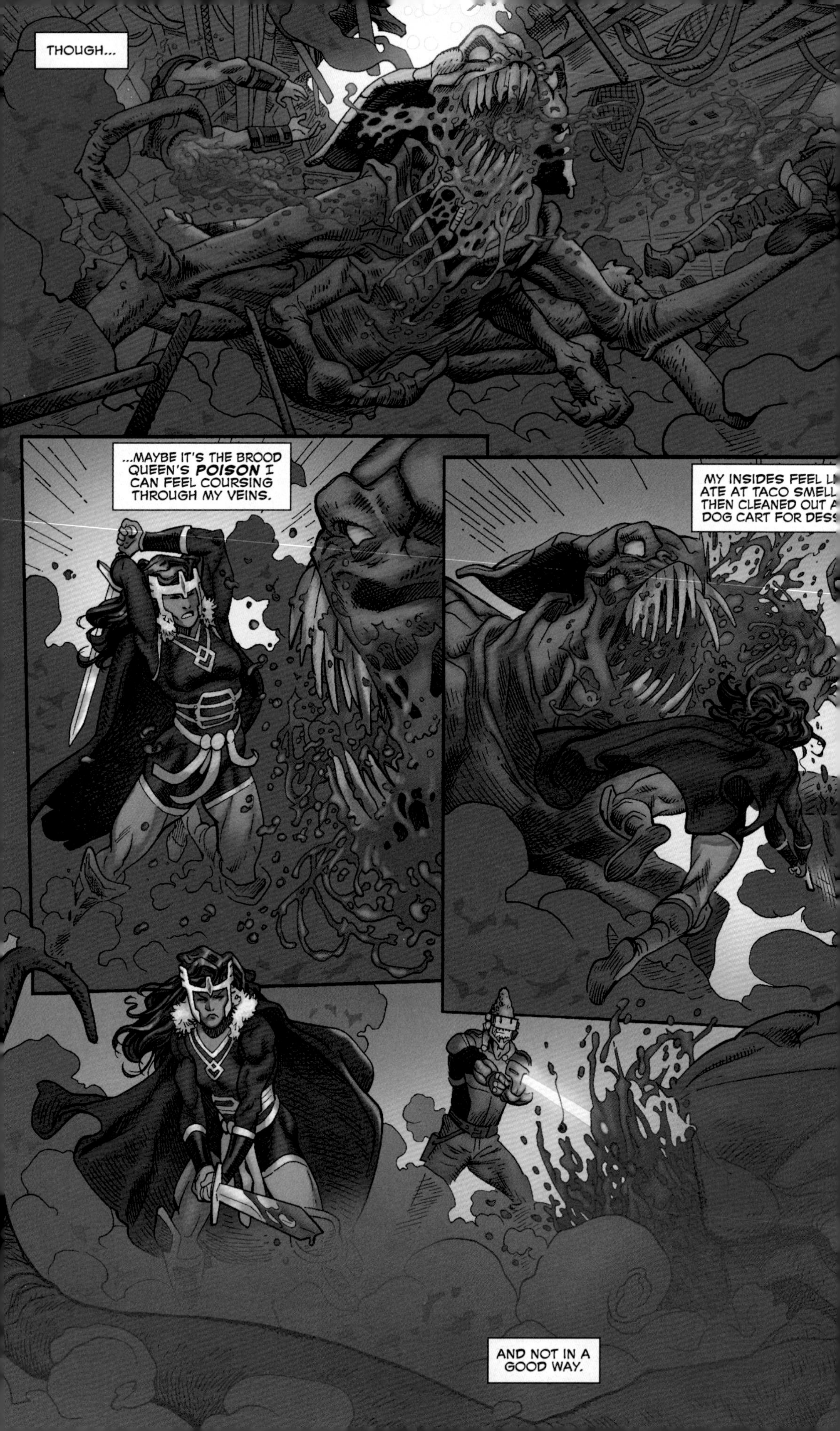
THOUGH...
...MAYBE IT'S THE BROOD QUEEN'S POISON I CAN FEEL COURSING THROUGH MY VEINS.
MY INSIDES FEEL LI
ATE AT TACO SMELL
THEN CLEANED OUT A
DOG CART FOR DES
AND NOT IN A GOOD WAY.

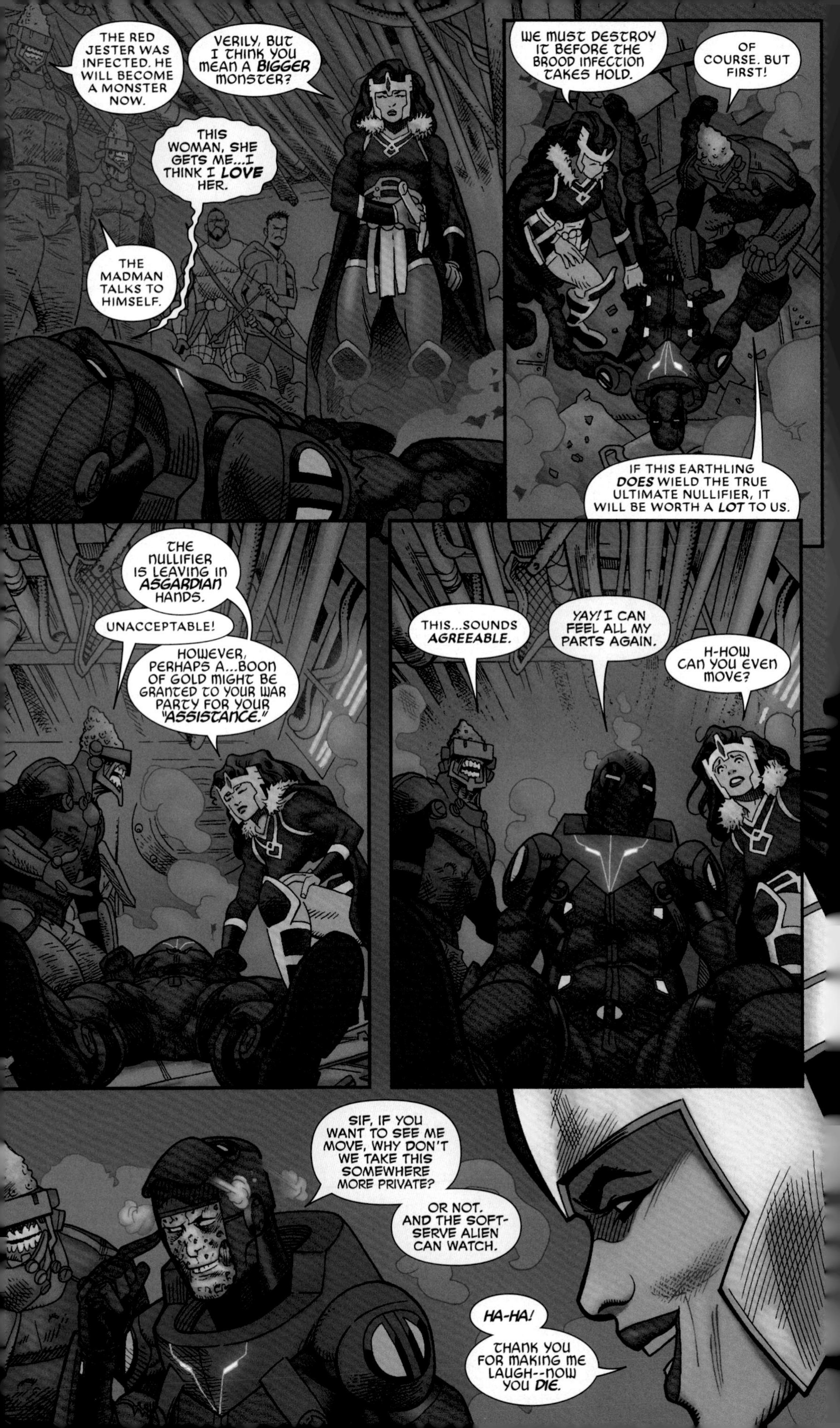
THE RED JESTER WAS INFECTED. HE WILL BECOME A MONSTER NOW.
VERILY, BUT I THINK YOU MEAN A BIGGER MONSTER?
THIS WOMAN, SHE GETS ME...I THINK I LOVE HER.
THE MADMAN TALKS TO HIMSELF.
WE MUST DESTROY IT BEFORE THE BROOD INFECTION TAKES HOLD.
OF COURSE. BUT FIRST!
IF THIS EARTHLING DOES WIELD THE TRUE ULTIMATE NULLIFIER, IT WILL BE WORTH A LOT TO US.
THE NULLIFIER IS LEAVING IN ASGARDIAN HANDS.
UNACCEPTABLE!
HOWEVER, PERHAPS A...BOON OF GOLD MIGHT BE GRANTED TO YOUR WAR PARTY FOR YOUR "ASSISTANCE."
THIS...SOUNDS AGREEABLE.
YAY! I CAN FEEL ALL MY PARTS AGAIN.
H-HOW CAN YOU EVEN MOVE?
SIF, IF YOU WANT TO SEE ME MOVE, WHY DON'T WE TAKE THIS SOMEWHERE MORE PRIVATE?
OR NOT. AND THE SOFT-SERVE ALIEN CAN WATCH.
HA-HA!
THANK YOU FOR MAKING ME LAUGH--NOW YOU DIE.

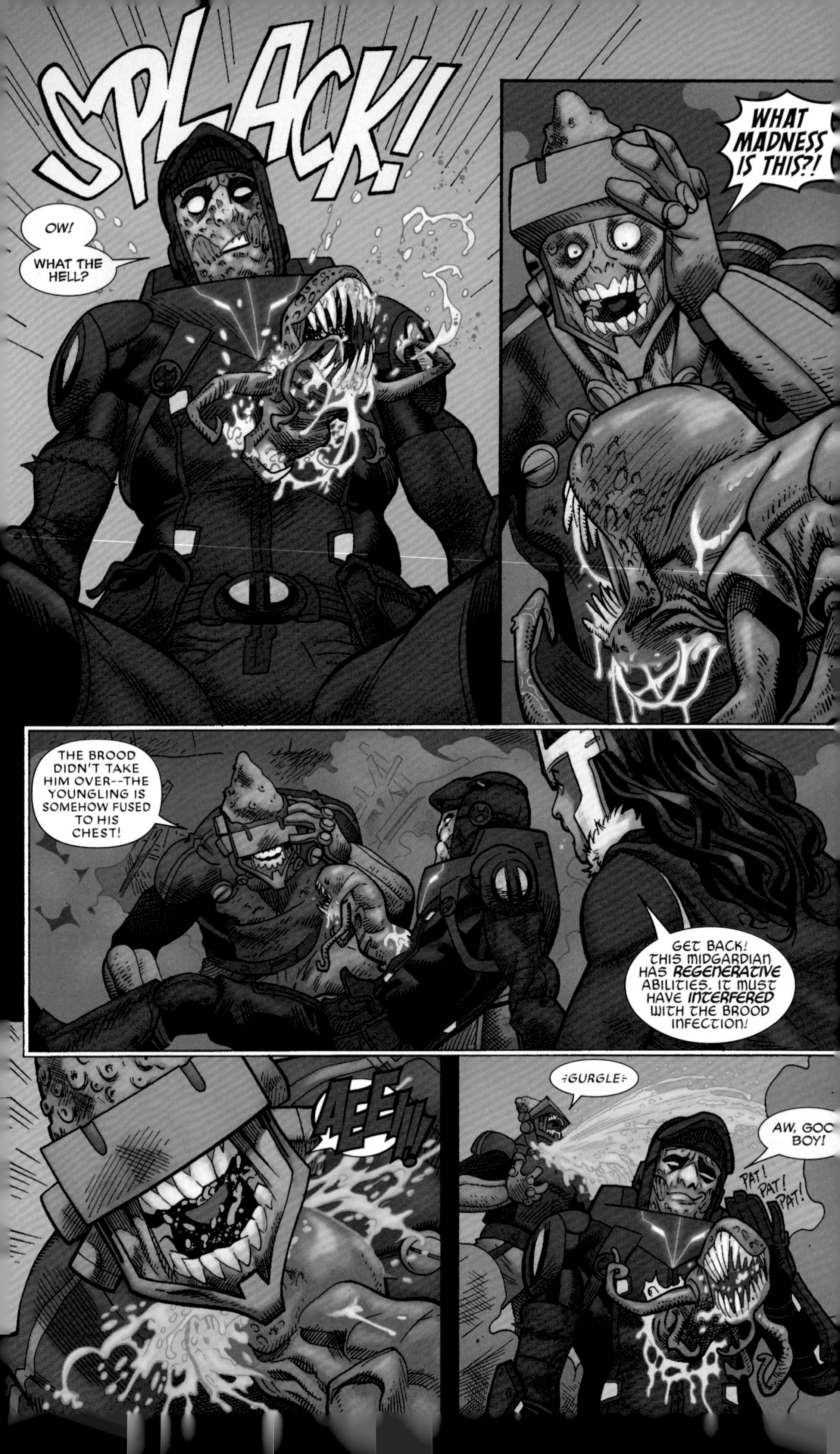
SPLACK!
OW!
WHAT THE HELL?
WHAT MADNESS IS THIS?!
THE BROOD DIDN'T TAKE HIM OVER--THE YOUNGLING IS SOMEHOW FUSED TO HIS CHEST!
GET BACK! THIS MIDGARDIAN HAS REGENERATIVE ABILITIES. IT MUST HAVE INTERFERED WITH THE BROOD INFECTION!
AEE!!!
GURGLE
AW, GOO BOY!
PAT! PAT! PAT!

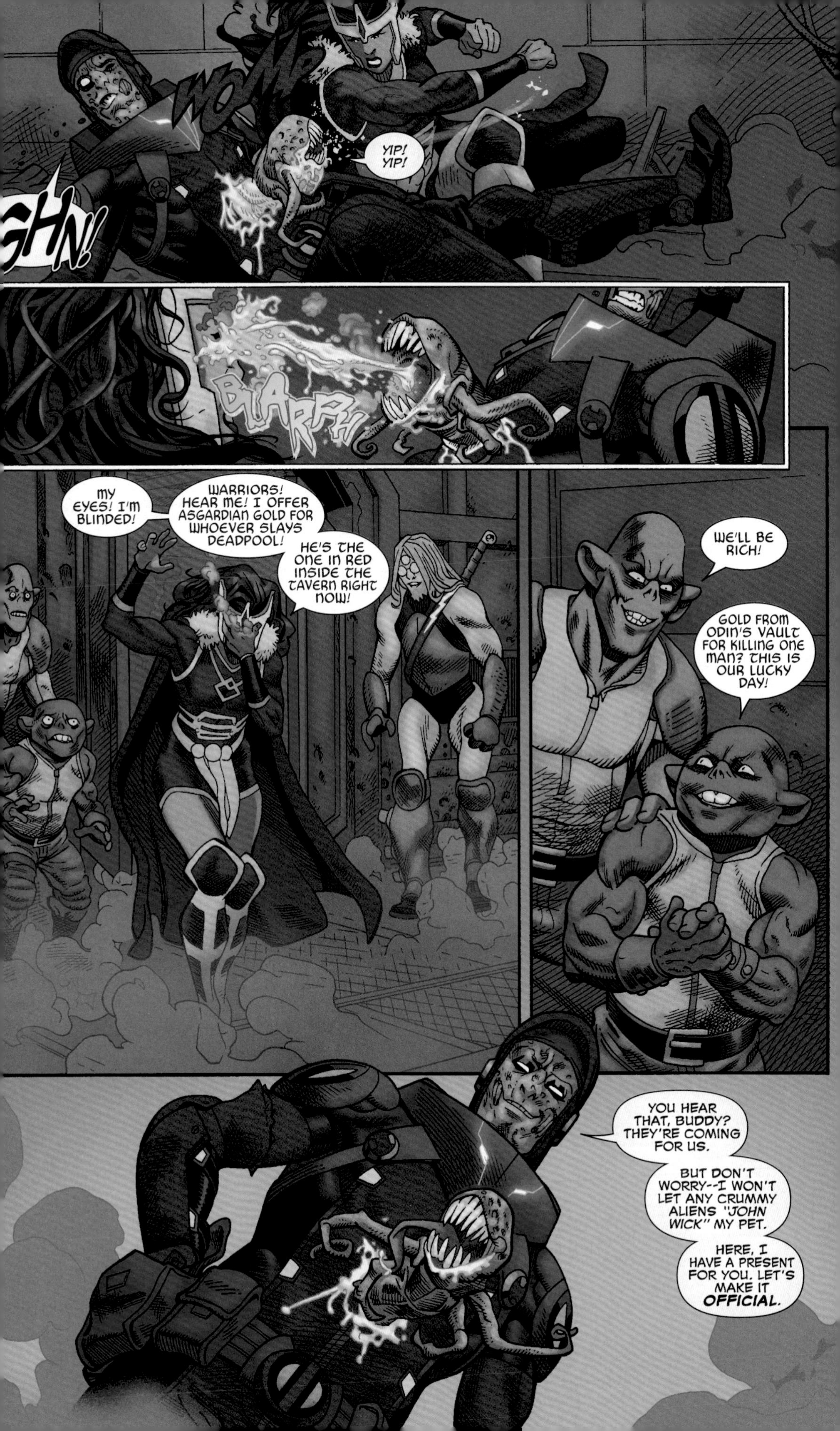
WOMP
YIP! YIP!
GHN!
BLARRGH
MY EYES! I'M BLINDED!
WARRIORS! HEAR ME! I OFFER ASGARDIAN GOLD FOR WHOEVER SLAYS DEADPOOL!
HE'S THE ONE IN RED INSIDE THE TAVERN RIGHT NOW!
WE'LL BE RICH!
GOLD FROM ODIN'S VAULT FOR KILLING ONE MAN? THIS IS OUR LUCKY DAY!
YOU HEAR THAT, BUDDY? THEY'RE COMING FOR US.
BUT DON'T WORRY--I WON'T LET ANY CRUMMY ALIENS "JOHN WICK" MY PET.
HERE, I HAVE A PRESENT FOR YOU. LET'S MAKE IT OFFICIAL.

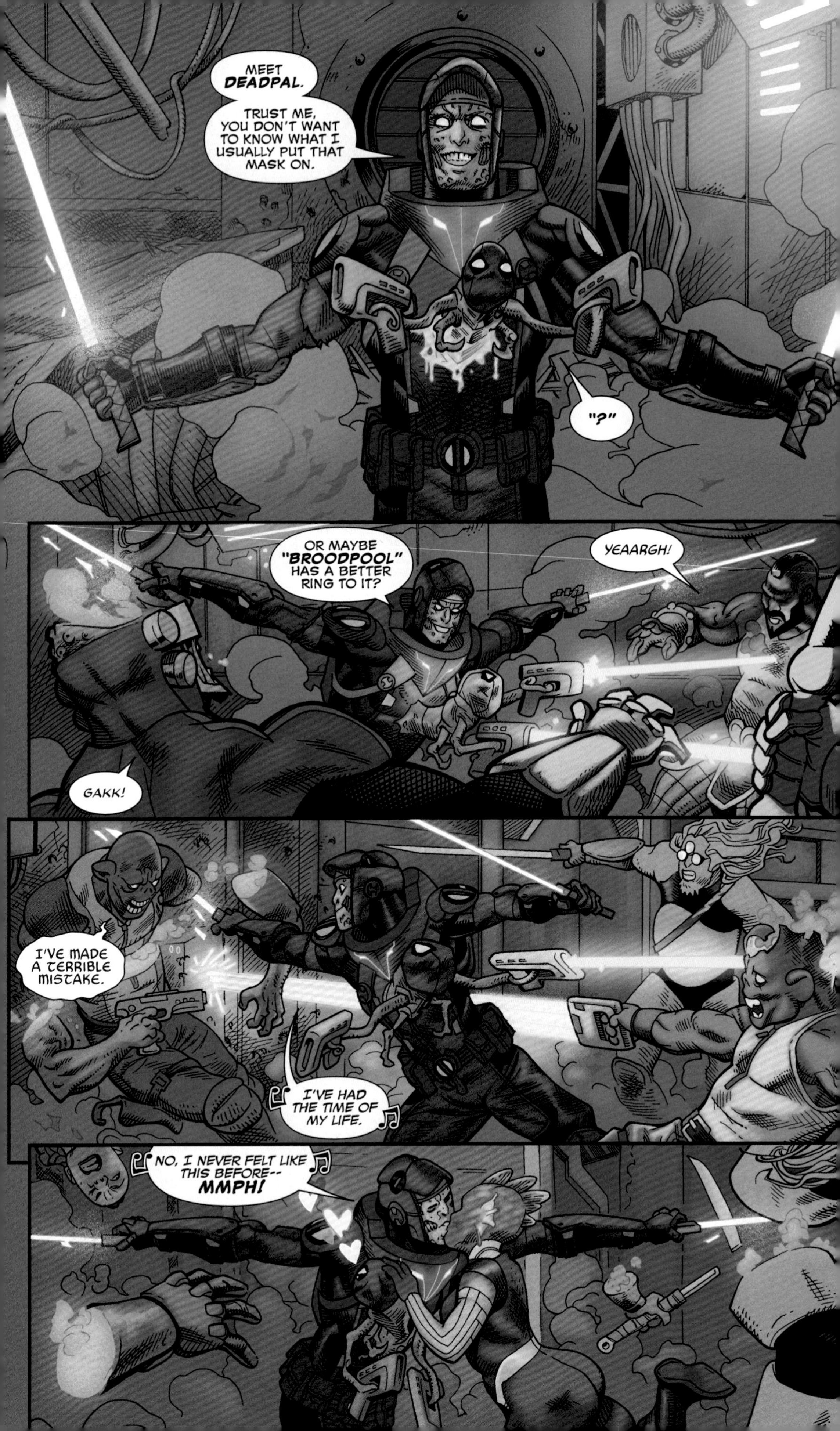
MEET DEADPAL.
TRUST ME, YOU DON'T WANT TO KNOW WHAT I USUALLY PUT THAT MASK ON.
"?"
OR MAYBE "BROODPOOL" HAS A BETTER RING TO IT?
YEAARGH!
GAKK!
I'VE MADE A TERRIBLE MISTAKE.
I'VE HAD THE TIME OF MY LIFE.
NO, I NEVER FELT LIKE THIS BEFORE-- MMPH!

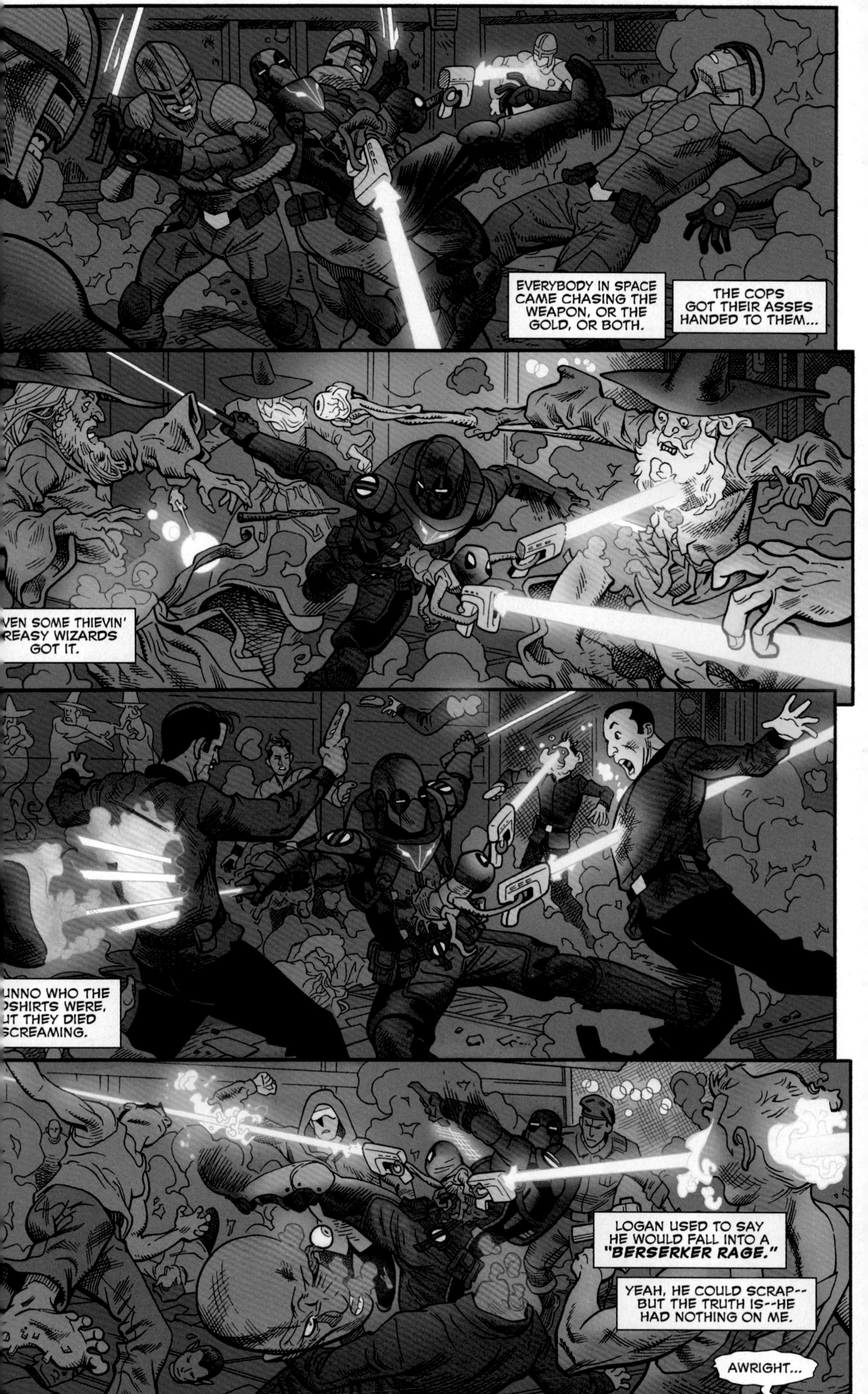
EVERYBODY IN SPACE CAME CHASING THE WEAPON, OR THE GOLD, OR BOTH.
THE COPS GOT THEIR ASSES HANDED TO THEM...
VEN SOME THIEVIN' REASY WIZARDS GOT IT.
UNNO WHO THE DSHIRTS WERE, UT THEY DIED SCREAMING.
LOGAN USED TO SAY HE WOULD FALL INTO A "BERSERKER RAGE."
YEAH, HE COULD SCRAP-- BUT THE TRUTH IS--HE HAD NOTHING ON ME.
AWRIGHT...

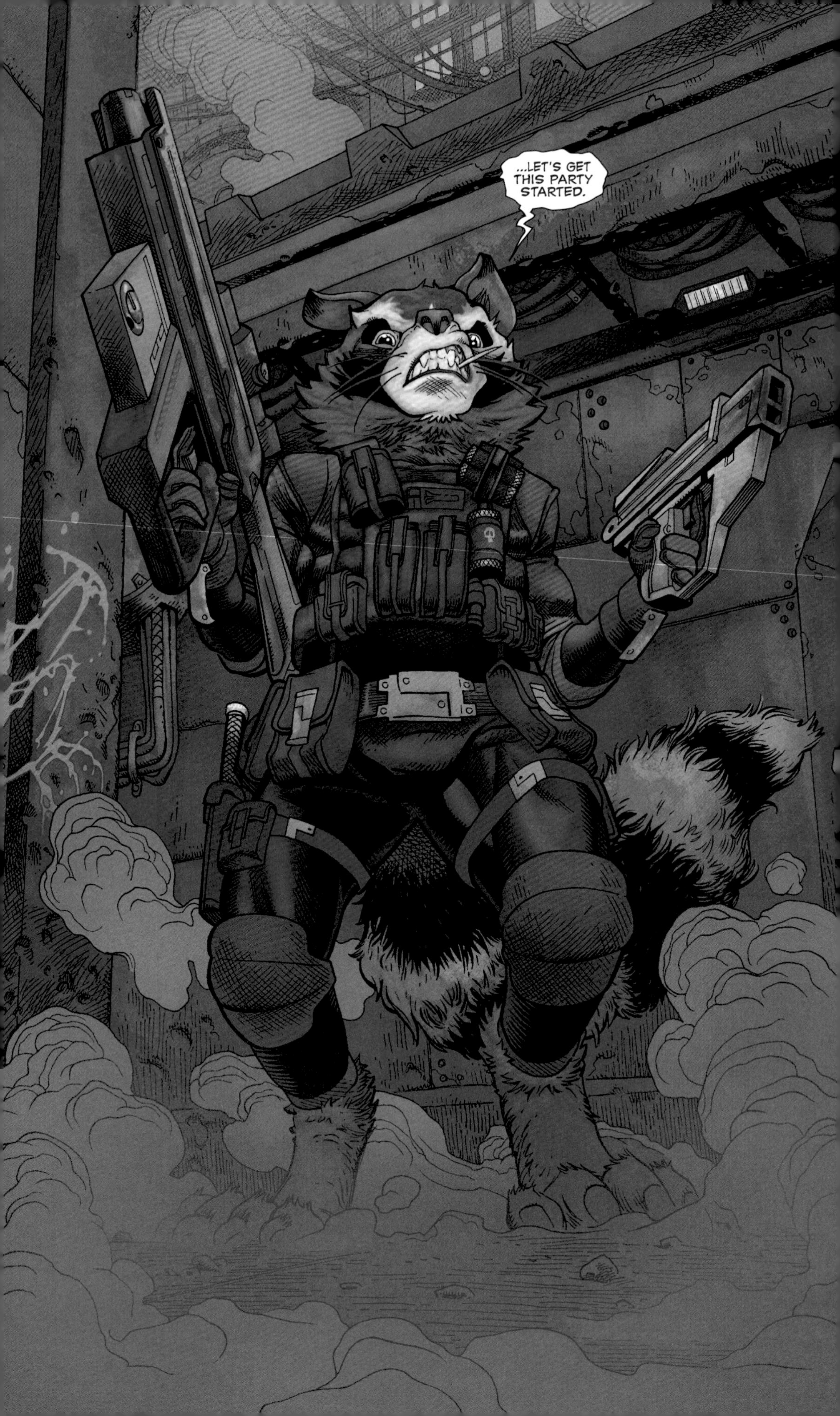
...LET'S GET THIS PARTY STARTED.

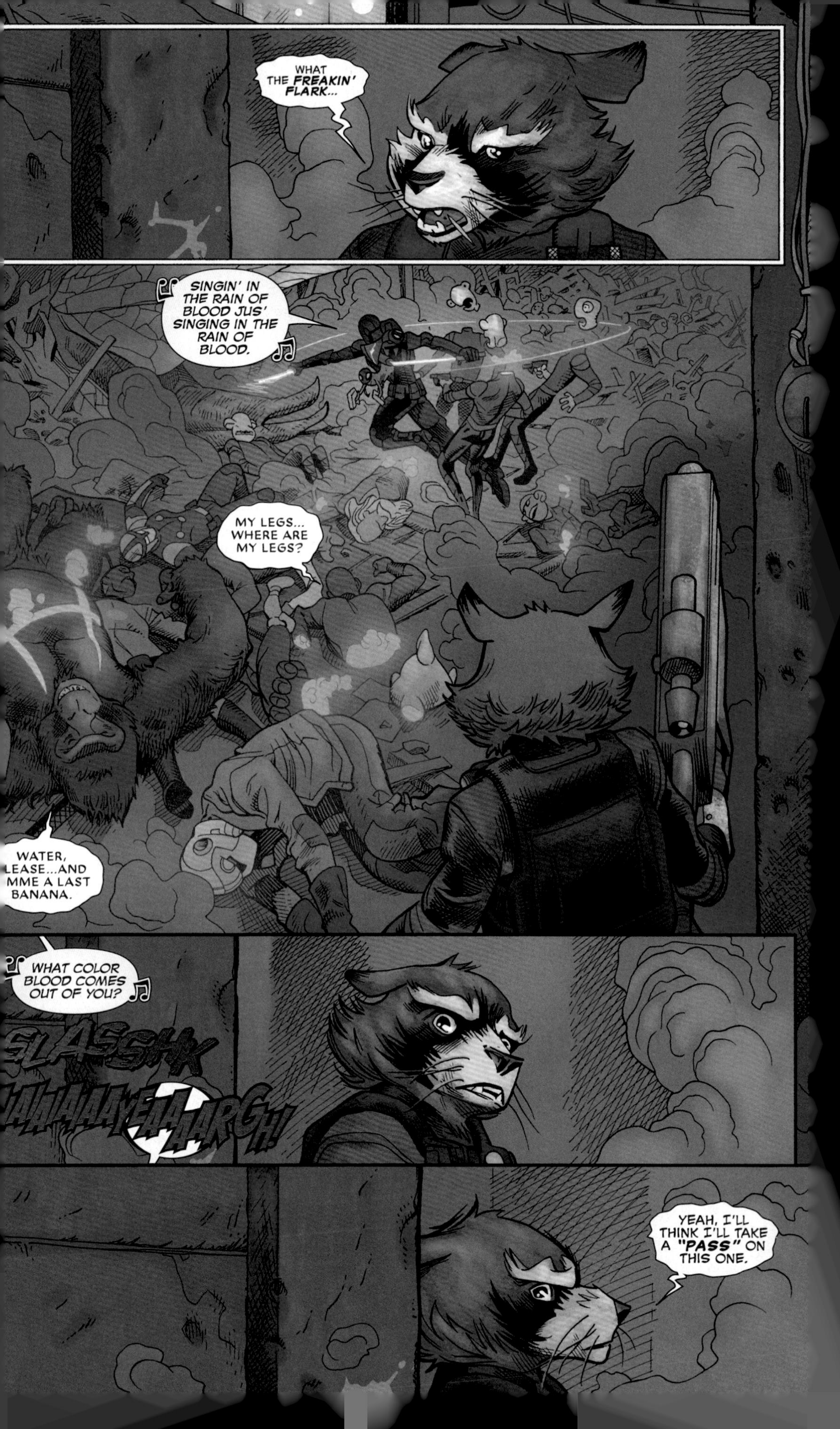
WHAT THE FREAKIN' FLARK...
SINGIN' IN THE RAIN OF BLOOD JUS' SINGING IN THE RAIN OF BLOOD.
MY LEGS... WHERE ARE MY LEGS?
WATER, LEASE...AND MME A LAST BANANA.
WHAT COLOR BLOOD COMES OUT OF YOU?
SLASSHK
AAAAAAYEAAARGH!
YEAH, I'LL THINK I'LL TAKE A "PASS" ON THIS ONE.

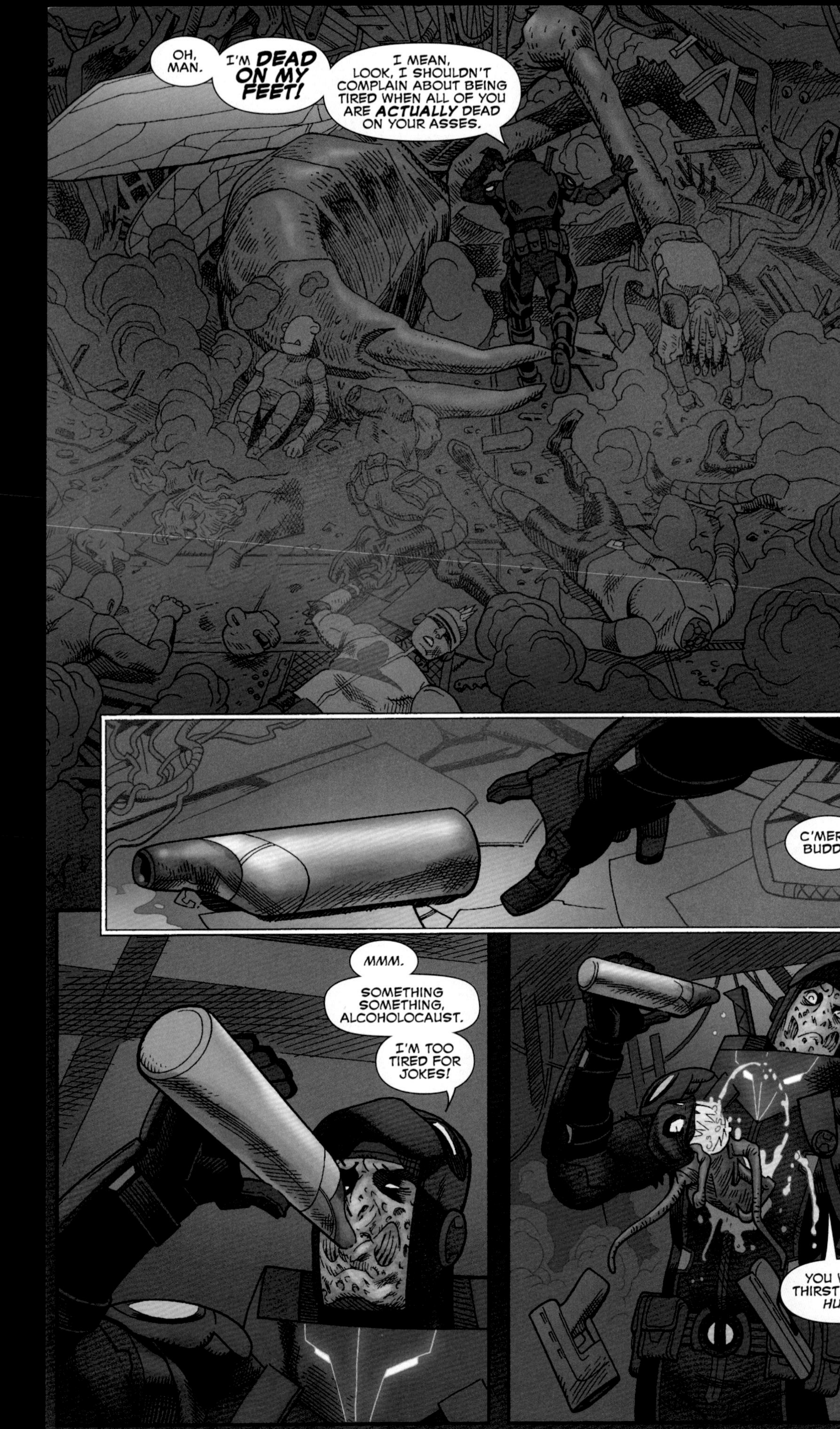
OH, MAN.
I'M **DEAD ON MY FEET!**
I MEAN, LOOK, I SHOULDN'T COMPLAIN ABOUT BEING TIRED WHEN ALL OF YOU ARE **ACTUALLY** DEAD ON YOUR ASSES.
C'MER
BUDD
MMM.
SOMETHING SOMETHING, ALCOHOLOCAUST.
I'M TOO TIRED FOR JOKES!
YOU W
THIRST
HU

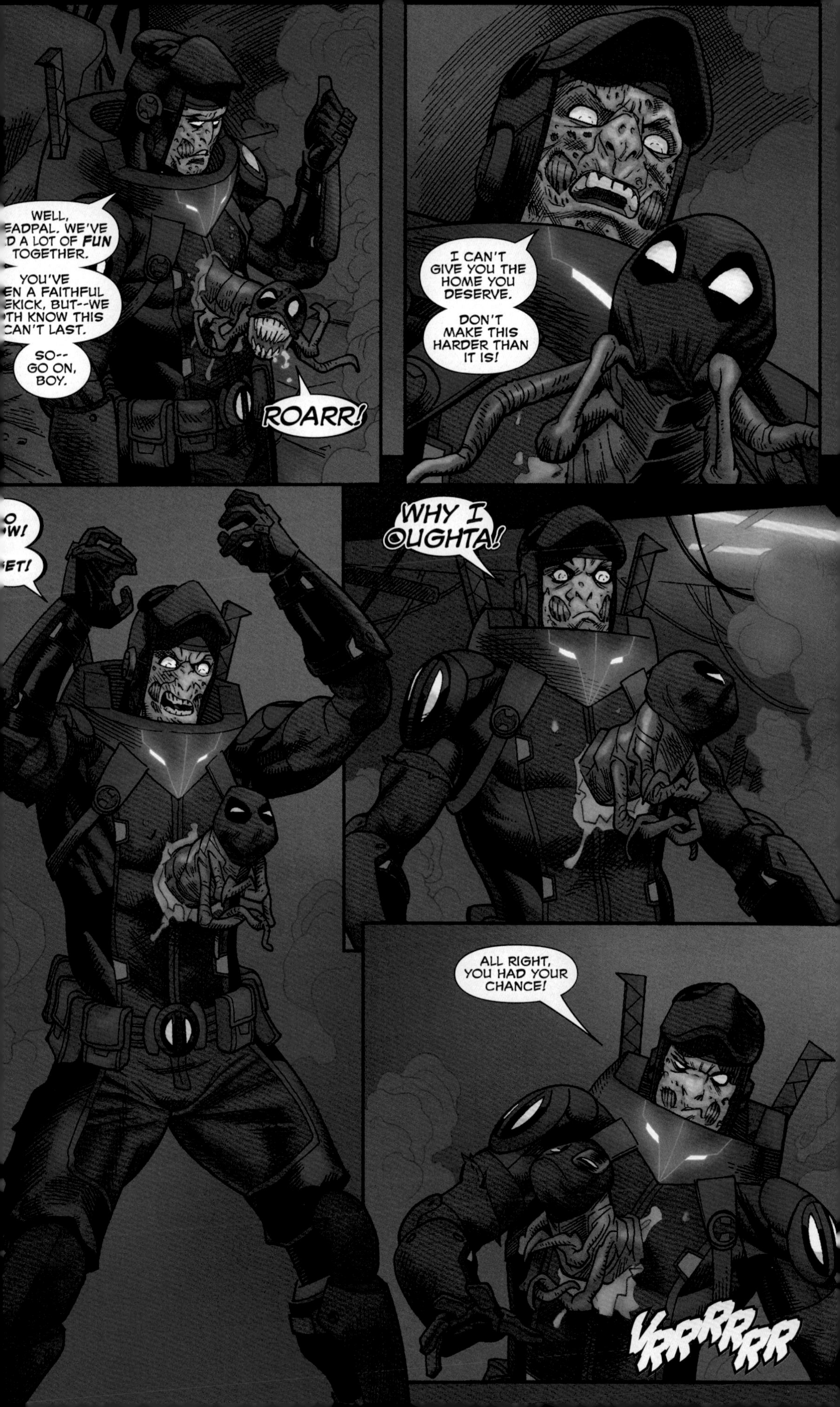

WELL, EADPAL. WE'VE D A LOT OF FUN TOGETHER.
YOU'VE EN A FAITHFUL EKICK, BUT--WE TH KNOW THIS CAN'T LAST.
SO-- GO ON, BOY.
ROARR!
I CAN'T GIVE YOU THE HOME YOU DESERVE.
DON'T MAKE THIS HARDER THAN IT IS!
WHY I OUGHTA!
ALL RIGHT, YOU HAD YOUR CHANCE!
VRRRRRR

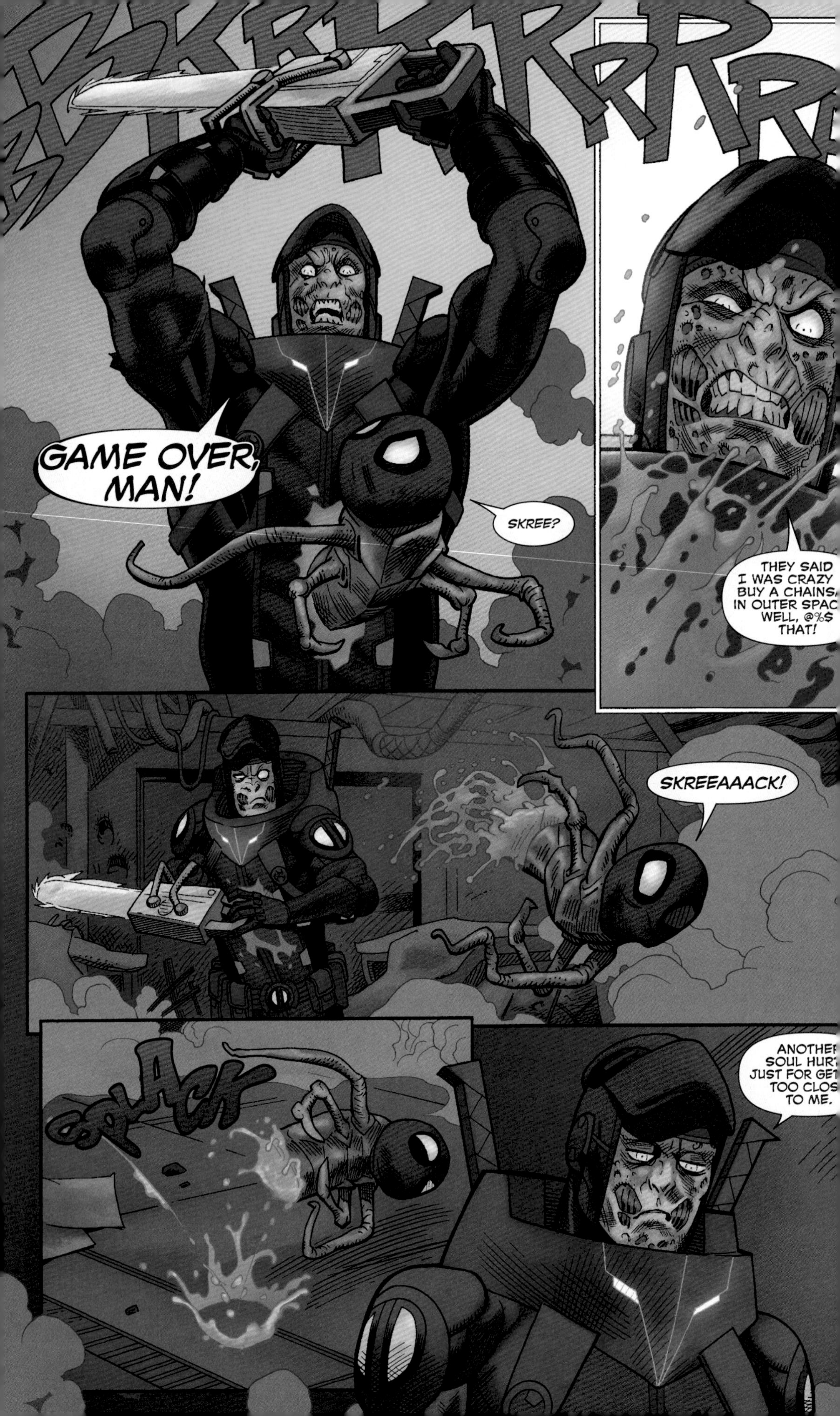
BBKRKRRRRR
GAME OVER, MAN!
SKREE?
THEY SAID I WAS CRAZY BUY A CHAINS IN OUTER SPAC WELL, @%$ THAT!
SKREEAAACK!
SPLACK
ANOTHE SOUL HUR JUST FOR GE TOO CLOS TO ME.

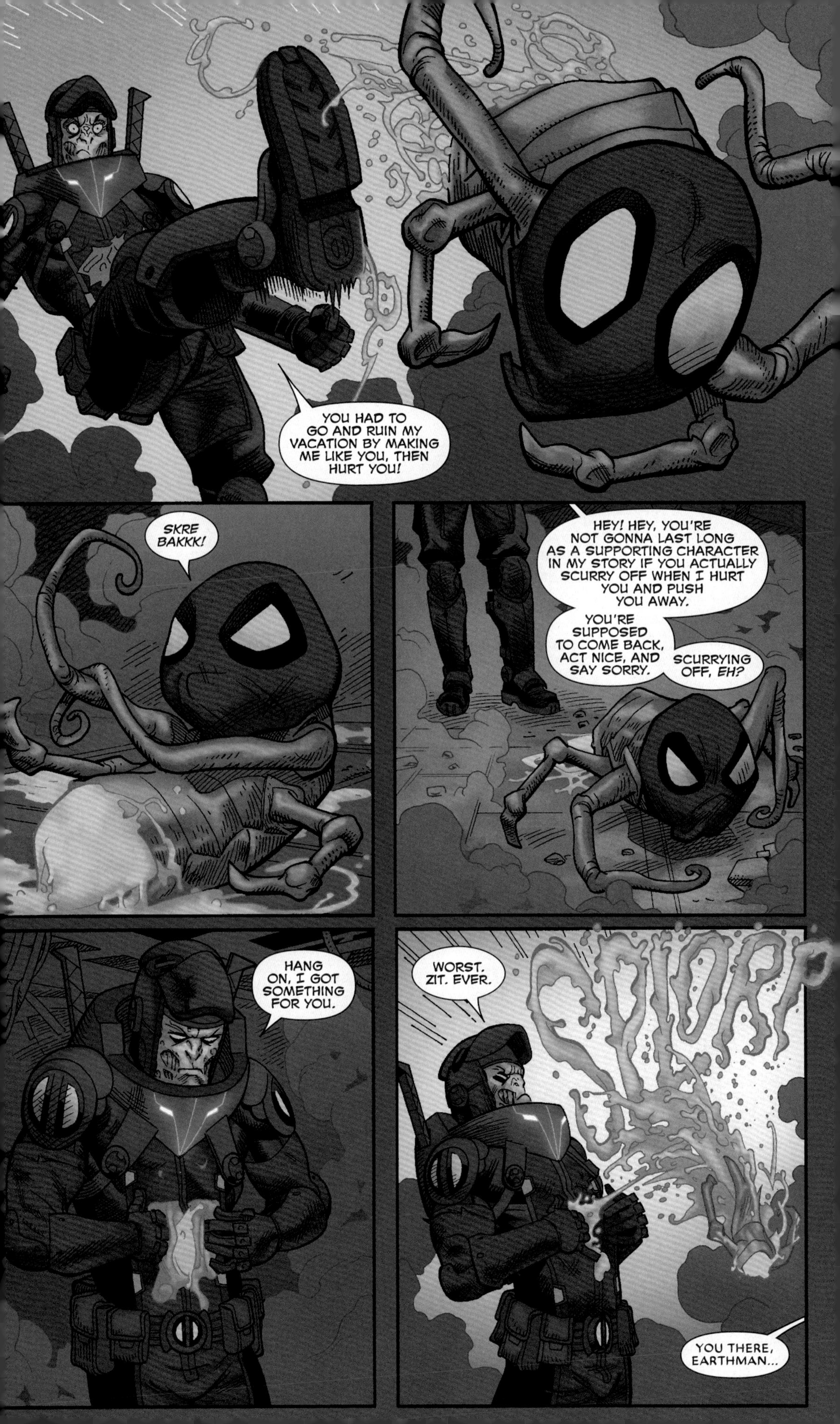
YOU HAD TO GO AND RUIN MY VACATION BY MAKING ME LIKE YOU, THEN HURT YOU!
SKRE BAKKK!
HEY! HEY, YOU'RE NOT GONNA LAST LONG AS A SUPPORTING CHARACTER IN MY STORY IF YOU ACTUALLY SCURRY OFF WHEN I HURT YOU AND PUSH YOU AWAY.
YOU'RE SUPPOSED TO COME BACK, ACT NICE, AND SAY SORRY.
SCURRYING OFF, *EH?*
HANG ON, I GOT SOMETHING FOR YOU.
WORST. ZIT. EVER.
SPLORP
YOU THERE, EARTHMAN...

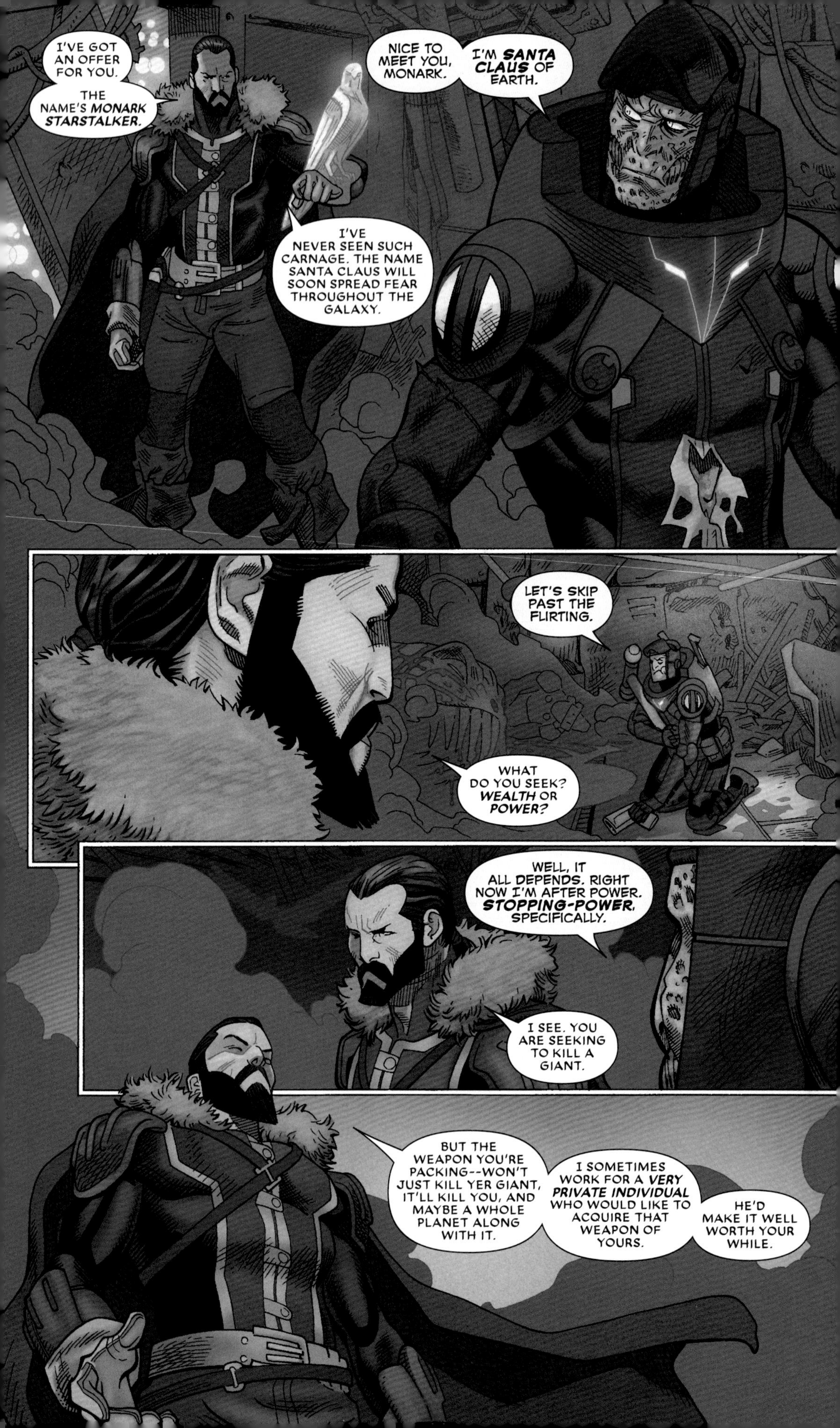
I'VE GOT AN OFFER FOR YOU.
THE NAME'S *MONARK STARSTALKER.*
NICE TO MEET YOU, MONARK.
I'M *SANTA CLAUS* OF EARTH.
I'VE NEVER SEEN SUCH CARNAGE. THE NAME SANTA CLAUS WILL SOON SPREAD FEAR THROUGHOUT THE GALAXY.
LET'S SKIP PAST THE FLIRTING.
WHAT DO YOU SEEK? *WEALTH* OR *POWER?*
WELL, IT ALL **DEPENDS.** RIGHT NOW I'M AFTER POWER. ***STOPPING-POWER,*** SPECIFICALLY.
I SEE. YOU ARE SEEKING TO KILL A GIANT.
BUT THE WEAPON YOU'RE PACKING--WON'T JUST KILL YER GIANT, IT'LL KILL YOU, AND MAYBE A WHOLE PLANET ALONG WITH IT.
I SOMETIMES WORK FOR A ***VERY PRIVATE INDIVIDUAL*** WHO WOULD LIKE TO ACQUIRE THAT WEAPON OF YOURS.
HE'D MAKE IT WELL WORTH YOUR WHILE.

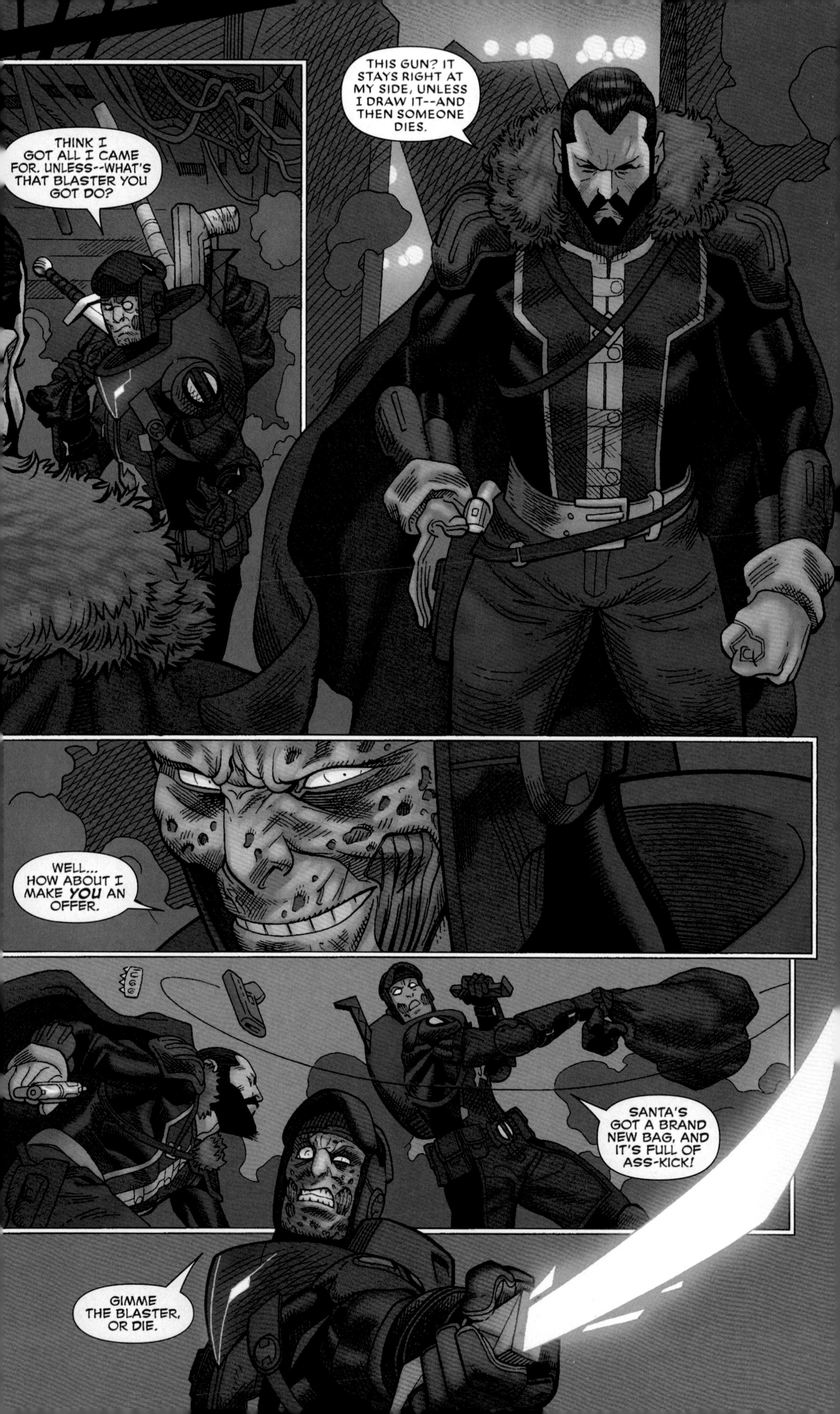
THINK I GOT ALL I CAME FOR. UNLESS--WHAT'S THAT BLASTER YOU GOT DO?
THIS GUN? IT STAYS RIGHT AT MY SIDE, UNLESS I DRAW IT--AND THEN SOMEONE DIES.
WELL... HOW ABOUT I MAKE *YOU* AN OFFER.
SANTA'S GOT A BRAND NEW BAG, AND IT'S FULL OF ASS-KICK!
GIMME THE BLASTER, OR DIE.

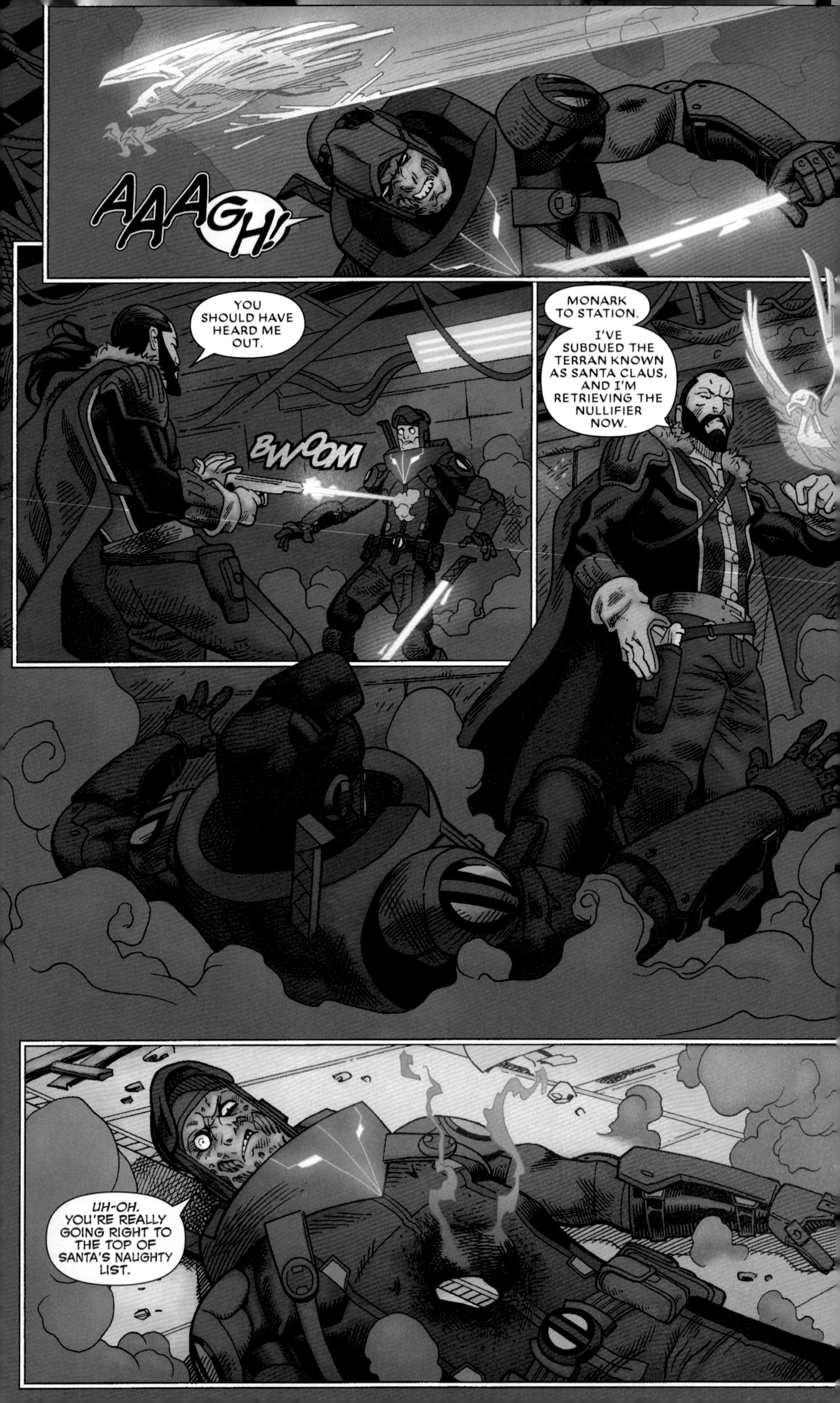

AAAGH!
YOU SHOULD HAVE HEARD ME OUT.
BWOOM
MONARK TO STATION.
I'VE SUBDUED THE TERRAN KNOWN AS SANTA CLAUS, AND I'M RETRIEVING THE NULLIFIER NOW.
UH-OH. YOU'RE REALLY GOING RIGHT TO THE TOP OF SANTA'S NAUGHTY LIST.

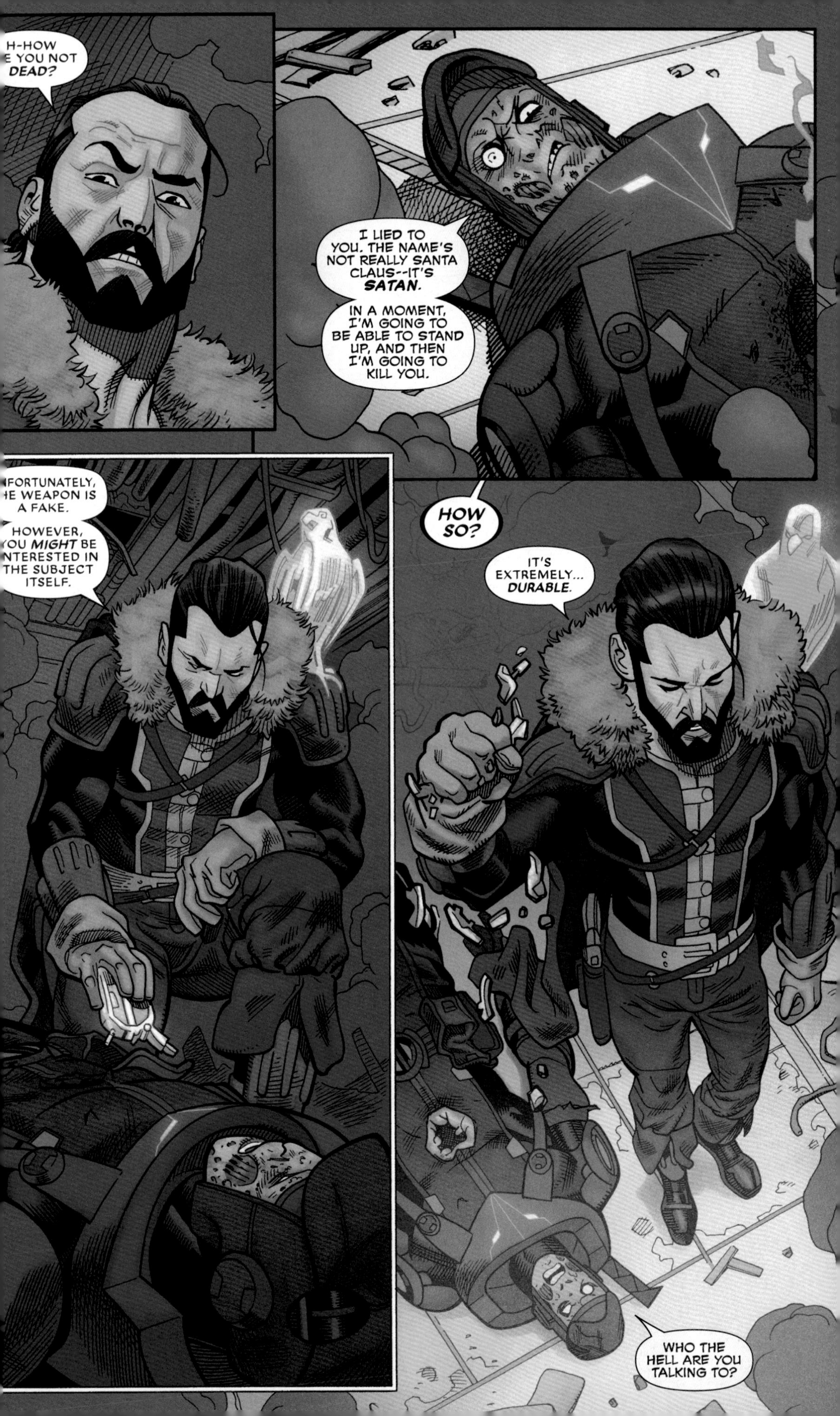
H-HOW
E YOU NOT DEAD?
I LIED TO YOU. THE NAME'S NOT REALLY SANTA CLAUS--IT'S **SATAN**.
IN A MOMENT, I'M GOING TO BE ABLE TO STAND UP, AND THEN I'M GOING TO KILL YOU.
FORTUNATELY, HE WEAPON IS A FAKE.
HOWEVER, YOU *MIGHT* BE INTERESTED IN THE SUBJECT ITSELF.
HOW SO?
IT'S EXTREMELY... *DURABLE*.
WHO THE HELL ARE YOU TALKING TO?

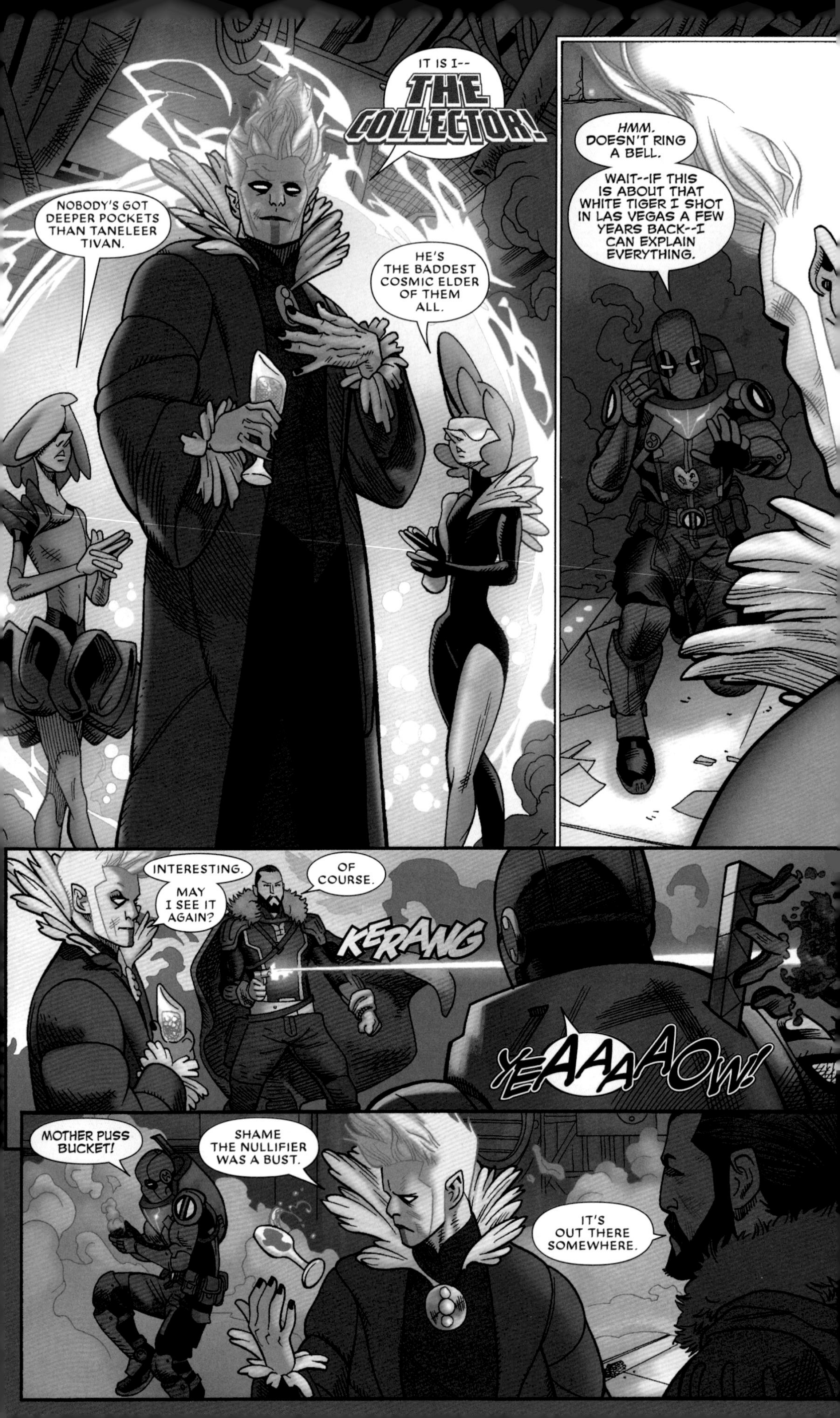
IT IS I--
THE COLLECTOR!
NOBODY'S GOT DEEPER POCKETS THAN TANELEER TIVAN.
HE'S THE BADDEST COSMIC ELDER OF THEM ALL.
HMM. DOESN'T RING A BELL.
WAIT--IF THIS IS ABOUT THAT WHITE TIGER I SHOT IN LAS VEGAS A FEW YEARS BACK--I CAN EXPLAIN EVERYTHING.
INTERESTING.
MAY I SEE IT AGAIN?
OF COURSE.
KERANG
YEAAAAAOW!
MOTHER PUSS BUCKET!
SHAME THE NULLIFIER WAS A BUST.
IT'S OUT THERE SOMEWHERE.

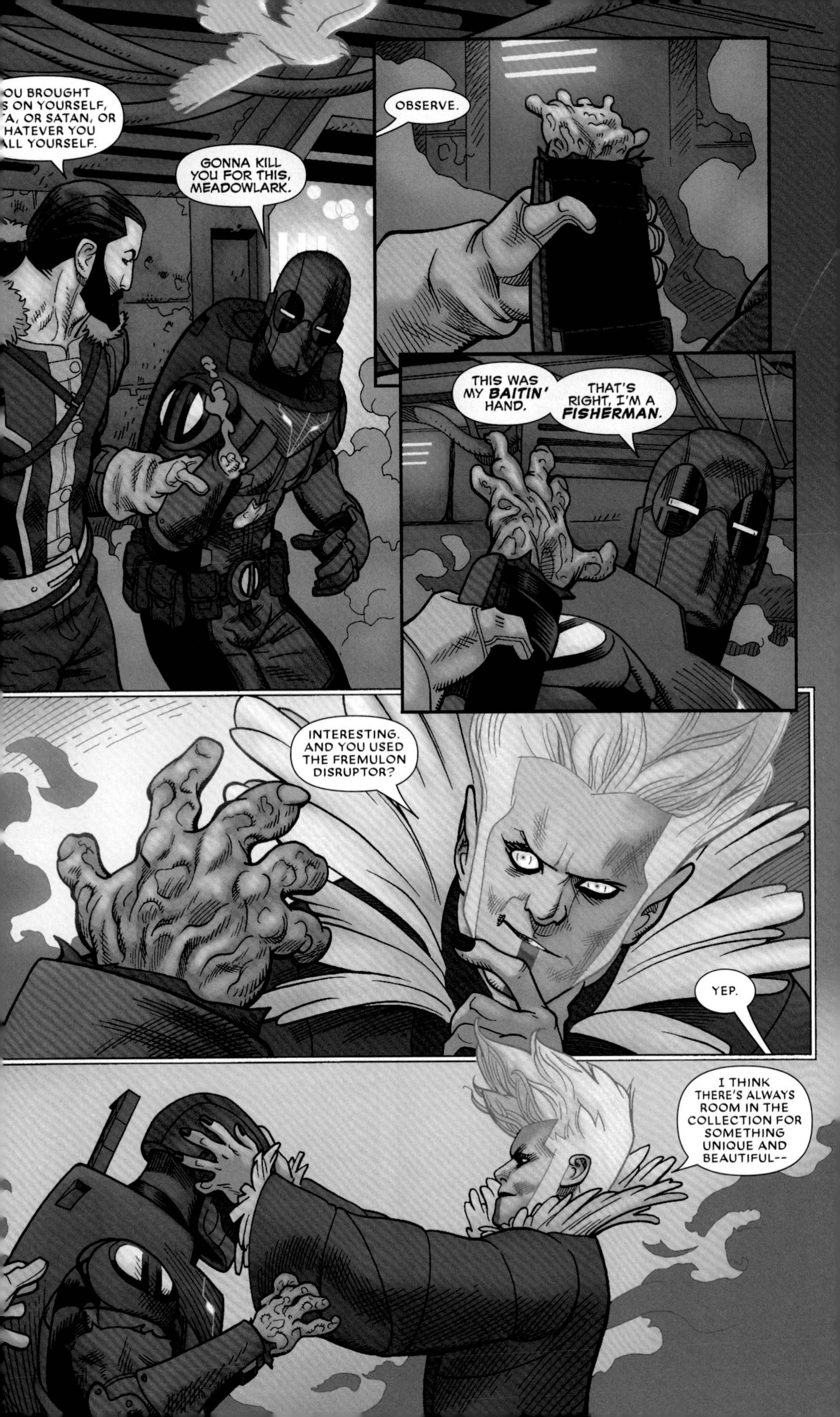
OU BROUGHT S ON YOURSELF, 'A, OR SATAN, OR HATEVER YOU ALL YOURSELF.
GONNA KILL YOU FOR THIS, MEADOWLARK.
OBSERVE.
THIS WAS MY BAITIN' HAND.
THAT'S RIGHT, I'M A FISHERMAN.
INTERESTING. AND YOU USED THE FREMULON DISRUPTOR?
YEP.
I THINK THERE'S ALWAYS ROOM IN THE COLLECTION FOR SOMETHING UNIQUE AND BEAUTIFUL--

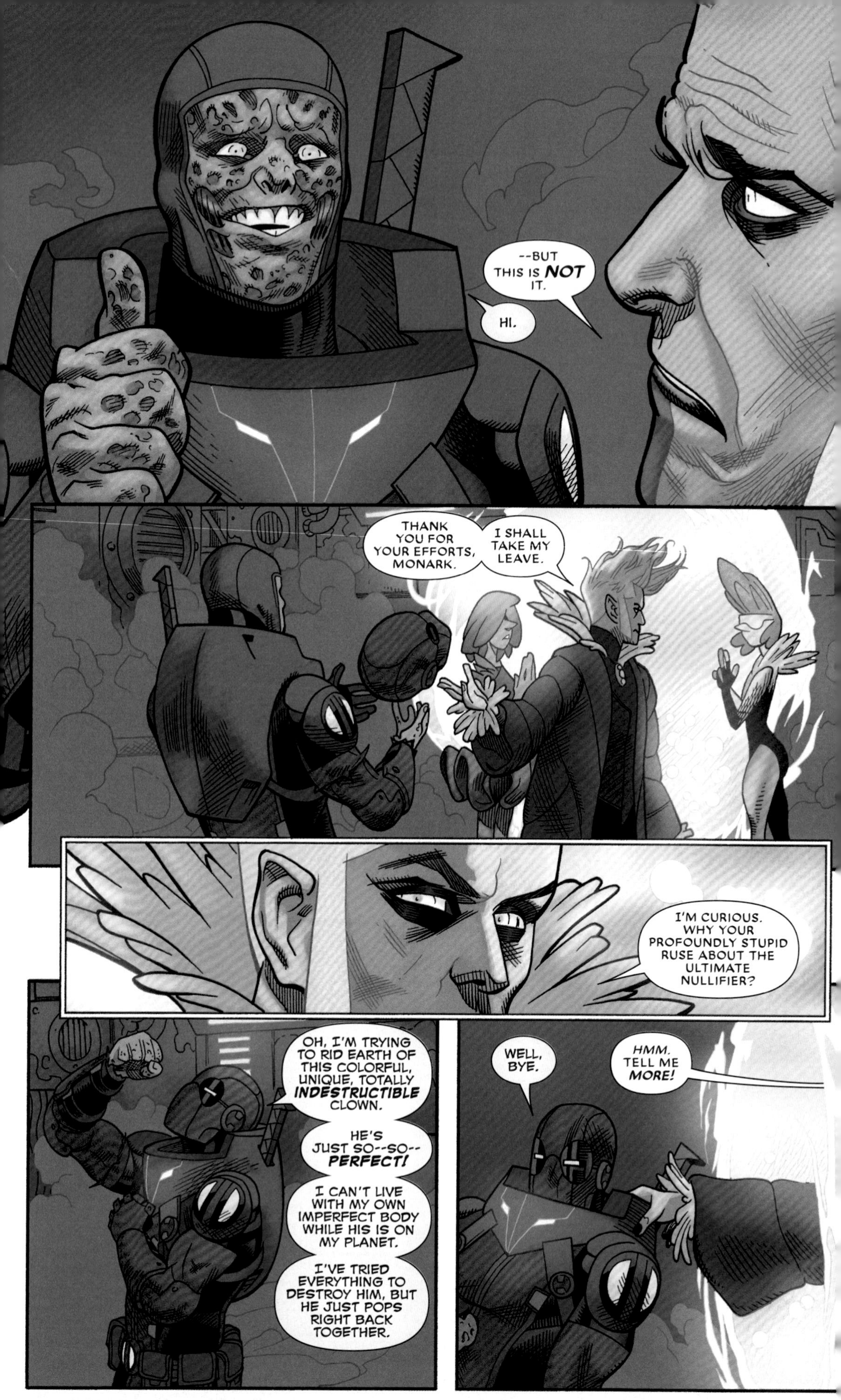
HI.
--BUT THIS IS NOT IT.
THANK YOU FOR YOUR EFFORTS, MONARK.
I SHALL TAKE MY LEAVE.
I'M CURIOUS. WHY YOUR PROFOUNDLY STUPID RUSE ABOUT THE ULTIMATE NULLIFIER?
OH, I'M TRYING TO RID EARTH OF THIS COLORFUL, UNIQUE, TOTALLY INDESTRUCTIBLE CLOWN.
HE'S JUST SO--SO--PERFECT!
I CAN'T LIVE WITH MY OWN IMPERFECT BODY WHILE HIS IS ON MY PLANET.
I'VE TRIED EVERYTHING TO DESTROY HIM, BUT HE JUST POPS RIGHT BACK TOGETHER.
HMM. TELL ME MORE!
WELL, BYE.

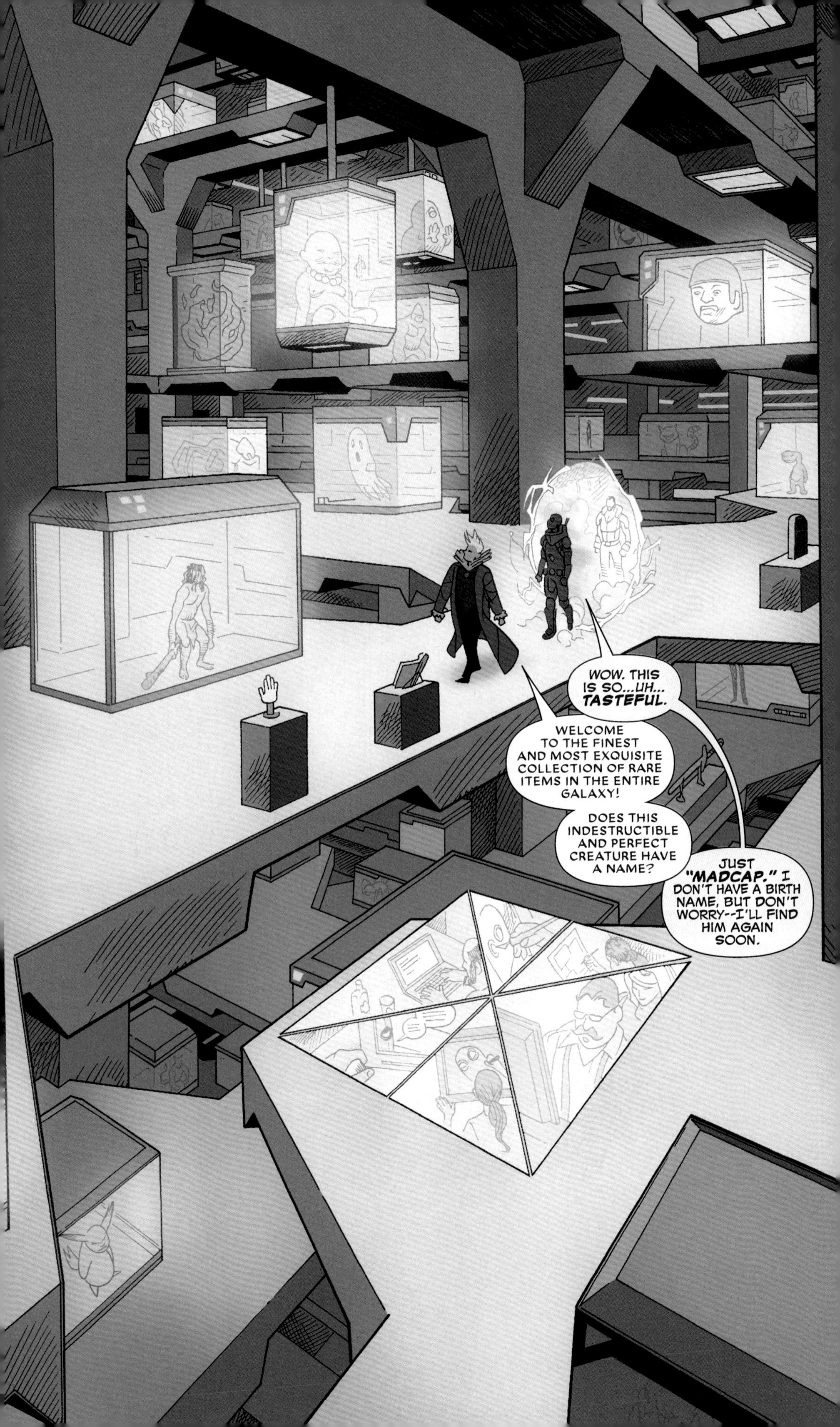
WOW. THIS IS SO...UH... ***TASTEFUL.***
WELCOME TO THE FINEST AND MOST EXQUISITE COLLECTION OF RARE ITEMS IN THE ENTIRE GALAXY!
DOES THIS INDESTRUCTIBLE AND PERFECT CREATURE HAVE A NAME?
JUST ***"MADCAP."*** I DON'T HAVE A BIRTH NAME, BUT DON'T WORRY--I'LL FIND HIM AGAIN SOON.

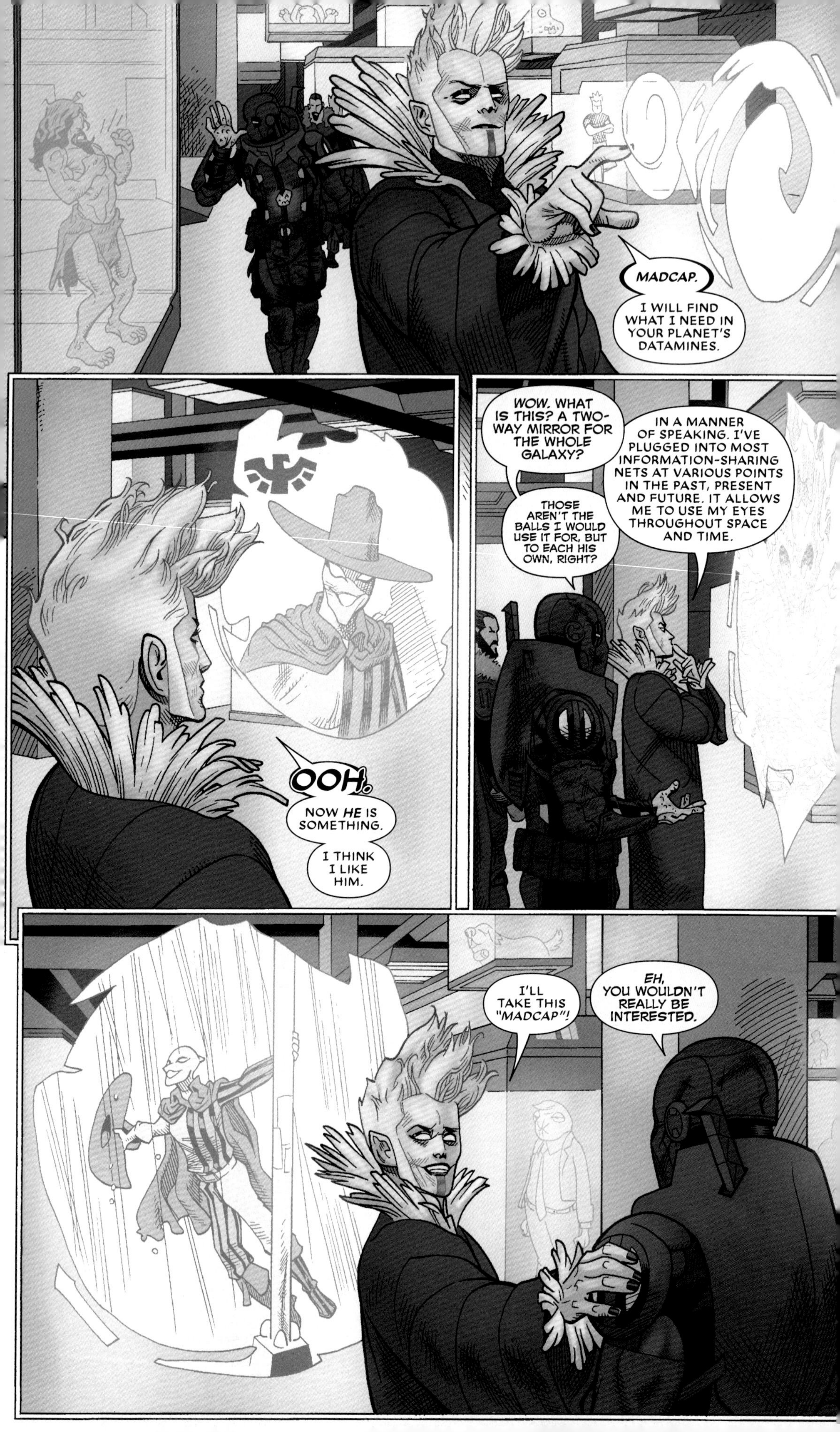

MADCAP.
I WILL FIND WHAT I NEED IN YOUR PLANET'S DATAMINES.
OOH.
NOW HE IS SOMETHING.
I THINK I LIKE HIM.
WOW. WHAT IS THIS? A TWO-WAY MIRROR FOR THE WHOLE GALAXY?
IN A MANNER OF SPEAKING. I'VE PLUGGED INTO MOST INFORMATION-SHARING NETS AT VARIOUS POINTS IN THE PAST, PRESENT AND FUTURE. IT ALLOWS ME TO USE MY EYES THROUGHOUT SPACE AND TIME.
THOSE AREN'T THE BALLS I WOULD USE IT FOR, BUT TO EACH HIS OWN, RIGHT?
I'LL TAKE THIS "MADCAP"!
EH, YOU WOULDN'T REALLY BE INTERESTED.

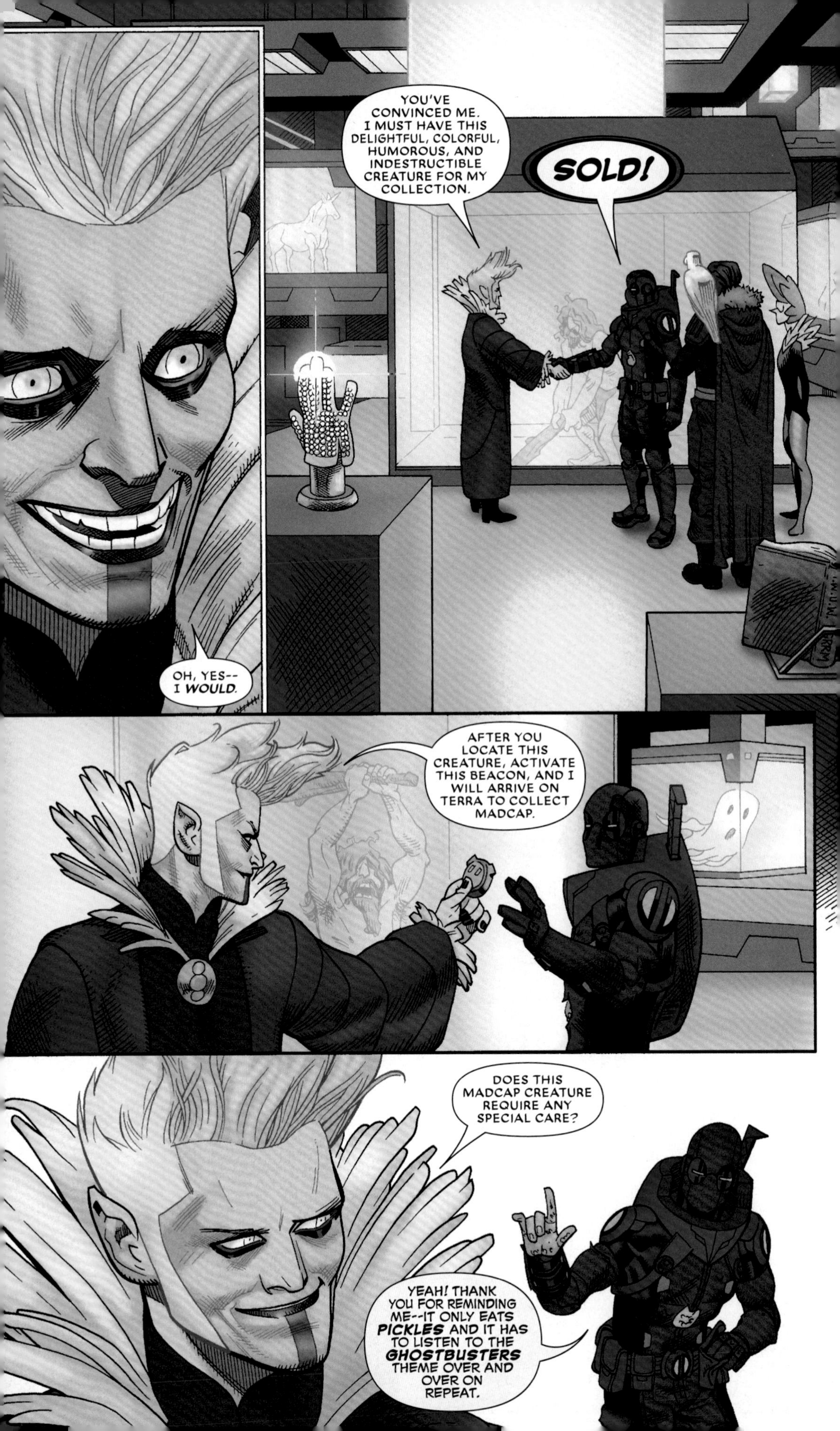
YOU'VE CONVINCED ME. I MUST HAVE THIS DELIGHTFUL, COLORFUL, HUMOROUS, AND INDESTRUCTIBLE CREATURE FOR MY COLLECTION.
SOLD!
OH, YES-- I *WOULD*.
AFTER YOU LOCATE THIS CREATURE, ACTIVATE THIS BEACON, AND I WILL ARRIVE ON TERRA TO COLLECT MADCAP.
DOES THIS MADCAP CREATURE REQUIRE ANY SPECIAL CARE?
YEAH! THANK YOU FOR REMINDING ME--IT ONLY EATS **PICKLES** AND IT HAS TO LISTEN TO THE ***GHOSTBUSTERS*** THEME OVER AND OVER ON REPEAT.

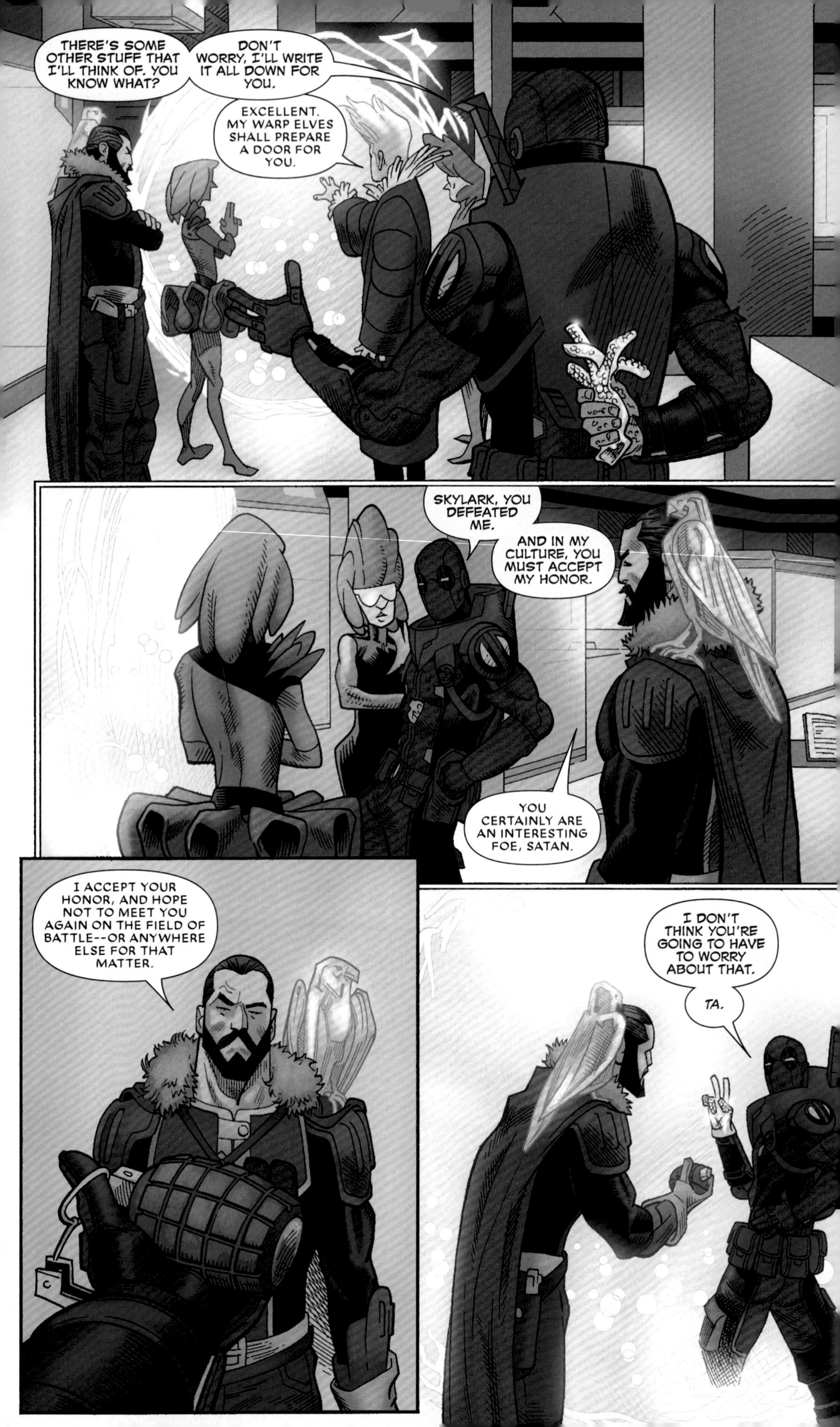
THERE'S SOME OTHER STUFF THAT I'LL THINK OF. YOU KNOW WHAT?
DON'T WORRY, I'LL WRITE IT ALL DOWN FOR YOU.
EXCELLENT. MY WARP ELVES SHALL PREPARE A DOOR FOR YOU.
SKYLARK, YOU DEFEATED ME.
AND IN MY CULTURE, YOU MUST ACCEPT MY HONOR.
YOU CERTAINLY ARE AN INTERESTING FOE, SATAN.
I ACCEPT YOUR HONOR, AND HOPE NOT TO MEET YOU AGAIN ON THE FIELD OF BATTLE--OR ANYWHERE ELSE FOR THAT MATTER.
I DON'T THINK YOU'RE GOING TO HAVE TO WORRY ABOUT THAT.
TA.

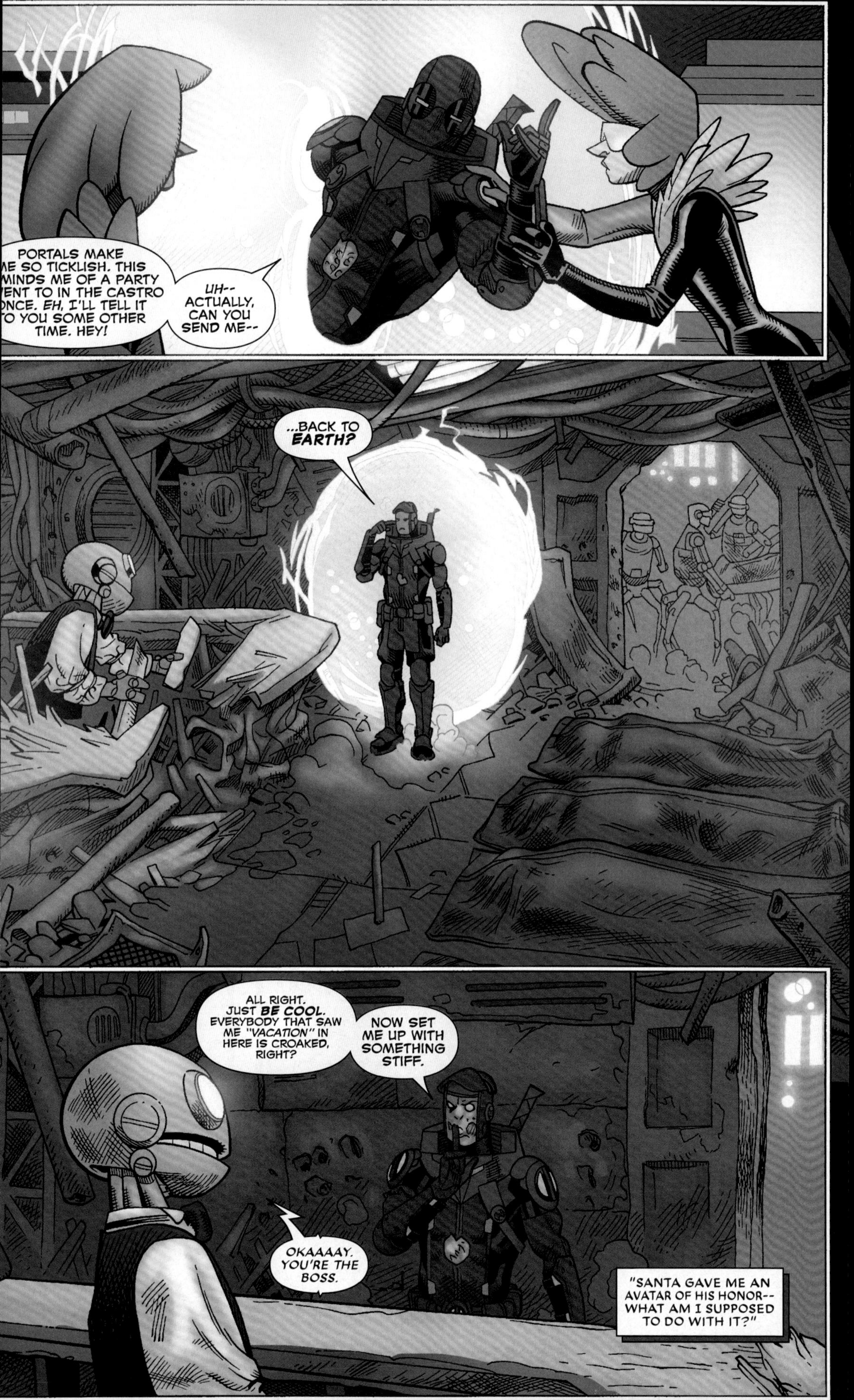
PORTALS MAKE ME SO TICKLISH. THIS MINDS ME OF A PARTY ENT TO IN THE CASTRO NCE. EH, I'LL TELL IT O YOU SOME OTHER TIME. HEY!
UH-- ACTUALLY, CAN YOU SEND ME--
...BACK TO EARTH?
ALL RIGHT. JUST BE COOL. EVERYBODY THAT SAW ME "VACATION" IN HERE IS CROAKED, RIGHT?
NOW SET ME UP WITH SOMETHING STIFF.
OKAAAAY. YOU'RE THE BOSS.
"SANTA GAVE ME AN AVATAR OF HIS HONOR-- WHAT AM I SUPPOSED TO DO WITH IT?"

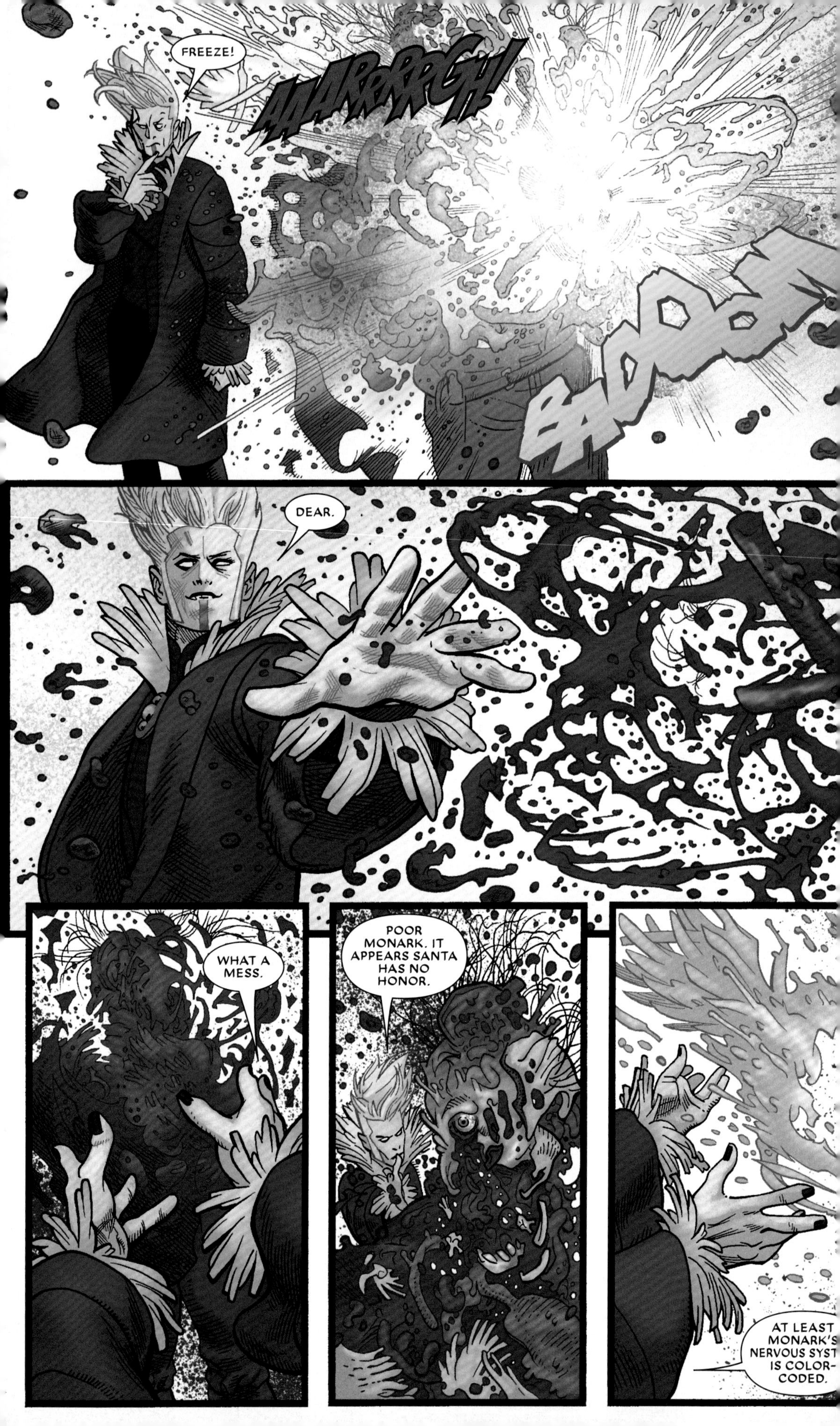

FREEZE!
AAAARRRRRGH!
BADOOM
DEAR.
WHAT A MESS.
POOR MONARK. IT APPEARS SANTA HAS NO HONOR.
AT LEAST MONARK'S NERVOUS SYST IS COLOR-CODED.

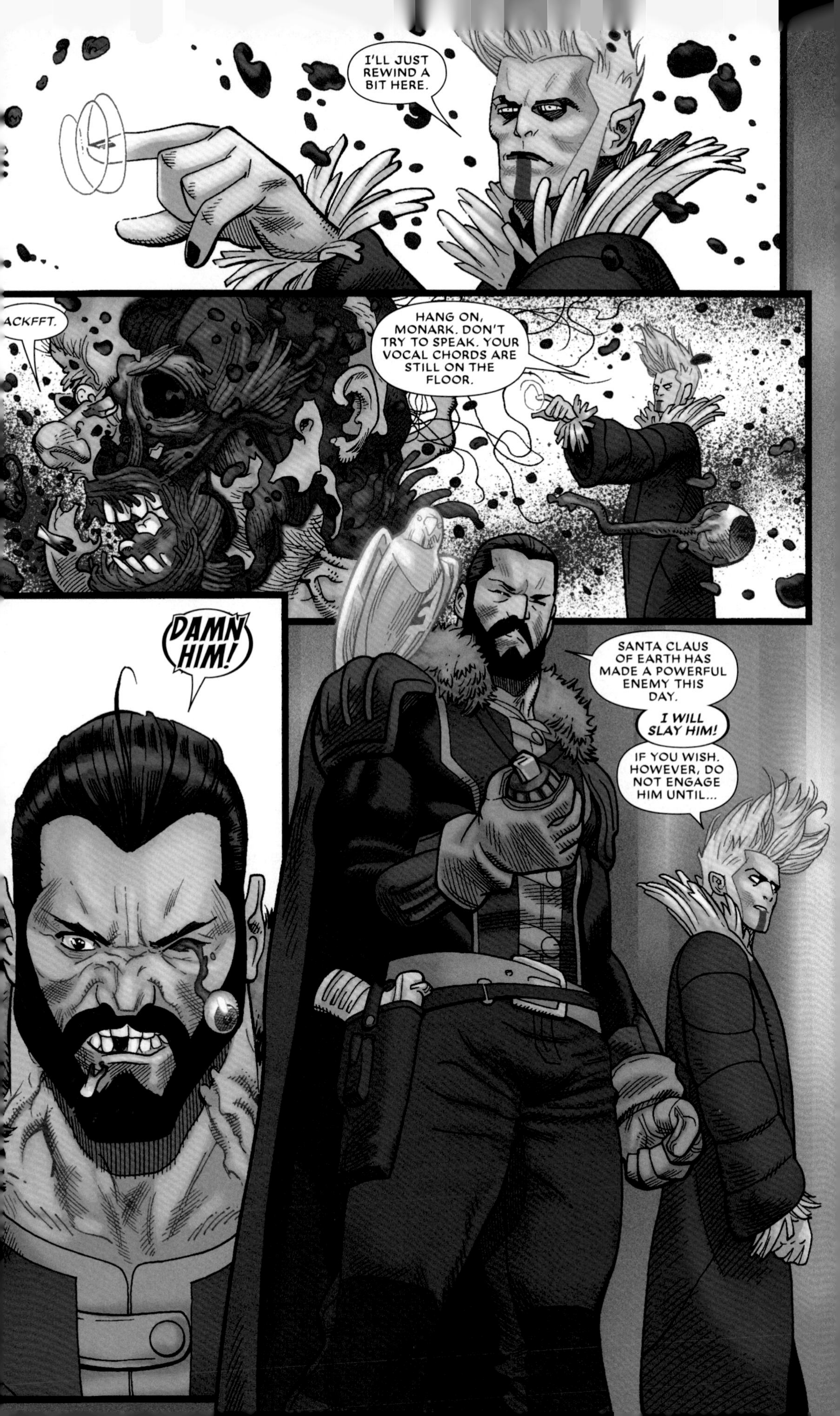
I'LL JUST REWIND A BIT HERE.
ACKFFT.
HANG ON, MONARK. DON'T TRY TO SPEAK. YOUR VOCAL CHORDS ARE STILL ON THE FLOOR.
DAMN HIM!
SANTA CLAUS OF EARTH HAS MADE A POWERFUL ENEMY THIS DAY.
I WILL SLAY HIM!
IF YOU WISH. HOWEVER, DO NOT ENGAGE HIM UNTIL...

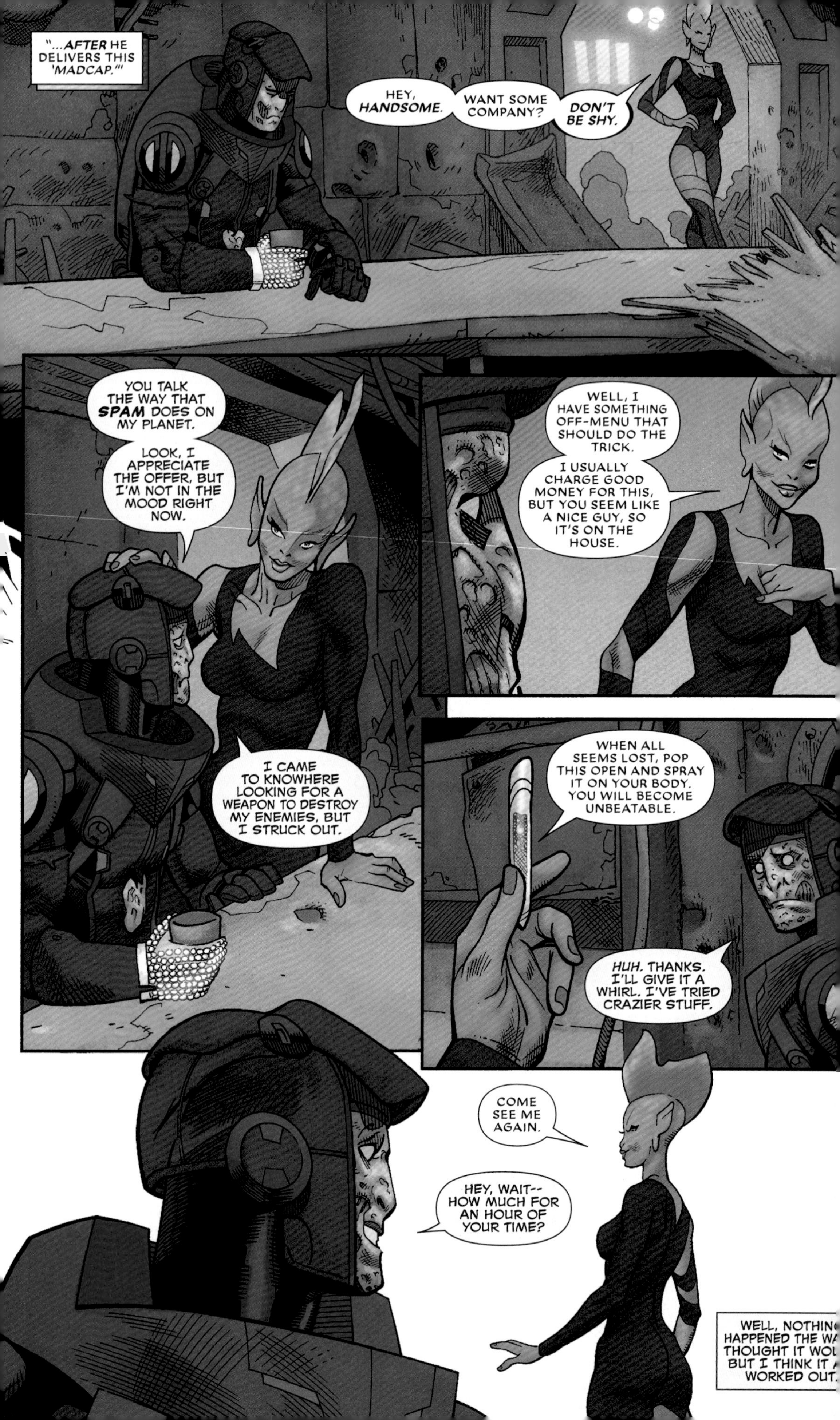

"...*AFTER* HE DELIVERS THIS 'MADCAP.'"
HEY, *HANDSOME.*
WANT SOME COMPANY?
DON'T BE SHY.
YOU TALK THE WAY THAT *SPAM* DOES ON MY PLANET.
LOOK, I APPRECIATE THE OFFER, BUT I'M NOT IN THE MOOD RIGHT NOW.
I CAME TO KNOWHERE LOOKING FOR A WEAPON TO DESTROY MY ENEMIES, BUT I STRUCK OUT.
WELL, I HAVE SOMETHING OFF-MENU THAT SHOULD DO THE TRICK.
I USUALLY CHARGE GOOD MONEY FOR THIS, BUT YOU SEEM LIKE A NICE GUY, SO IT'S ON THE HOUSE.
WHEN ALL SEEMS LOST, POP THIS OPEN AND SPRAY IT ON YOUR BODY. YOU WILL BECOME UNBEATABLE.
HUH. THANKS. I'LL GIVE IT A WHIRL. I'VE TRIED CRAZIER STUFF.
COME SEE ME AGAIN.
HEY, WAIT-- HOW MUCH FOR AN HOUR OF YOUR TIME?

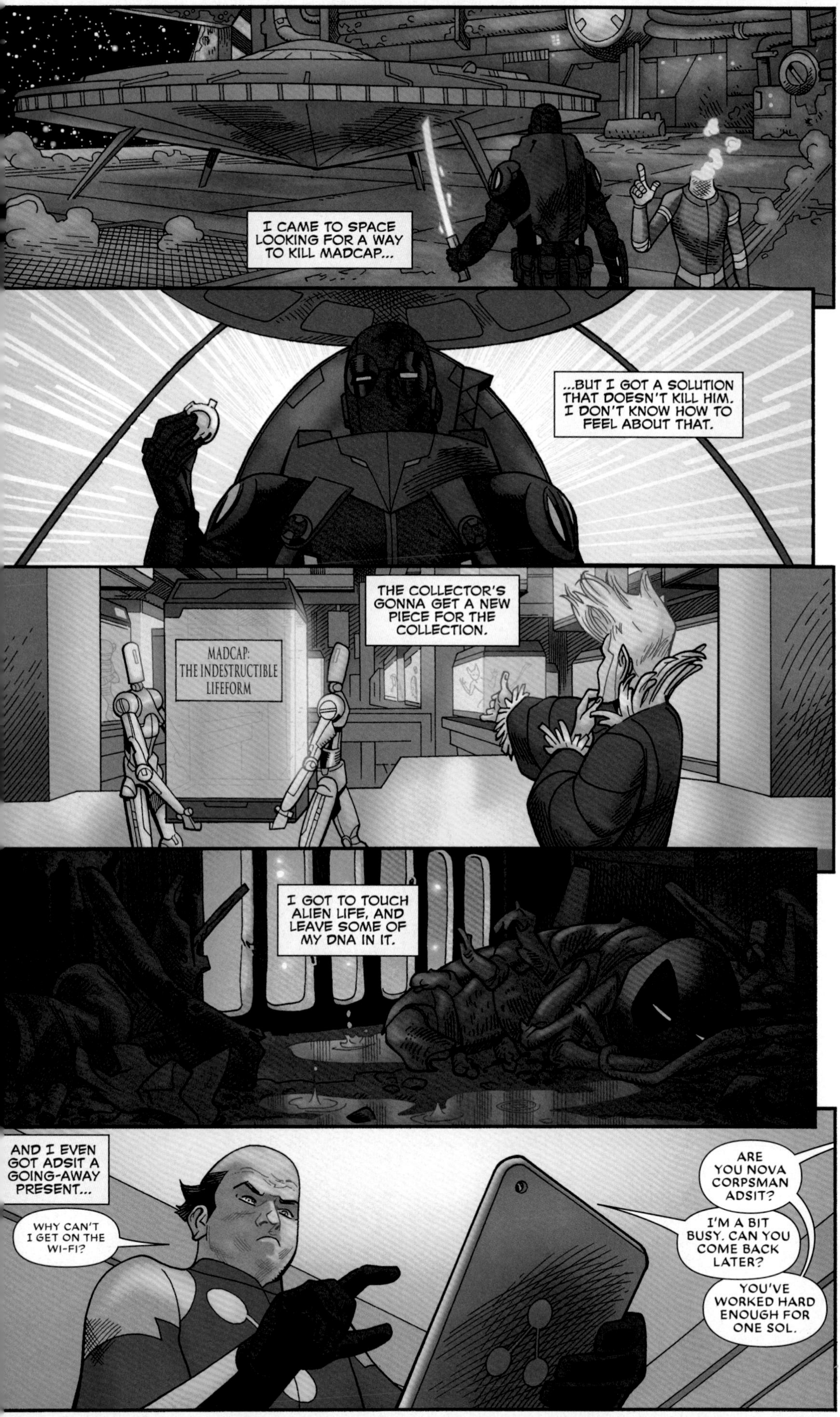
I CAME TO SPACE LOOKING FOR A WAY TO KILL MADCAP...
...BUT I GOT A SOLUTION THAT DOESN'T KILL HIM. I DON'T KNOW HOW TO FEEL ABOUT THAT.
MADCAP: THE INDESTRUCTIBLE LIFEFORM
THE COLLECTOR'S GONNA GET A NEW PIECE FOR THE COLLECTION.
I GOT TO TOUCH ALIEN LIFE, AND LEAVE SOME OF MY DNA IN IT.
AND I EVEN GOT ADSIT A GOING-AWAY PRESENT...
WHY CAN'T I GET ON THE WI-FI?
ARE YOU NOVA CORPSMAN ADSIT?
I'M A BIT BUSY. CAN YOU COME BACK LATER?
YOU'VE WORKED HARD ENOUGH FOR ONE SOL.

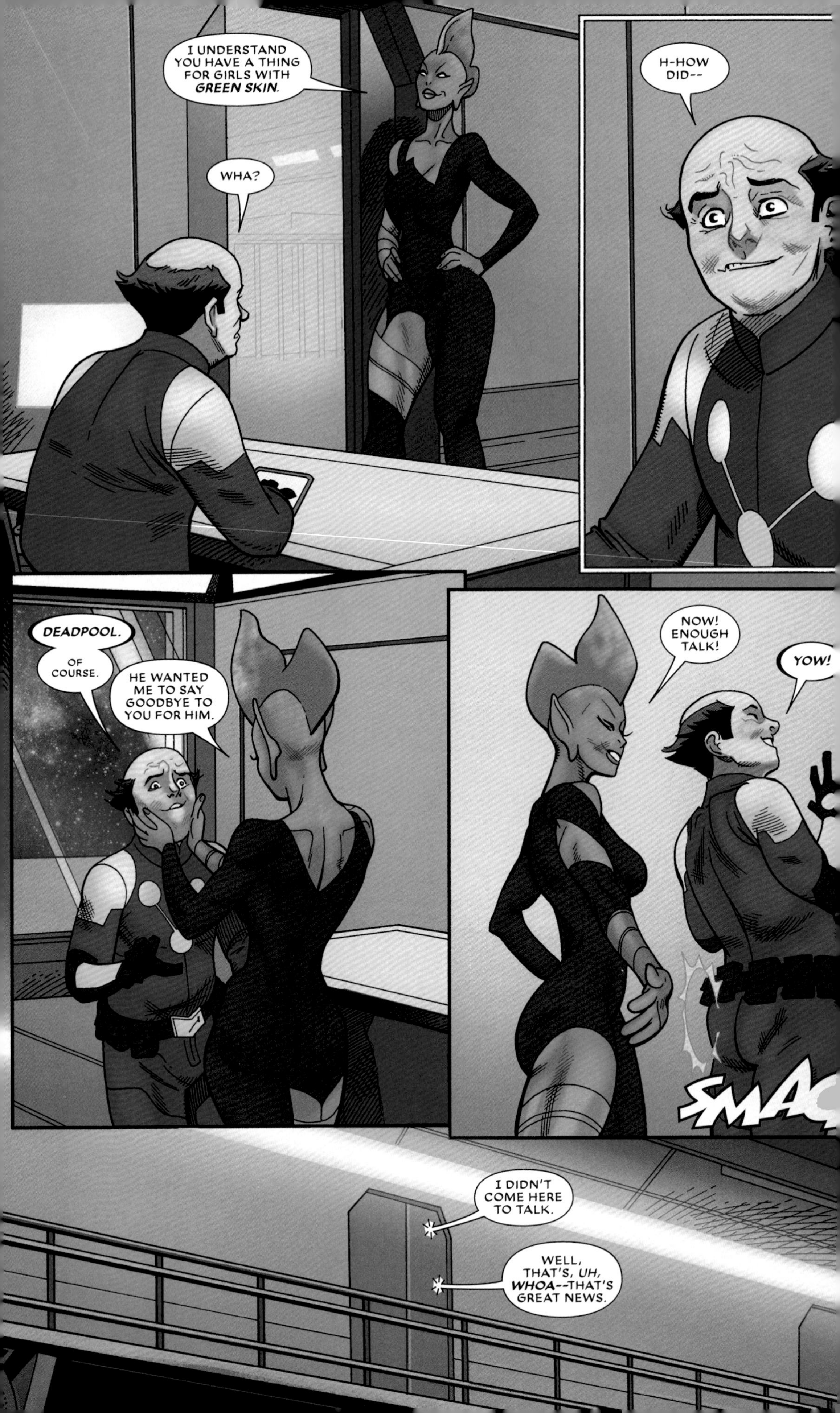
I UNDERSTAND YOU HAVE A THING FOR GIRLS WITH GREEN SKIN.
WHA?
H-HOW DID--
DEADPOOL.
OF COURSE.
HE WANTED ME TO SAY GOODBYE TO YOU FOR HIM.
NOW! ENOUGH TALK!
YOW!
SMAC
I DIDN'T COME HERE TO TALK.
WELL, THAT'S, UH, WHOA--THAT'S GREAT NEWS.

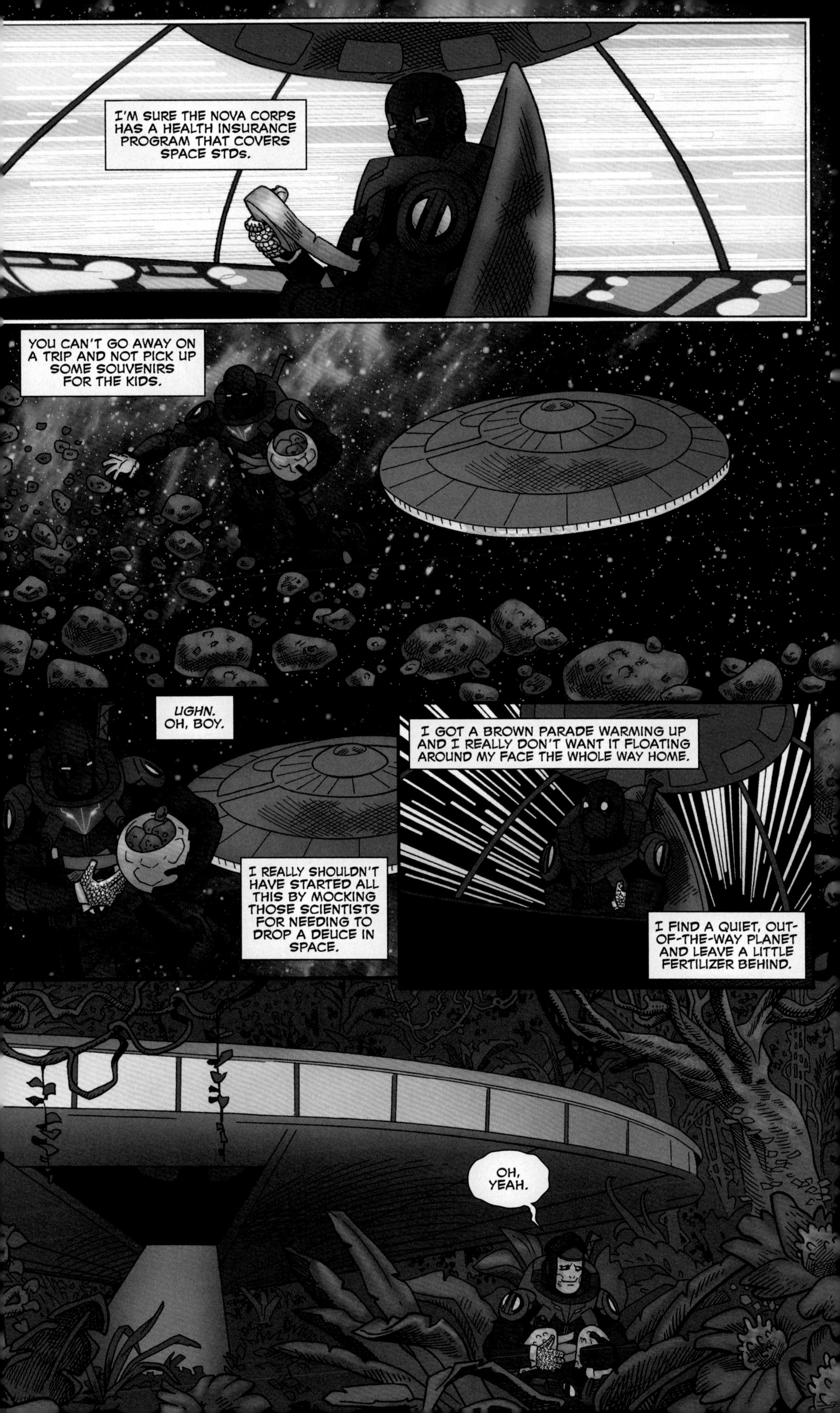
I'M SURE THE NOVA CORPS HAS A HEALTH INSURANCE PROGRAM THAT COVERS SPACE STDs.
YOU CAN'T GO AWAY ON A TRIP AND NOT PICK UP SOME SOUVENIRS FOR THE KIDS.
UGHN. OH, BOY.
I REALLY SHOULDN'T HAVE STARTED ALL THIS BY MOCKING THOSE SCIENTISTS FOR NEEDING TO DROP A DEUCE IN SPACE.
I GOT A BROWN PARADE WARMING UP AND I REALLY DON'T WANT IT FLOATING AROUND MY FACE THE WHOLE WAY HOME.
I FIND A QUIET, OUT-OF-THE-WAY PLANET AND LEAVE A LITTLE FERTILIZER BEHIND.
OH, YEAH.

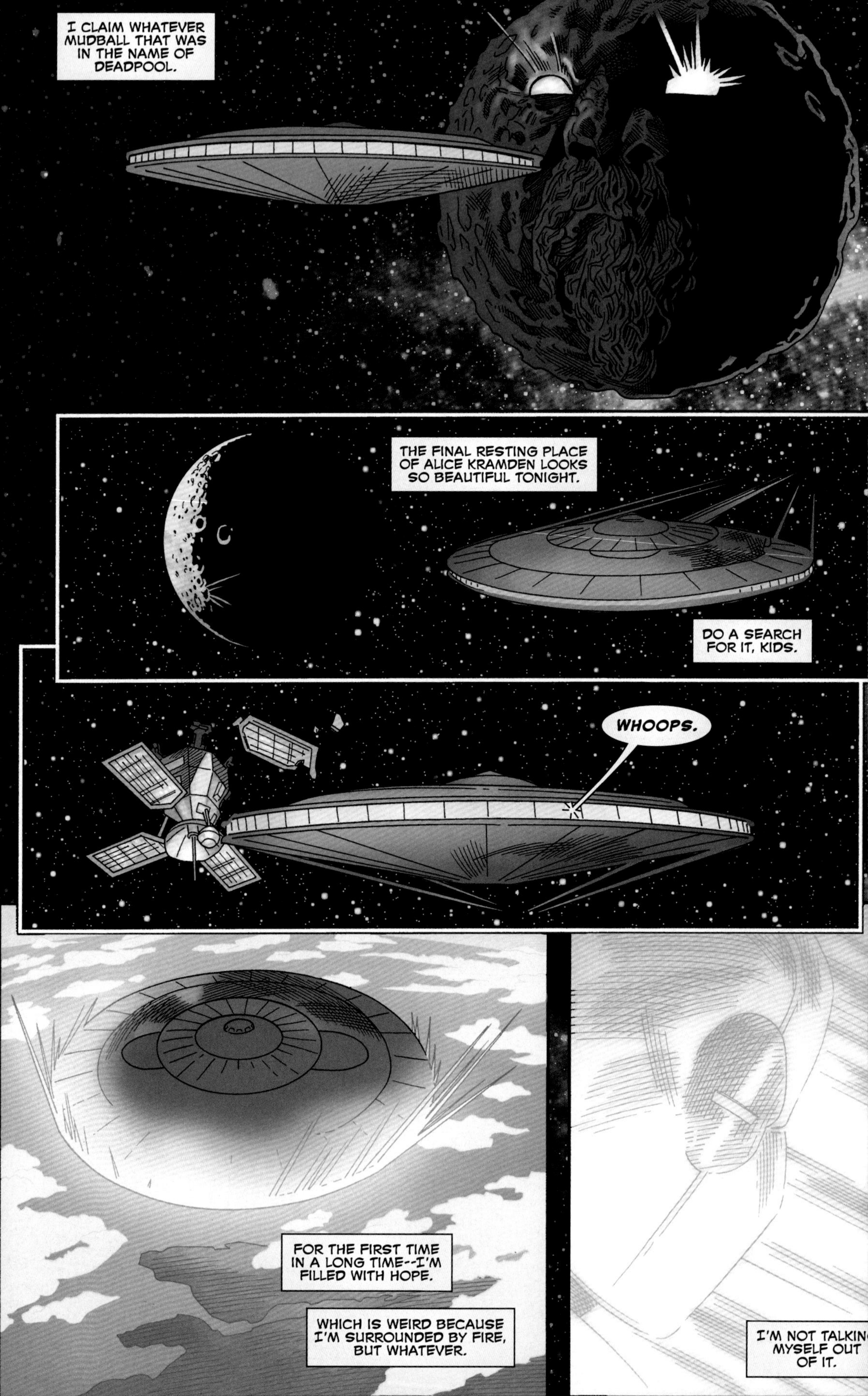
I CLAIM WHATEVER MUDBALL THAT WAS IN THE NAME OF DEADPOOL.
THE FINAL RESTING PLACE OF ALICE KRAMDEN LOOKS SO BEAUTIFUL TONIGHT.
DO A SEARCH FOR IT, KIDS.
WHOOPS.
FOR THE FIRST TIME IN A LONG TIME--I'M FILLED WITH HOPE.
WHICH IS WEIRD BECAUSE I'M SURROUNDED BY FIRE, BUT WHATEVER.
I'M NOT TALKIN MYSELF OUT OF IT.

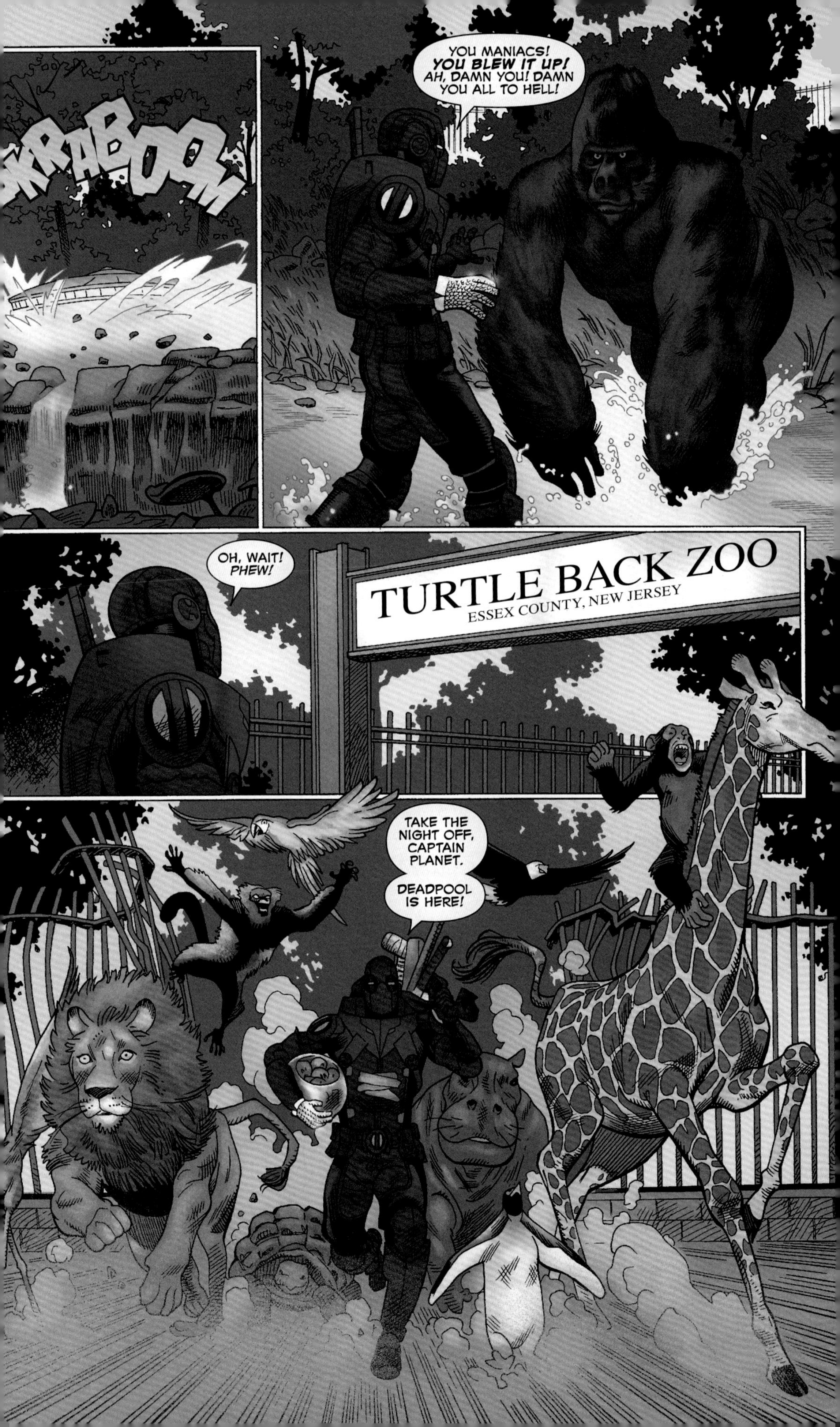
KRABOOM
YOU MANIACS! YOU BLEW IT UP! AH, DAMN YOU! DAMN YOU ALL TO HELL!
OH, WAIT! PHEW!
TURTLE BACK ZOO
ESSEX COUNTY, NEW JERSEY
TAKE THE NIGHT OFF, CAPTAIN PLANET.
DEADPOOL IS HERE!

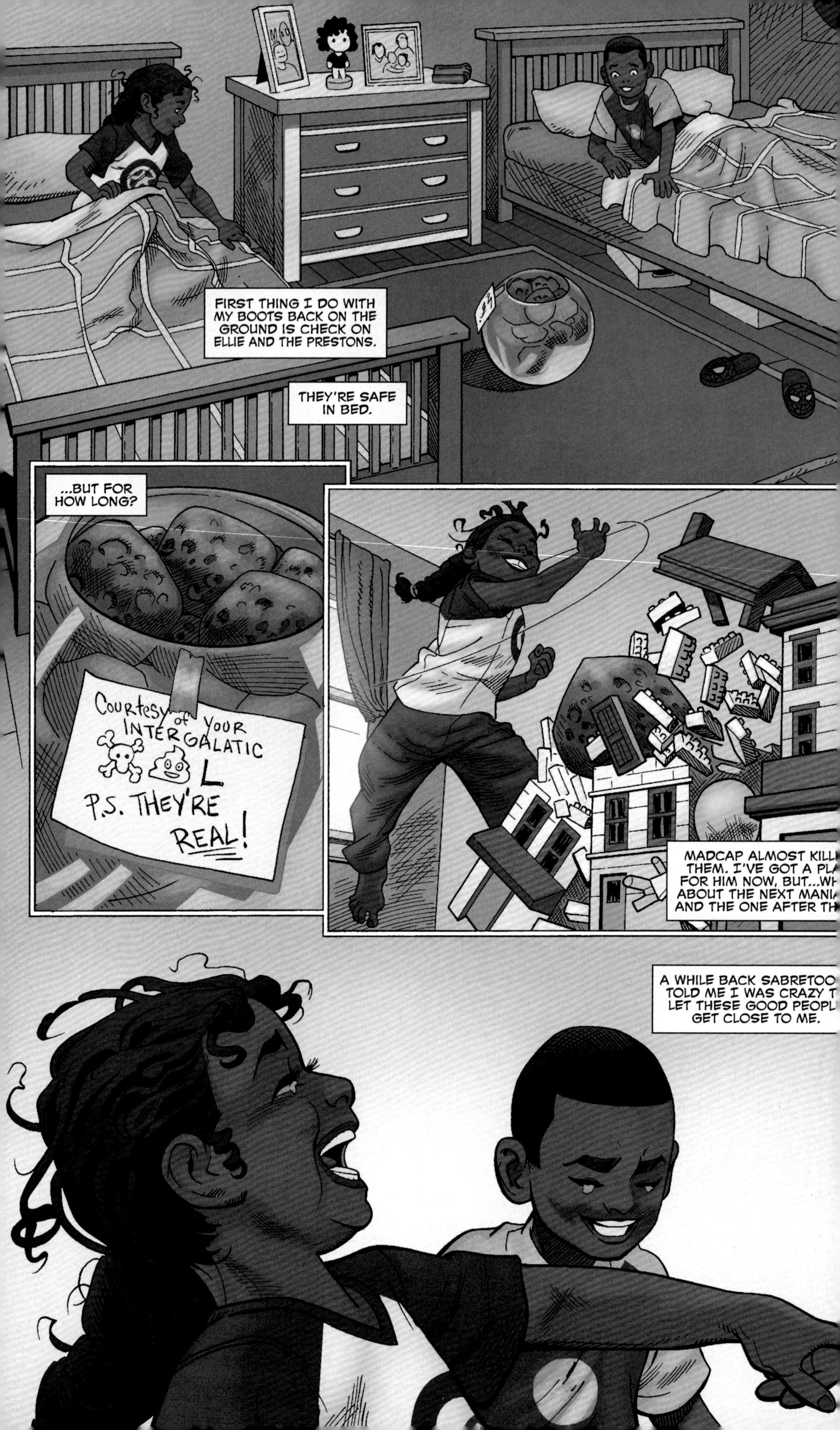
FIRST THING I DO WITH MY BOOTS BACK ON THE GROUND IS CHECK ON ELLIE AND THE PRESTONS.
THEY'RE SAFE IN BED.
...BUT FOR HOW LONG?
Courtesy of your INTERGALATIC
L
P.S. THEY'RE REAL!
MADCAP ALMOST KILL THEM. I'VE GOT A PLA FOR HIM NOW, BUT...WH ABOUT THE NEXT MANI AND THE ONE AFTER TH
A WHILE BACK SABRETOO TOLD ME I WAS CRAZY T LET THESE GOOD PEOPL GET CLOSE TO ME.

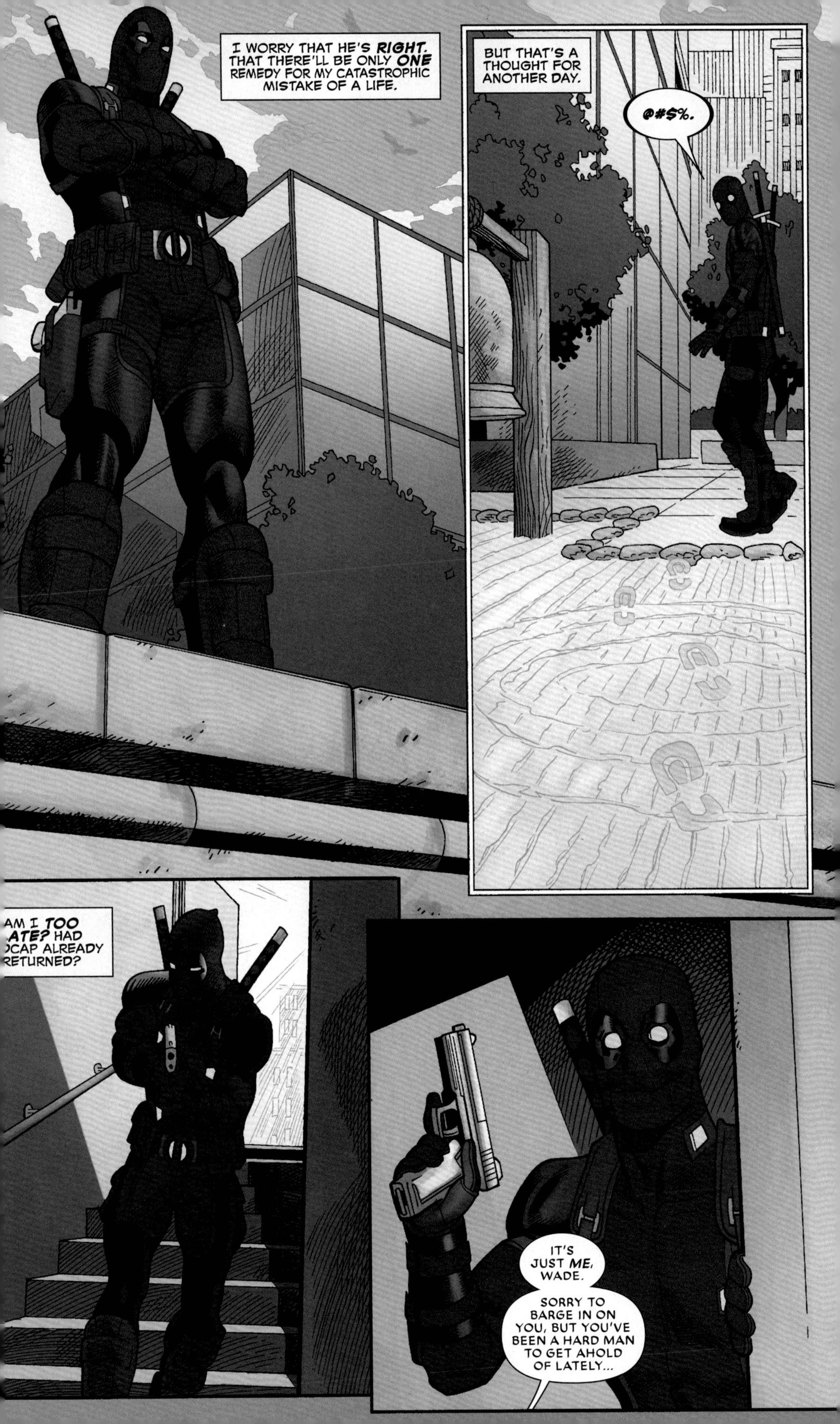
I WORRY THAT HE'S *RIGHT*. THAT THERE'LL BE ONLY *ONE* REMEDY FOR MY CATASTROPHIC MISTAKE OF A LIFE.
BUT THAT'S A THOUGHT FOR ANOTHER DAY.
@#$%.
AM I *TOO* ATE? HAD OCAP ALREADY RETURNED?
IT'S JUST *ME*, WADE.
SORRY TO BARGE IN ON YOU, BUT YOU'VE BEEN A HARD MAN TO GET AHOLD OF LATELY...

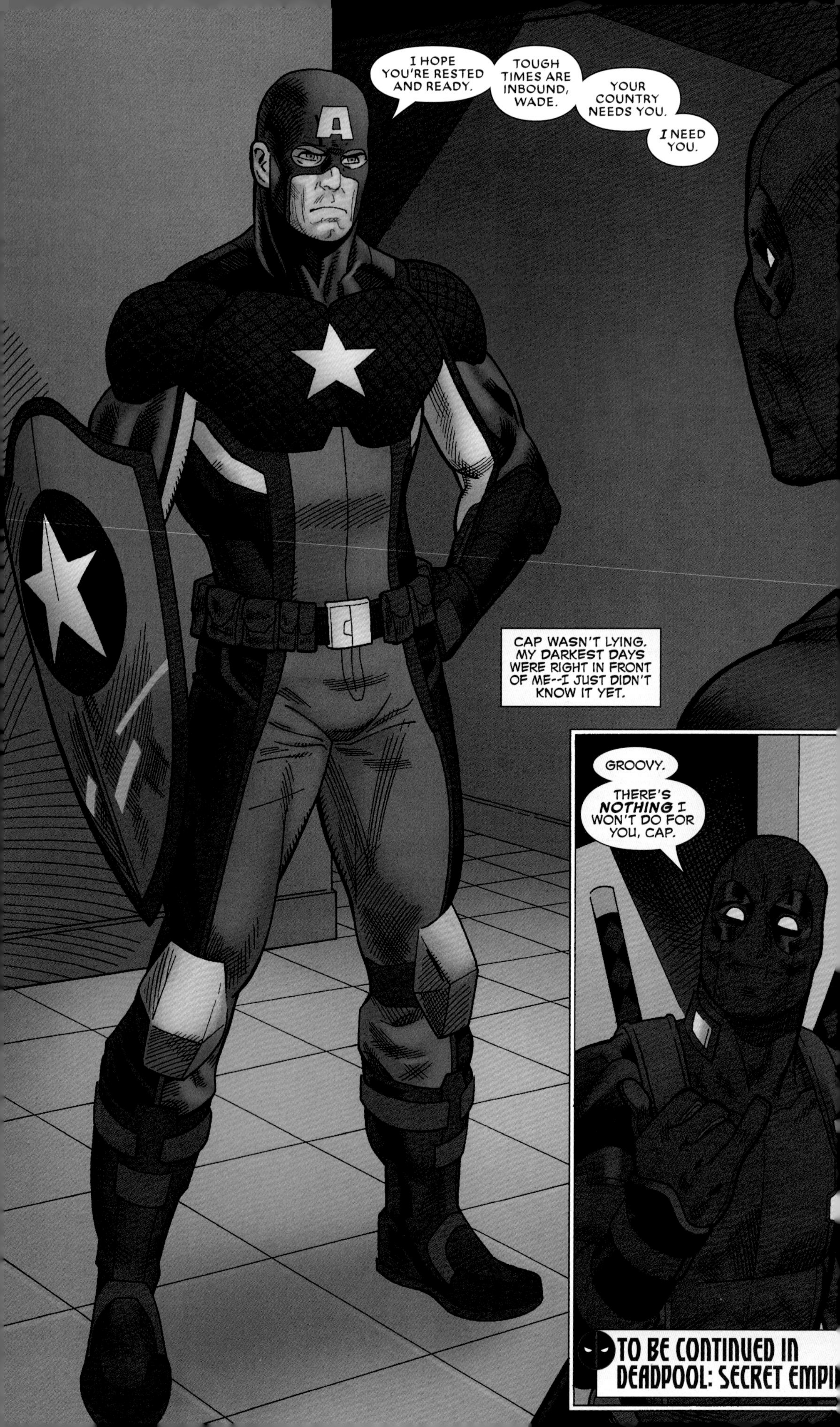
I HOPE YOU'RE RESTED AND READY.
TOUGH TIMES ARE INBOUND, WADE.
YOUR COUNTRY NEEDS YOU.
I NEED YOU.
CAP WASN'T LYING. MY DARKEST DAYS WERE RIGHT IN FRONT OF ME--I JUST DIDN'T KNOW IT YET.
GROOVY.
THERE'S NOTHING I WON'T DO FOR YOU, CAP.
TO BE CONTINUED IN DEADPOOL: SECRET EMPI

Hey there, 'Pool Partiers!

Welcome to the madness that is the *Deadpool* #SecretComic Variant covers! As you may know, variant covers are a pretty common thing in the comics industry right now — special additional covers usually created by top-tier artists that sometimes end up being more rare than the main cover of the series. We in the Deadpool office wanted to get into this variant cover game...but we decided to turn the whole thing on its head.

The following 20 pages of comic book were originally printed as 20 variant covers over 20 issues of the ongoing *Deadpool* series. Each issue, those intrepid fans who sought out these extra-special issues got one page more of the ongoing story of Deadpool's cover adventure, along with the chance to meet one of the most important characters in Marvel history — one who affects every single issue we've published for the last number of years.

This technically isn't the first time they've been collected — they were in *Deadpool: The Adamantium Collection* first. But... come on. I think anyone who is physically able to carry that massive book deserved to get a little treat, am I right? For those of us without bodybuilding arms, this is our first chance to see the full story of the *Deadpool* #SecretComic issue #1 in one place.

Oh, what's that? You noticed that I said "issue #1"? It is true — we are still doing #SecretComic variants as of this writing! Issue #2 is well under way and will likely be included in some future collection...but don't wait! Track down the originals today and you can be in on the secret before anyone else!

Be seeing you!

Deadpool's Pal,
Jordan D. White

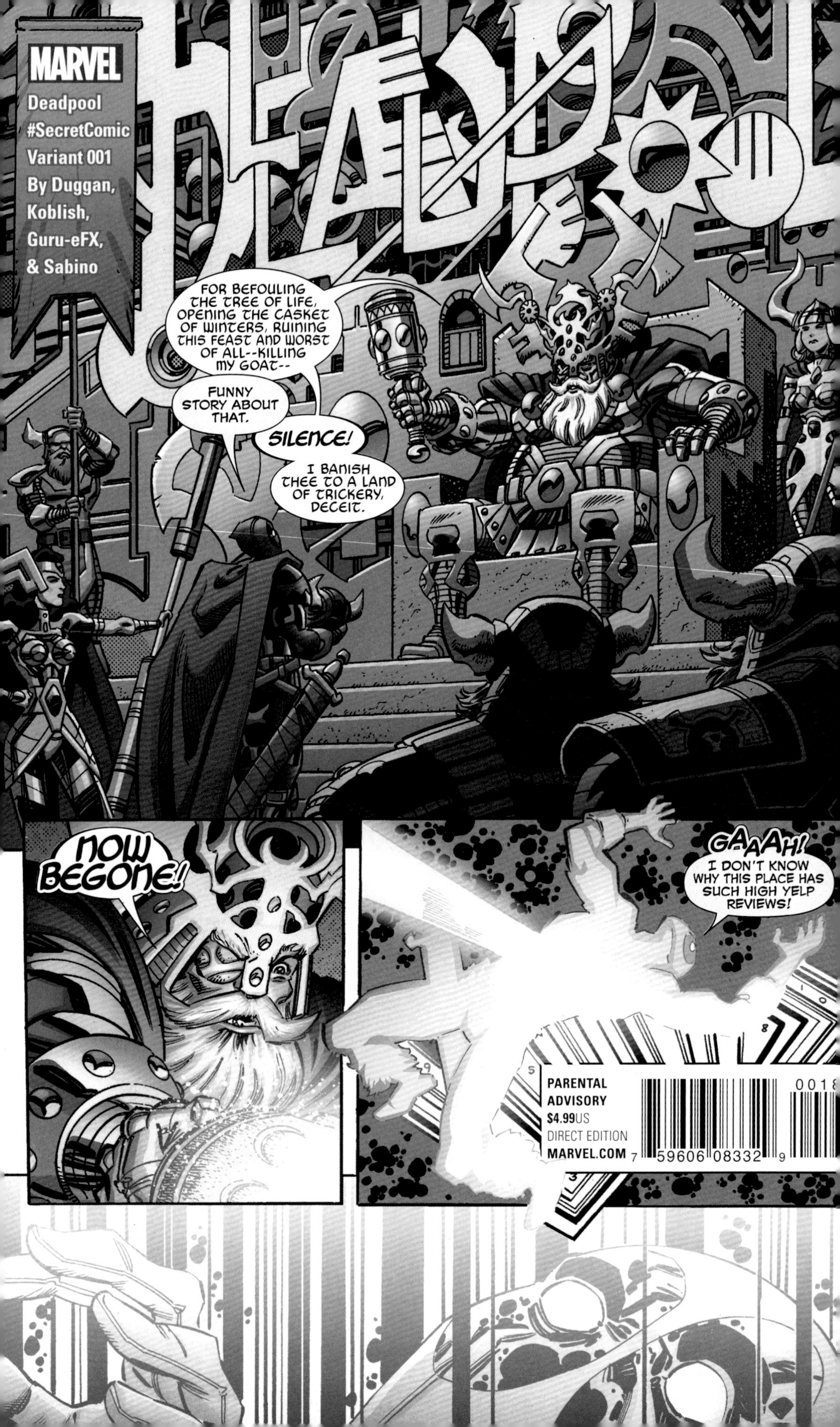
MARVEL
Deadpool #SecretComic Variant 001
By Duggan, Koblish, Guru-eFX, & Sabino
FOR BEFOULING THE TREE OF LIFE, OPENING THE CASKET OF WINTERS, RUINING THIS FEAST AND WORST OF ALL--KILLING MY GOAT--
FUNNY STORY ABOUT THAT.
SILENCE!
I BANISH THEE TO A LAND OF TRICKERY, DECEIT.
NOW BEGONE!
GAAAH!
I DON'T KNOW WHY THIS PLACE HAS SUCH HIGH YELP REVIEWS!
PARENTAL ADVISORY
$4.99US
DIRECT EDITION
MARVEL.COM

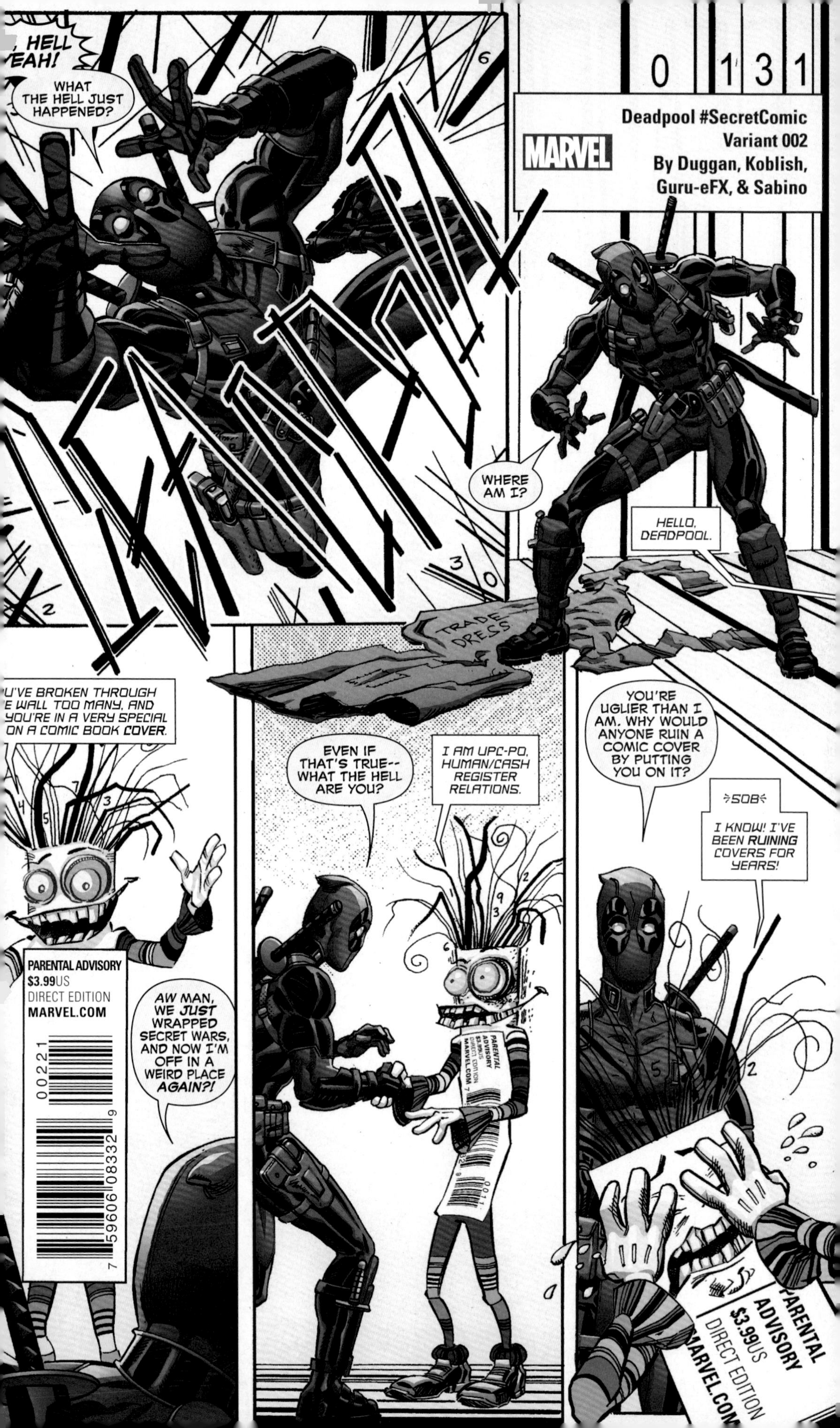
0 131
Deadpool #SecretComic
Variant 002
By Duggan, Koblish, Guru-eFX, & Sabino
MARVEL
, HELL YEAH!
WHAT THE HELL JUST HAPPENED?
WHERE AM I?
HELLO, DEADPOOL.
TRADE DRESS
U'VE BROKEN THROUGH E WALL TOO MANY, AND YOU'RE IN A VERY SPECIAL ON A COMIC BOOK COVER.
PARENTAL ADVISORY
$3.99US
DIRECT EDITION
MARVEL.COM
AW MAN, WE JUST WRAPPED SECRET WARS, AND NOW I'M OFF IN A WEIRD PLACE AGAIN?!
EVEN IF THAT'S TRUE-- WHAT THE HELL ARE YOU?
I AM UPC-PO, HUMAN/CASH REGISTER RELATIONS.
YOU'RE UGLIER THAN I AM. WHY WOULD ANYONE RUIN A COMIC COVER BY PUTTING YOU ON IT?
SOB
I KNOW! I'VE BEEN RUINING COVERS FOR YEARS!
PARENTAL ADVISORY
$3.99US
DIRECT EDITION
MARVEL.COM

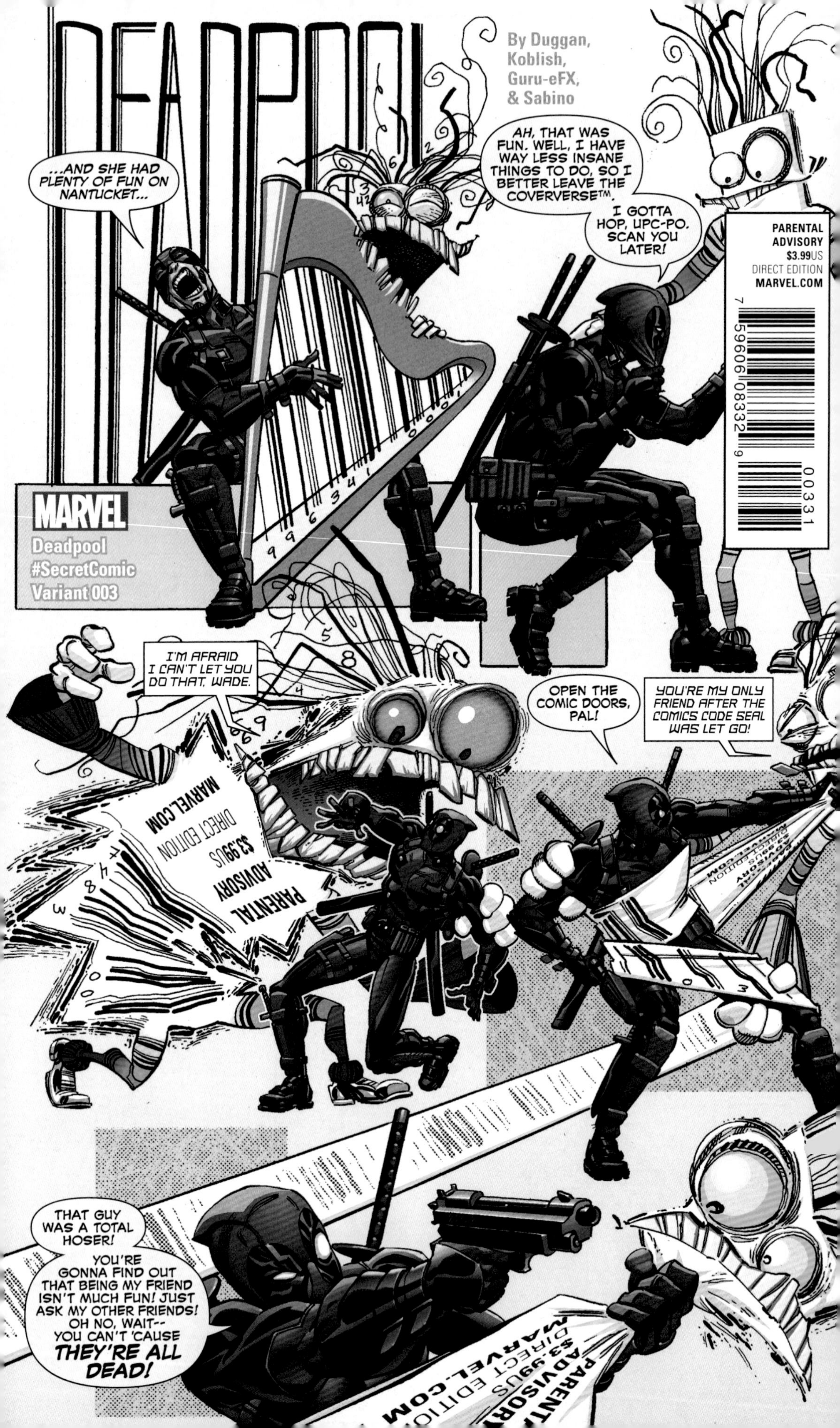
DEADPOOL
By Duggan,
Koblish,
Guru-eFX,
& Sabino
...AND SHE HAD PLENTY OF FUN ON NANTUCKET...
AH, THAT WAS FUN. WELL, I HAVE WAY LESS INSANE THINGS TO DO, SO I BETTER LEAVE THE COVERVERSE™.
I GOTTA HOP, UPC-PO. SCAN YOU LATER!
PARENTAL ADVISORY
$3.99US
DIRECT EDITION
MARVEL.COM
MARVEL
Deadpool
#SecretComic
Variant 003
I'M AFRAID I CAN'T LET YOU DO THAT, WADE.
OPEN THE COMIC DOORS, PAL!
YOU'RE MY ONLY FRIEND AFTER THE COMICS CODE SEAL WAS LET GO!
THAT GUY WAS A TOTAL HOSER!
YOU'RE GONNA FIND OUT THAT BEING MY FRIEND ISN'T MUCH FUN! JUST ASK MY OTHER FRIENDS! OH NO, WAIT-- YOU CAN'T 'CAUSE THEY'RE ALL DEAD!

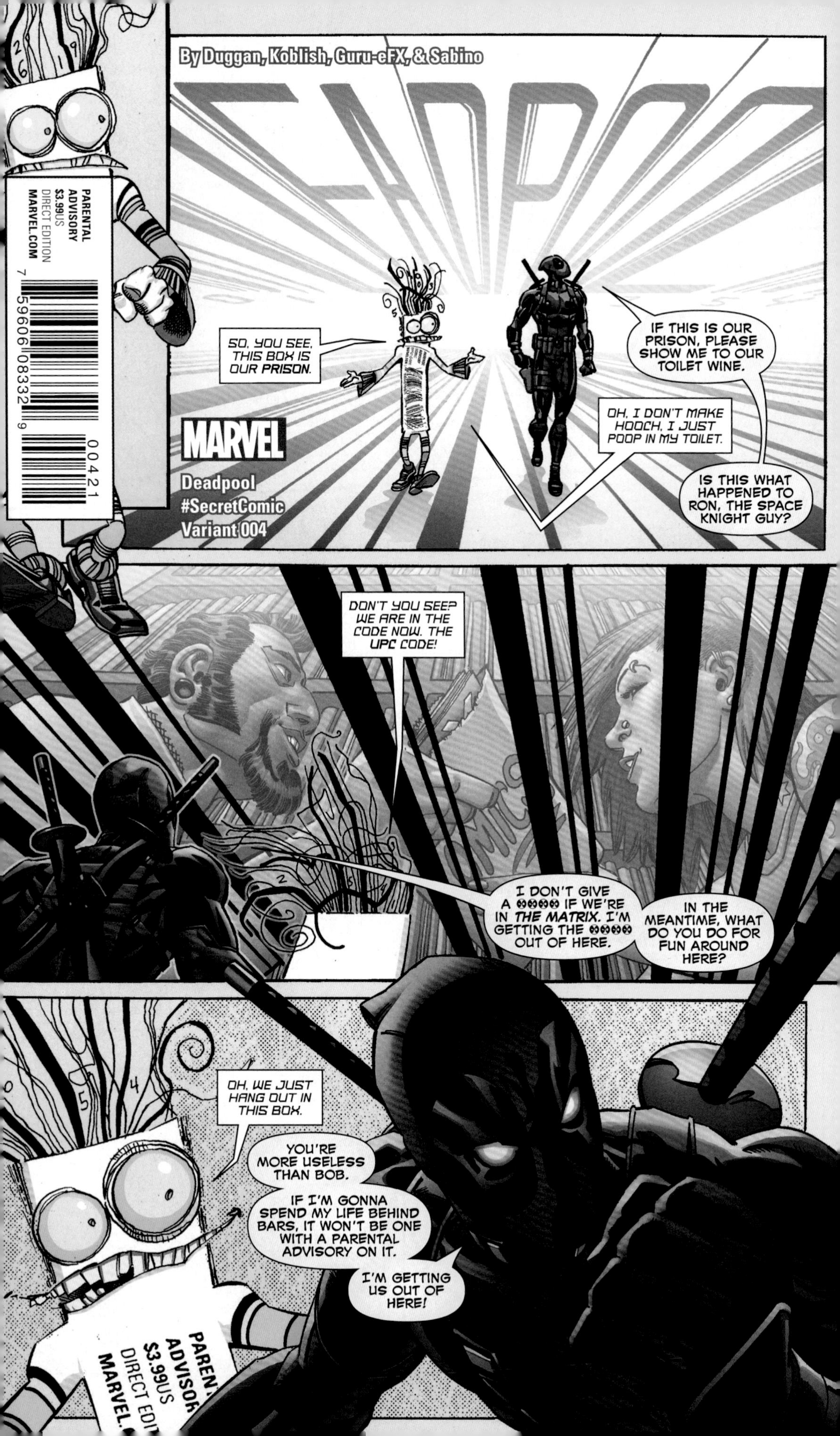
By Duggan, Koblish, Guru-eFX, & Sabino
PARENTAL ADVISORY $3.99US DIRECT EDITION MARVEL.COM
7 59606 08332 9 00421
MARVEL
Deadpool #SecretComic Variant 004
SO, YOU SEE, THIS BOX IS OUR PRISON.
IF THIS IS OUR PRISON, PLEASE SHOW ME TO OUR TOILET WINE.
OH, I DON'T MAKE HOOCH, I JUST POOP IN MY TOILET.
IS THIS WHAT HAPPENED TO RON, THE SPACE KNIGHT GUY?
DON'T YOU SEE? WE ARE IN THE CODE NOW. THE UPC CODE!
I DON'T GIVE A ⊗⊗⊗⊗ IF WE'RE IN THE MATRIX. I'M GETTING THE ⊗⊗⊗⊗ OUT OF HERE.
IN THE MEANTIME, WHAT DO YOU DO FOR FUN AROUND HERE?
OH, WE JUST HANG OUT IN THIS BOX.
YOU'RE MORE USELESS THAN BOB.
IF I'M GONNA SPEND MY LIFE BEHIND BARS, IT WON'T BE ONE WITH A PARENTAL ADVISORY ON IT.
I'M GETTING US OUT OF HERE!

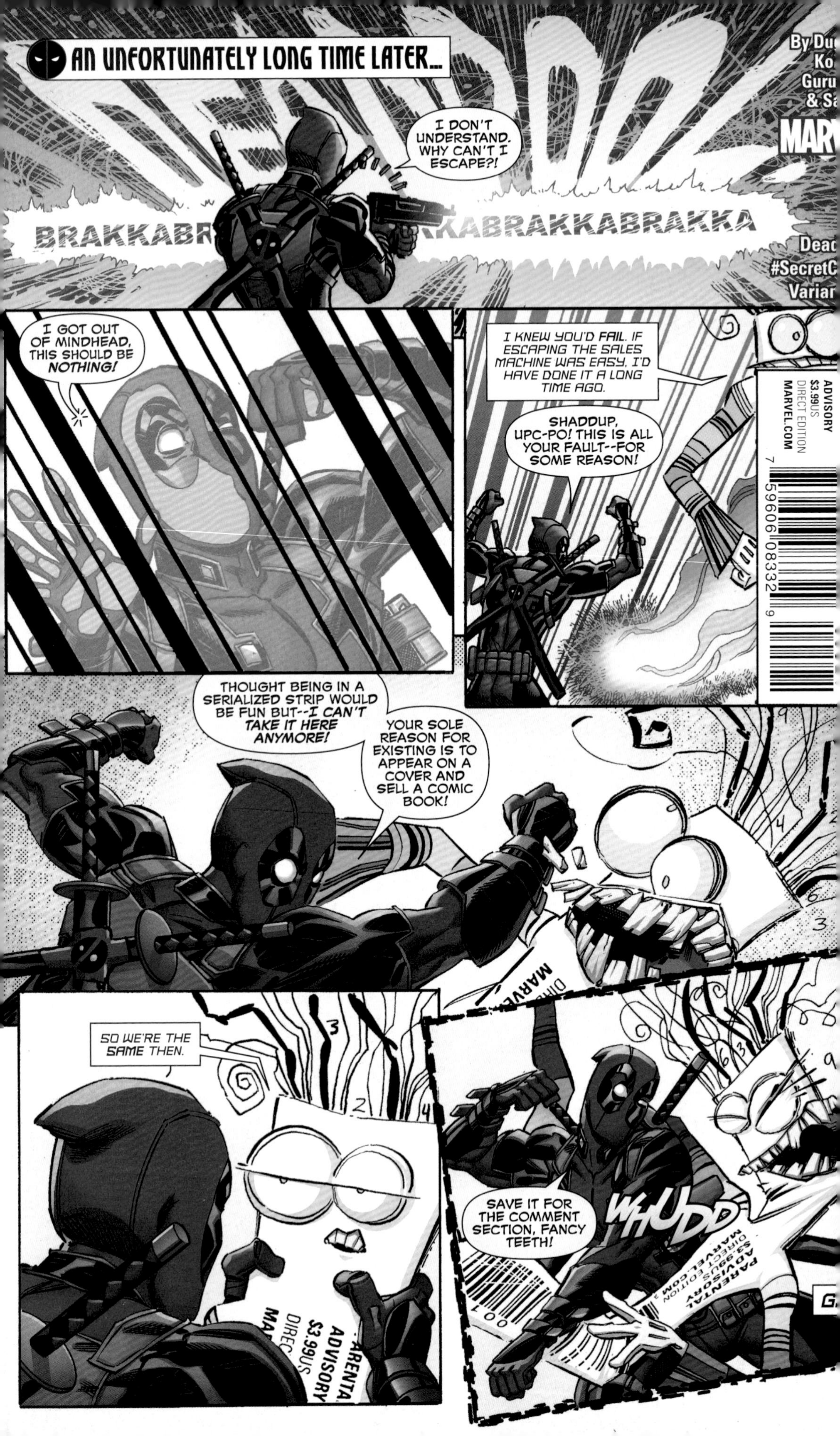

AN UNFORTUNATELY LONG TIME LATER...
I DON'T UNDERSTAND. WHY CAN'T I ESCAPE?!
BRAKKABR
KABRAKKABRAKKA
I GOT OUT OF MINDHEAD, THIS SHOULD BE NOTHING!
I KNEW YOU'D FAIL. IF ESCAPING THE SALES MACHINE WAS EASY, I'D HAVE DONE IT A LONG TIME AGO.
SHADDUP, UPC-PO! THIS IS ALL YOUR FAULT--FOR SOME REASON!
ADVISORY
$3.99US
DIRECT EDITION
MARVEL.COM
THOUGHT BEING IN A SERIALIZED STRIP WOULD BE FUN BUT--I CAN'T TAKE IT HERE ANYMORE!
YOUR SOLE REASON FOR EXISTING IS TO APPEAR ON A COVER AND SELL A COMIC BOOK!
SO WE'RE THE SAME THEN.
SAVE IT FOR THE COMMENT SECTION, FANCY TEETH!
WHUDD

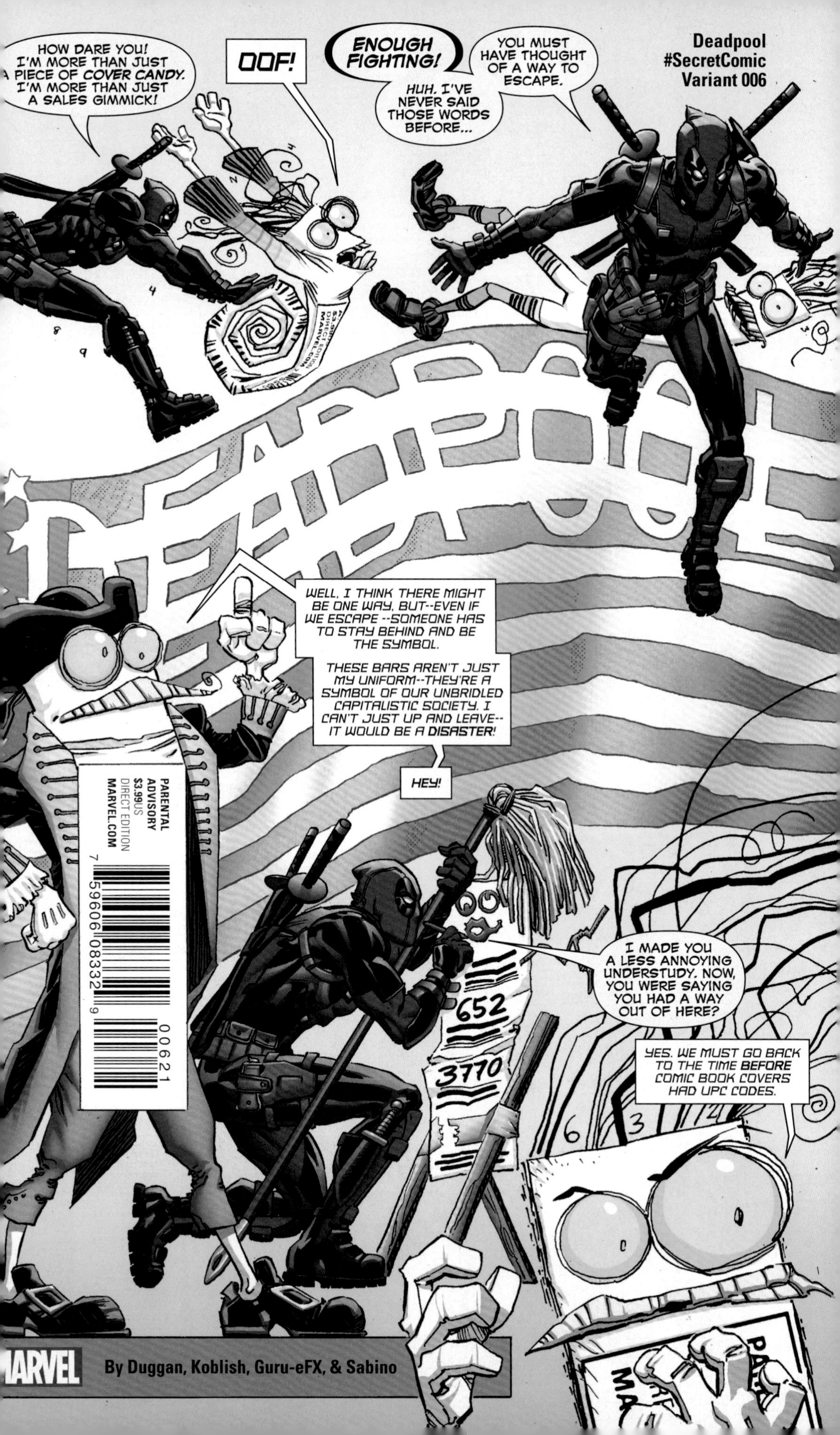
Deadpool
#SecretComic
Variant 006
HOW DARE YOU! I'M MORE THAN JUST A PIECE OF COVER CANDY. I'M MORE THAN JUST A SALES GIMMICK!
OOF!
ENOUGH FIGHTING!
HUH. I'VE NEVER SAID THOSE WORDS BEFORE...
YOU MUST HAVE THOUGHT OF A WAY TO ESCAPE.
WELL, I THINK THERE MIGHT BE ONE WAY, BUT--EVEN IF WE ESCAPE --SOMEONE HAS TO STAY BEHIND AND BE THE SYMBOL.
THESE BARS AREN'T JUST MY UNIFORM--THEY'RE A SYMBOL OF OUR UNBRIDLED CAPITALISTIC SOCIETY. I CAN'T JUST UP AND LEAVE--IT WOULD BE A DISASTER!
HEY!
PARENTAL ADVISORY
$3.99US
DIRECT EDITION
MARVEL.COM
I MADE YOU A LESS ANNOYING UNDERSTUDY. NOW, YOU WERE SAYING YOU HAD A WAY OUT OF HERE?
652
3770
YES. WE MUST GO BACK TO THE TIME BEFORE COMIC BOOK COVERS HAD UPC CODES.
MARVEL
By Duggan, Koblish, Guru-eFX, & Sabino

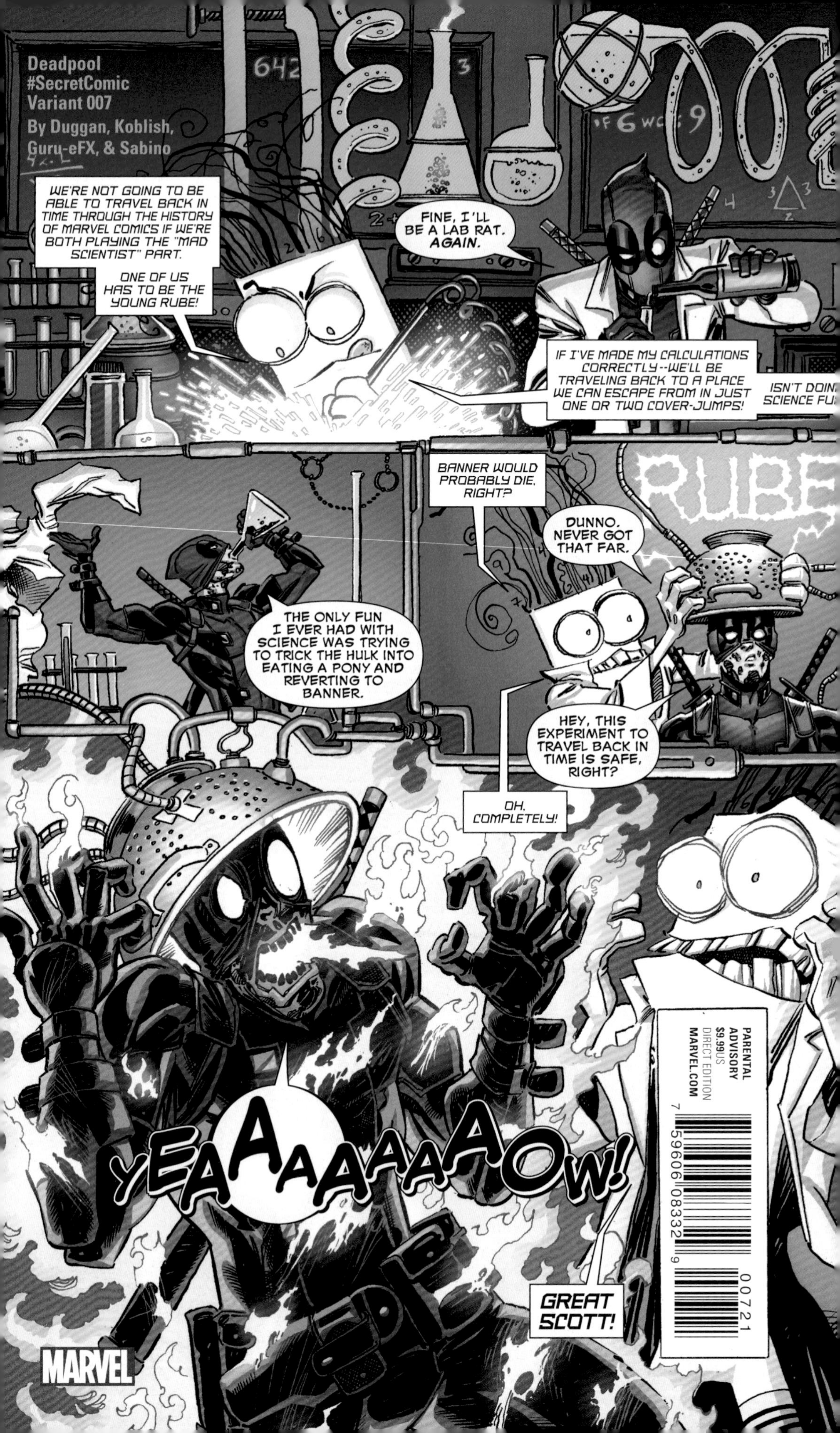

Deadpool
#SecretComic
Variant 007
By Duggan, Koblish, Guru-eFX, & Sabino
WE'RE NOT GOING TO BE ABLE TO TRAVEL BACK IN TIME THROUGH THE HISTORY OF MARVEL COMICS IF WE'RE BOTH PLAYING THE "MAD SCIENTIST" PART.
ONE OF US HAS TO BE THE YOUNG RUBE!
FINE, I'LL BE A LAB RAT. AGAIN.
IF I'VE MADE MY CALCULATIONS CORRECTLY--WE'LL BE TRAVELING BACK TO A PLACE WE CAN ESCAPE FROM IN JUST ONE OR TWO COVER-JUMPS!
THE ONLY FUN I EVER HAD WITH SCIENCE WAS TRYING TO TRICK THE HULK INTO EATING A PONY AND REVERTING TO BANNER.
BANNER WOULD PROBABLY DIE, RIGHT?
DUNNO. NEVER GOT THAT FAR.
RUBE
HEY, THIS EXPERIMENT TO TRAVEL BACK IN TIME IS SAFE, RIGHT?
OH, COMPLETELY!
YEAAAAAAAOW!
GREAT SCOTT!
PARENTAL ADVISORY
$9.99US
DIRECT EDITION
MARVEL.COM
MARVEL

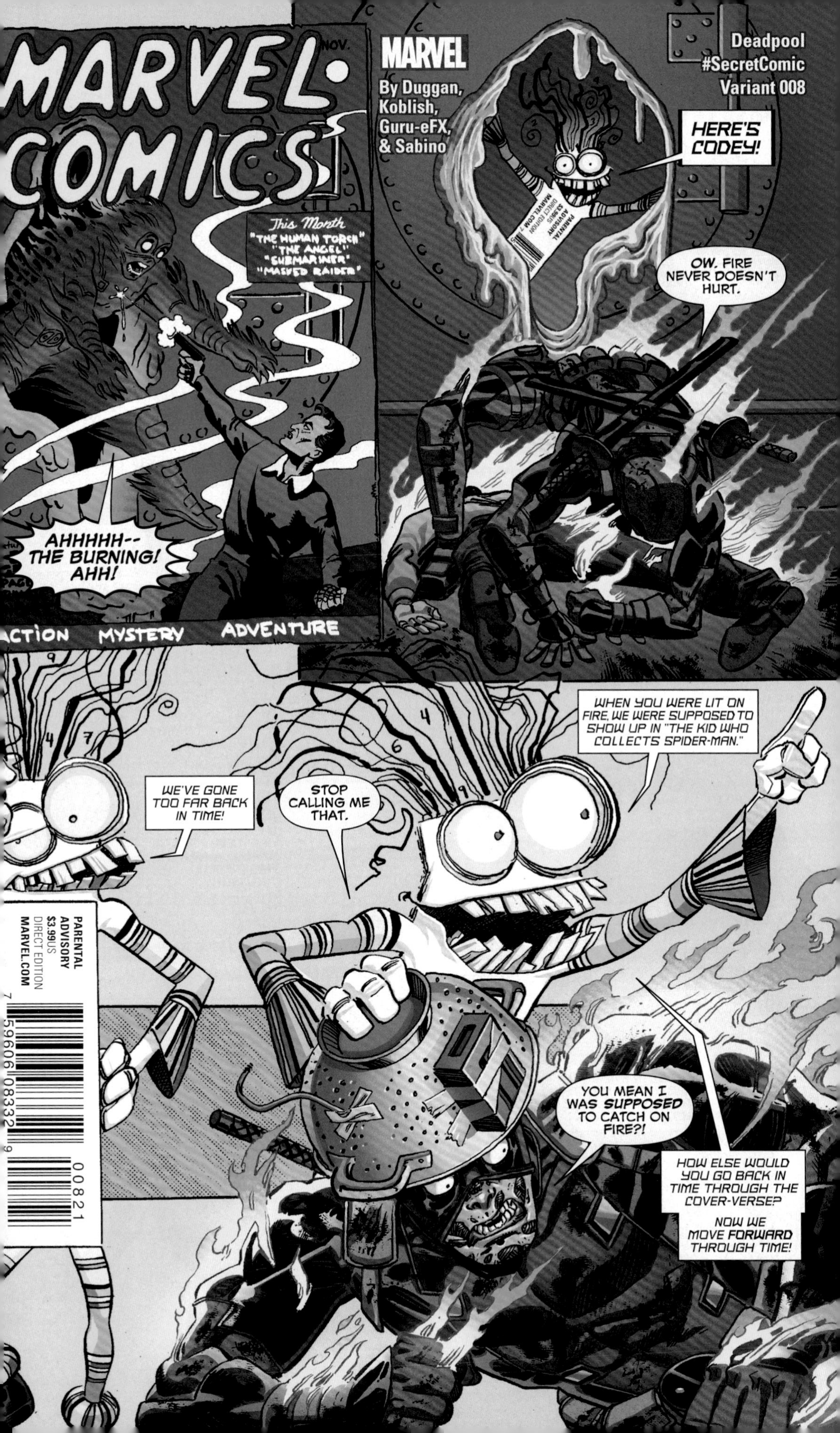

MARVEL
By Duggan, Koblish, Guru-eFX, & Sabino
Deadpool #SecretComic Variant 008
MARVEL COMICS
NOV.
This Month "THE HUMAN TORCH" "THE ANGEL" "SUBMARINER" "MASKED RAIDER"
AHHHHH-- THE BURNING! AHH!
ACTION MYSTERY ADVENTURE
HERE'S CODEY!
OW. FIRE NEVER DOESN'T HURT.
WE'VE GONE TOO FAR BACK IN TIME!
STOP CALLING ME THAT.
WHEN YOU WERE LIT ON FIRE, WE WERE SUPPOSED TO SHOW UP IN "THE KID WHO COLLECTS SPIDER-MAN."
YOU MEAN I WAS **SUPPOSED** TO CATCH ON FIRE?!
HOW ELSE WOULD YOU GO BACK IN TIME THROUGH THE COVER-VERSE?
NOW WE MOVE **FORWARD** THROUGH TIME!
PARENTAL ADVISORY $3.99US DIRECT EDITION MARVEL.COM

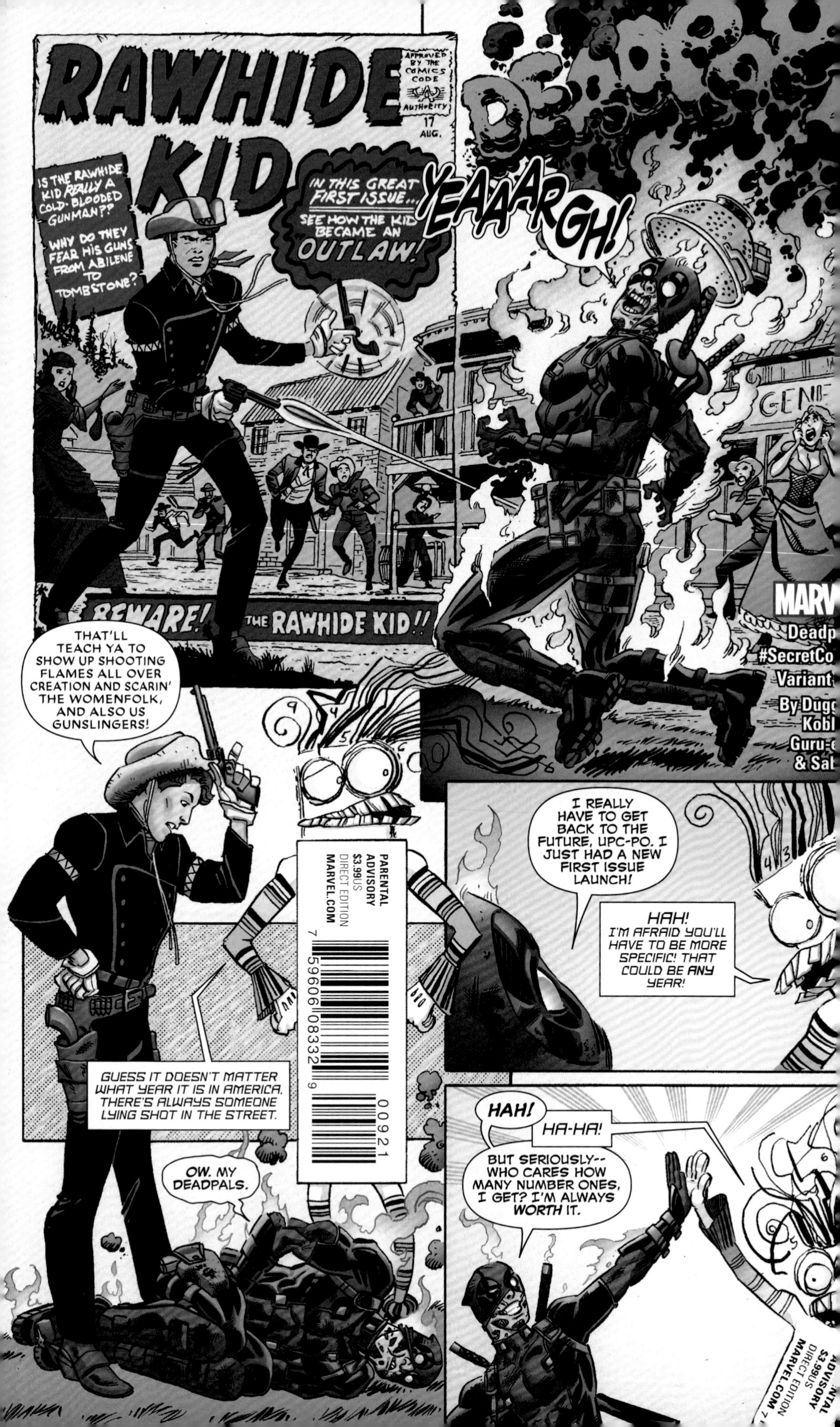
RAWHIDE KID
APPROVED BY THE COMICS CODE AUTHORITY
17 AUG.
IS THE RAWHIDE KID REALLY A COLD-BLOODED GUNMAN?? WHY DO THEY FEAR HIS GUNS FROM ABILENE TO TOMBSTONE?
IN THIS GREAT FIRST ISSUE... SEE HOW THE KID BECAME AN OUTLAW!
BEWARE! THE RAWHIDE KID!!
YEAAARGH!
THAT'LL TEACH YA TO SHOW UP SHOOTING FLAMES ALL OVER CREATION AND SCARIN' THE WOMENFOLK, AND ALSO US GUNSLINGERS!
GUESS IT DOESN'T MATTER WHAT YEAR IT IS IN AMERICA, THERE'S ALWAYS SOMEONE LYING SHOT IN THE STREET.
OW. MY DEADPALS.
PARENTAL ADVISORY
$3.99US
DIRECT EDITION
MARVEL.COM
I REALLY HAVE TO GET BACK TO THE FUTURE, UPC-PO. I JUST HAD A NEW FIRST ISSUE LAUNCH!
HAH! I'M AFRAID YOU'LL HAVE TO BE MORE SPECIFIC! THAT COULD BE ANY YEAR!
HAH!
HA-HA!
BUT SERIOUSLY-- WHO CARES HOW MANY NUMBER ONES, I GET? I'M ALWAYS WORTH IT.

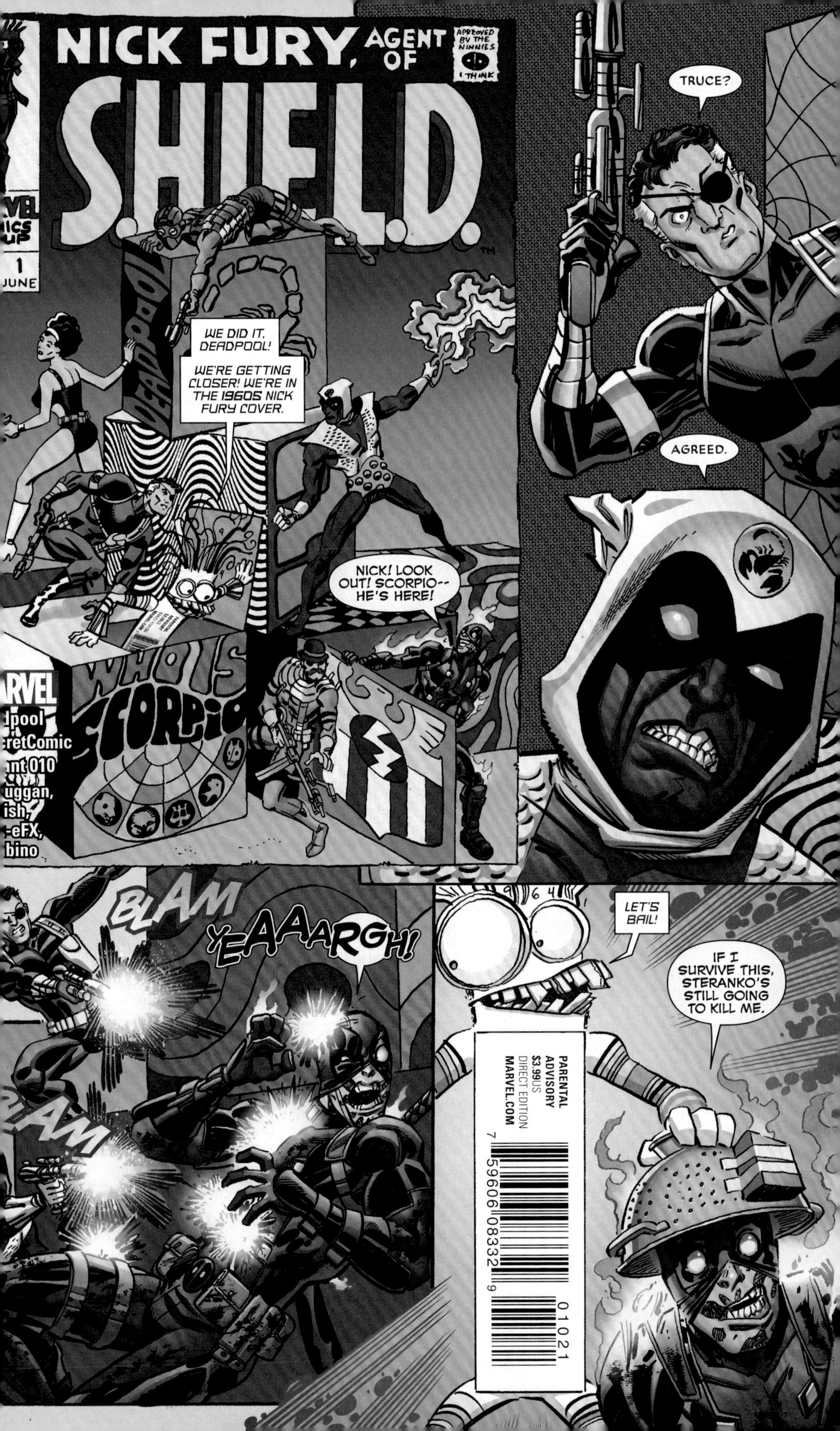
NICK FURY, AGENT OF
S.H.I.E.L.D.
APPROVED BY THE NINNIES I THINK
1
JUNE
WE DID IT, DEADPOOL!
WE'RE GETTING CLOSER! WE'RE IN THE 1960S NICK FURY COVER.
NICK! LOOK OUT! SCORPIO-- HE'S HERE!
WHO IS SCORPIO
TRUCE?
AGREED.
BLAM
YEAAAARGH!
BLAM
LET'S BAIL!
IF I SURVIVE THIS, STERANKO'S STILL GOING TO KILL ME.
PARENTAL ADVISORY
$3.99US
DIRECT EDITION
MARVEL.COM

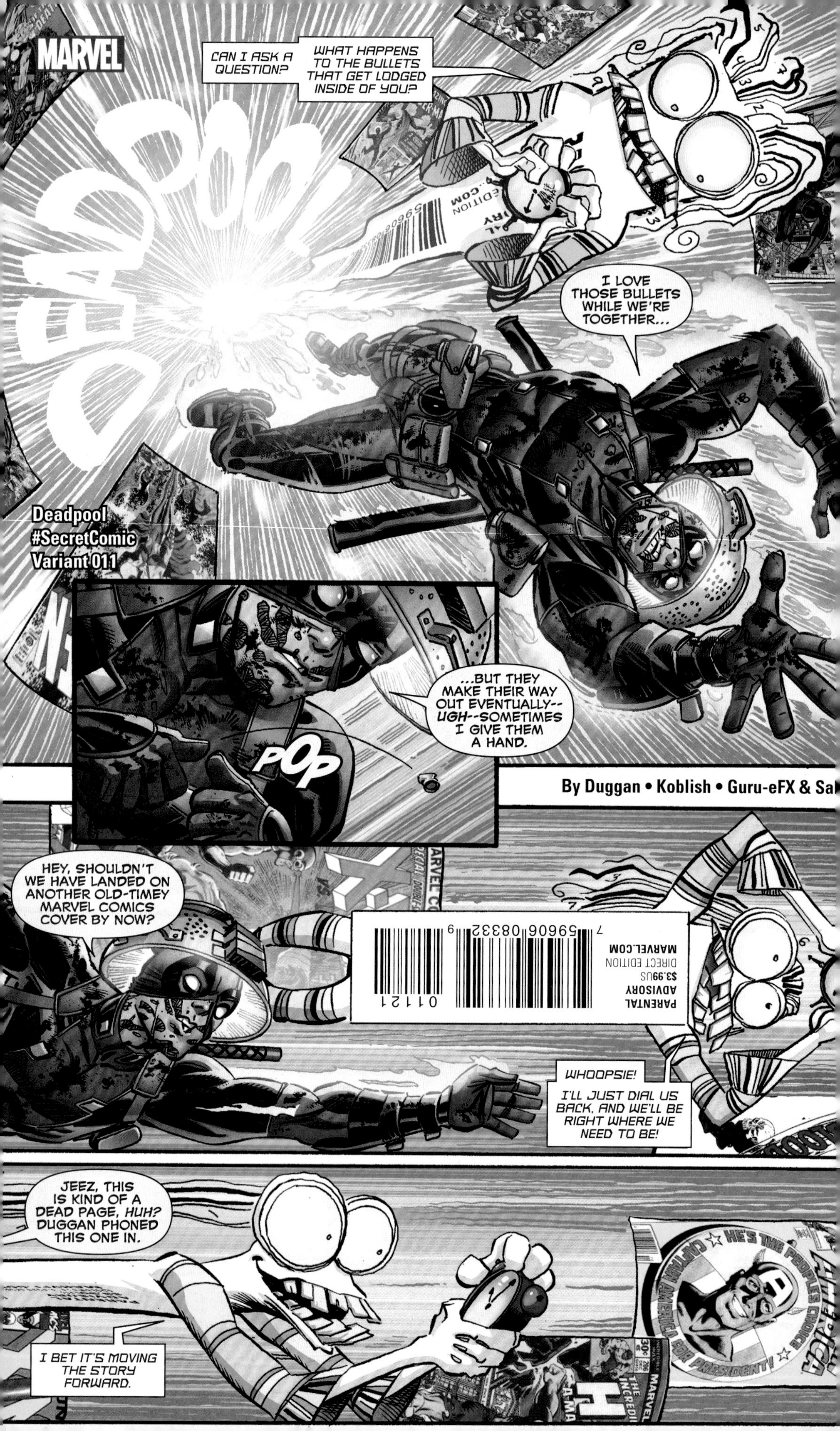
MARVEL
CAN I ASK A QUESTION?
WHAT HAPPENS TO THE BULLETS THAT GET LODGED INSIDE OF YOU?
I LOVE THOSE BULLETS WHILE WE'RE TOGETHER...
Deadpool #SecretComic Variant 011
...BUT THEY MAKE THEIR WAY OUT EVENTUALLY--UGH--SOMETIMES I GIVE THEM A HAND.
POP
By Duggan • Koblish • Guru-eFX & Sa
HEY, SHOULDN'T WE HAVE LANDED ON ANOTHER OLD-TIMEY MARVEL COMICS COVER BY NOW?
WHOOPSIE!
I'LL JUST DIAL US BACK, AND WE'LL BE RIGHT WHERE WE NEED TO BE!
JEEZ, THIS IS KIND OF A DEAD PAGE, HUH? DUGGAN PHONED THIS ONE IN.
I BET IT'S MOVING THE STORY FORWARD.
HE'S THE PEOPLE'S CHOICE
CAPTAIN AMERICA FOR PRESIDENT!

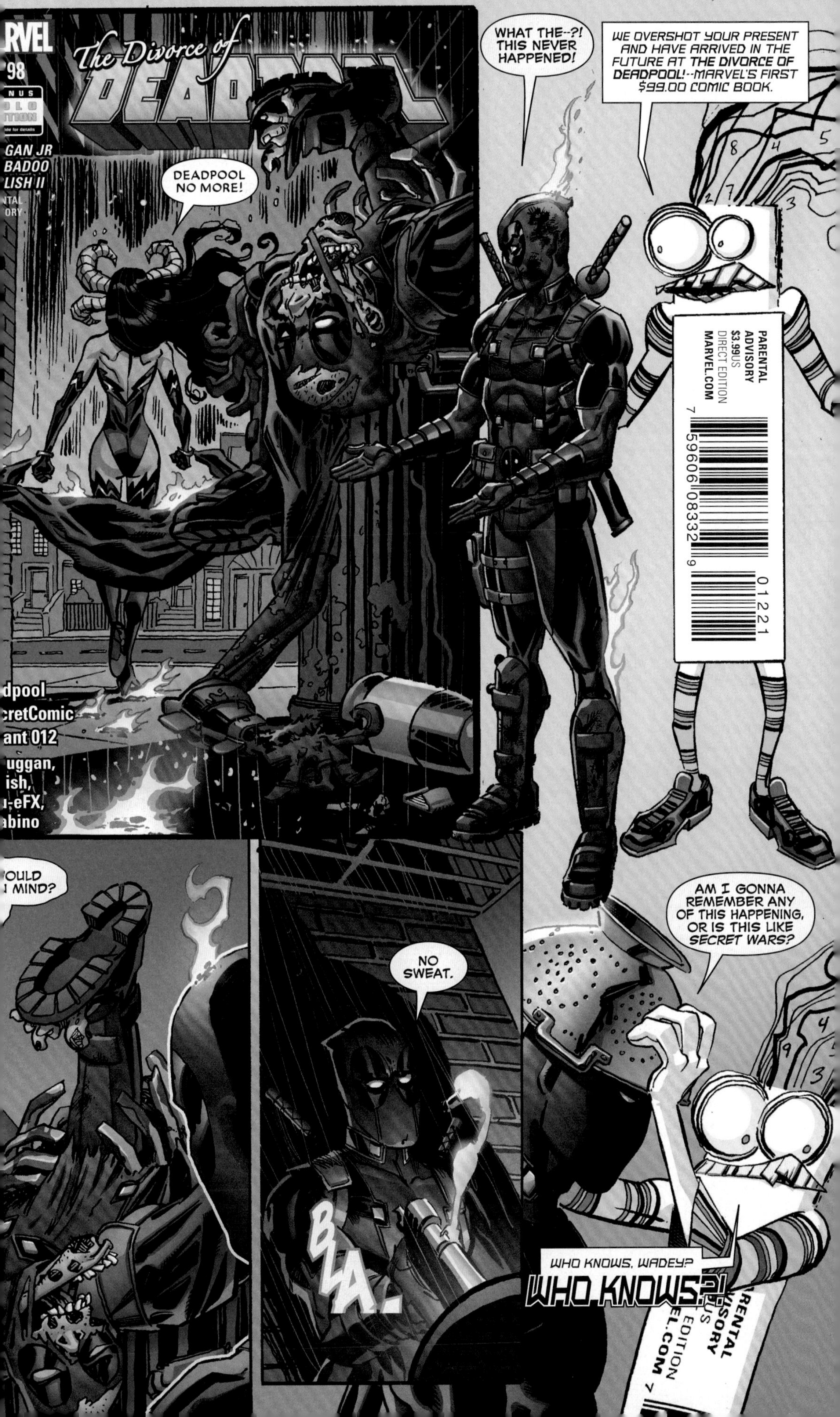

The Divorce of DEADPOOL
DEADPOOL NO MORE!
WHAT THE--?! THIS NEVER HAPPENED!
WE OVERSHOT YOUR PRESENT AND HAVE ARRIVED IN THE FUTURE AT THE DIVORCE OF DEADPOOL!--MARVEL'S FIRST $99.00 COMIC BOOK.
PARENTAL ADVISORY $3.99US DIRECT EDITION MARVEL.COM
NO SWEAT.
BLA.
AM I GONNA REMEMBER ANY OF THIS HAPPENING, OR IS THIS LIKE SECRET WARS?
WHO KNOWS, WADEY?
WHO KNOWS?!

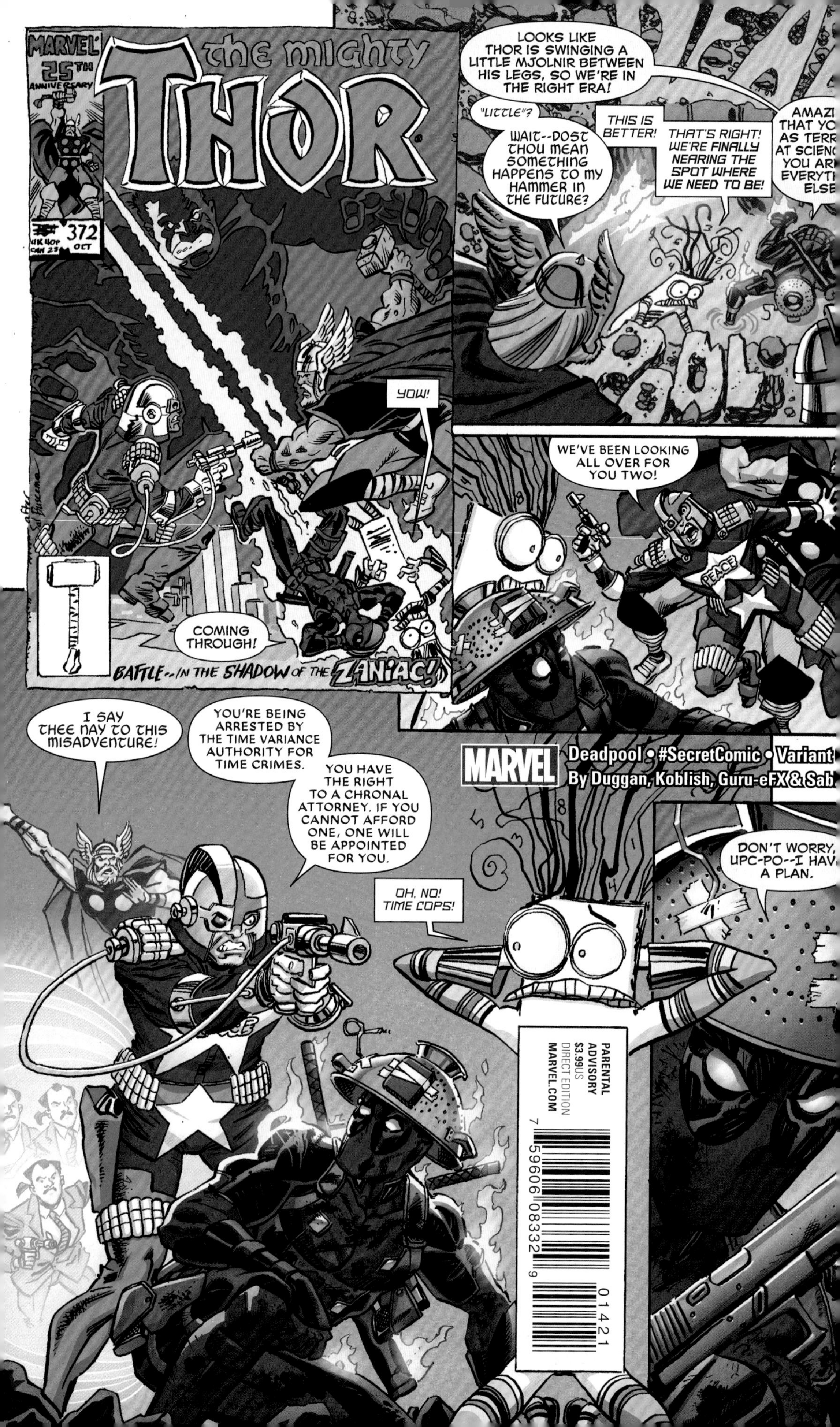
MARVEL 25TH ANNIVERSARY
the mighty THOR
372 OCT
LOOKS LIKE THOR IS SWINGING A LITTLE MJOLNIR BETWEEN HIS LEGS, SO WE'RE IN THE RIGHT ERA!
"LITTLE"?
WAIT--DOST THOU MEAN SOMETHING HAPPENS TO MY HAMMER IN THE FUTURE?
THIS IS BETTER!
THAT'S RIGHT! WE'RE FINALLY NEARING THE SPOT WHERE WE NEED TO BE!
AMAZI THAT YO AS TERR AT SCIEN YOU AR EVERYT ELSE
YOW!
COMING THROUGH!
BATTLE--IN THE SHADOW OF THE ZANIAC!
WE'VE BEEN LOOKING ALL OVER FOR YOU TWO!
PEACE
I SAY THEE NAY TO THIS MISADVENTURE!
YOU'RE BEING ARRESTED BY THE TIME VARIANCE AUTHORITY FOR TIME CRIMES.
YOU HAVE THE RIGHT TO A CHRONAL ATTORNEY. IF YOU CANNOT AFFORD ONE, ONE WILL BE APPOINTED FOR YOU.
MARVEL
Deadpool • #SecretComic • Variant
By Duggan, Koblish, Guru-eFX & Sab
OH, NO! TIME COPS!
DON'T WORRY, UPC-PO--I HAV A PLAN.
PARENTAL ADVISORY
$3.99US
DIRECT EDITION
MARVEL.COM

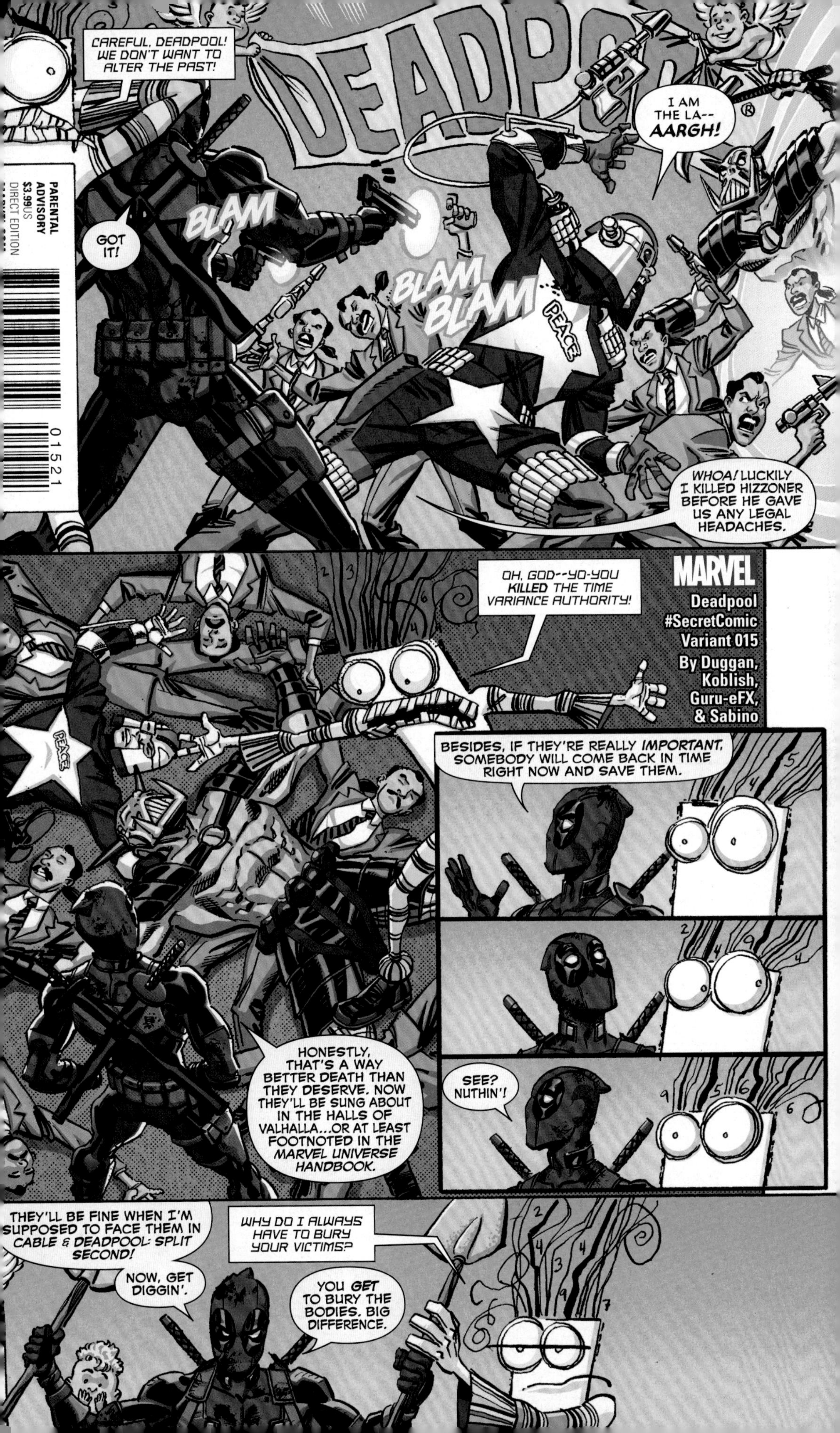

CAREFUL, DEADPOOL! WE DON'T WANT TO ALTER THE PAST!
DEADPOOL®
I AM THE LA-- AARGH!
PARENTAL ADVISORY
$3.99US
DIRECT EDITION
BLAM
GOT IT!
BLAM BLAM
PEACE
WHOA! LUCKILY I KILLED HIZZONER BEFORE HE GAVE US ANY LEGAL HEADACHES.
OH, GOD--YO-YOU KILLED THE TIME VARIANCE AUTHORITY!
MARVEL
Deadpool
#SecretComic
Variant 015
By Duggan,
Koblish,
Guru-eFX,
& Sabino
PEACE
BESIDES, IF THEY'RE REALLY IMPORTANT, SOMEBODY WILL COME BACK IN TIME RIGHT NOW AND SAVE THEM.
HONESTLY, THAT'S A WAY BETTER DEATH THAN THEY DESERVE. NOW THEY'LL BE SUNG ABOUT IN THE HALLS OF VALHALLA...OR AT LEAST FOOTNOTED IN THE MARVEL UNIVERSE HANDBOOK.
SEE? NUTHIN'!
THEY'LL BE FINE WHEN I'M SUPPOSED TO FACE THEM IN CABLE & DEADPOOL: SPLIT SECOND!
WHY DO I ALWAYS HAVE TO BURY YOUR VICTIMS?
NOW, GET DIGGIN'.
YOU GET TO BURY THE BODIES. BIG DIFFERENCE.

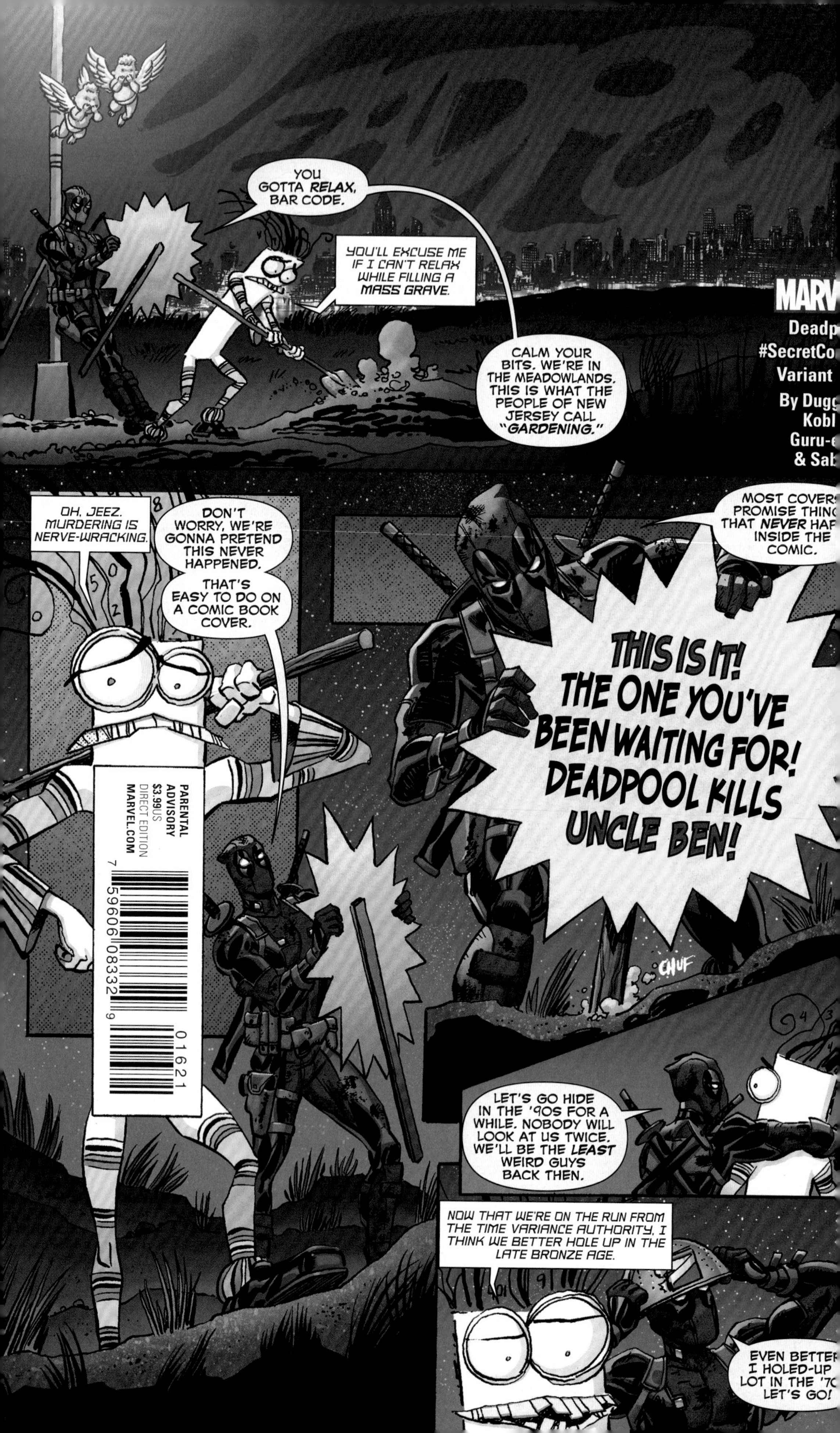

YOU GOTTA RELAX, BAR CODE.
YOU'LL EXCUSE ME IF I CAN'T RELAX WHILE FILLING A MASS GRAVE.
CALM YOUR BITS. WE'RE IN THE MEADOWLANDS. THIS IS WHAT THE PEOPLE OF NEW JERSEY CALL "GARDENING."
OH, JEEZ. MURDERING IS NERVE-WRACKING.
DON'T WORRY, WE'RE GONNA PRETEND THIS NEVER HAPPENED.
THAT'S EASY TO DO ON A COMIC BOOK COVER.
THIS IS IT! THE ONE YOU'VE BEEN WAITING FOR! DEADPOOL KILLS UNCLE BEN!
CHUF
LET'S GO HIDE IN THE '90S FOR A WHILE. NOBODY WILL LOOK AT US TWICE. WE'LL BE THE LEAST WEIRD GUYS BACK THEN.
NOW THAT WE'RE ON THE RUN FROM THE TIME VARIANCE AUTHORITY, I THINK WE BETTER HOLE UP IN THE LATE BRONZE AGE.
PARENTAL ADVISORY
$3.99US
DIRECT EDITION
MARVEL.COM

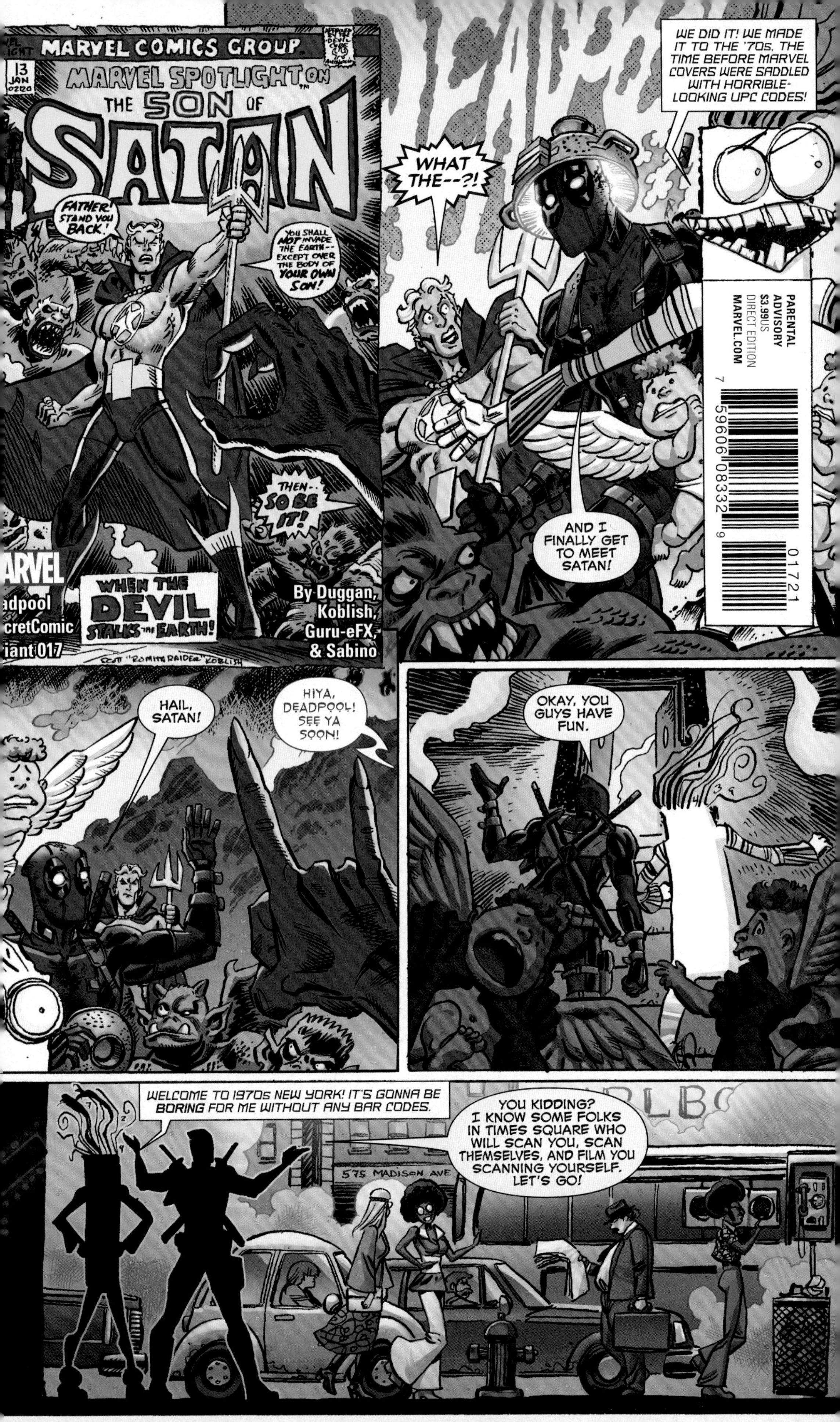
MARVEL COMICS GROUP
13 JAN 02120
MARVEL SPOTLIGHT ON THE SON OF SATAN
FATHER! STAND YOU BACK!
YOU SHALL NOT INVADE THE EARTH -- EXCEPT OVER THE BODY OF YOUR OWN SON!
THEN -- SO BE IT!
WHEN THE DEVIL STALKS THE EARTH!
MARVEL
adpool
cretComic
iant 017
By Duggan, Koblish, Guru-eFX, & Sabino
WE DID IT! WE MADE IT TO THE '70s, THE TIME BEFORE MARVEL COVERS WERE SADDLED WITH HORRIBLE-LOOKING UPC CODES!
WHAT THE--?!
PARENTAL ADVISORY
$3.99US
DIRECT EDITION
MARVEL.COM
AND I FINALLY GET TO MEET SATAN!
HAIL, SATAN!
HIYA, DEADPOOL! SEE YA SOON!
OKAY, YOU GUYS HAVE FUN.
WELCOME TO 1970s NEW YORK! IT'S GONNA BE BORING FOR ME WITHOUT ANY BAR CODES.
YOU KIDDING? I KNOW SOME FOLKS IN TIMES SQUARE WHO WILL SCAN YOU, SCAN THEMSELVES, AND FILM YOU SCANNING YOURSELF. LET'S GO!
575 MADISON AVE

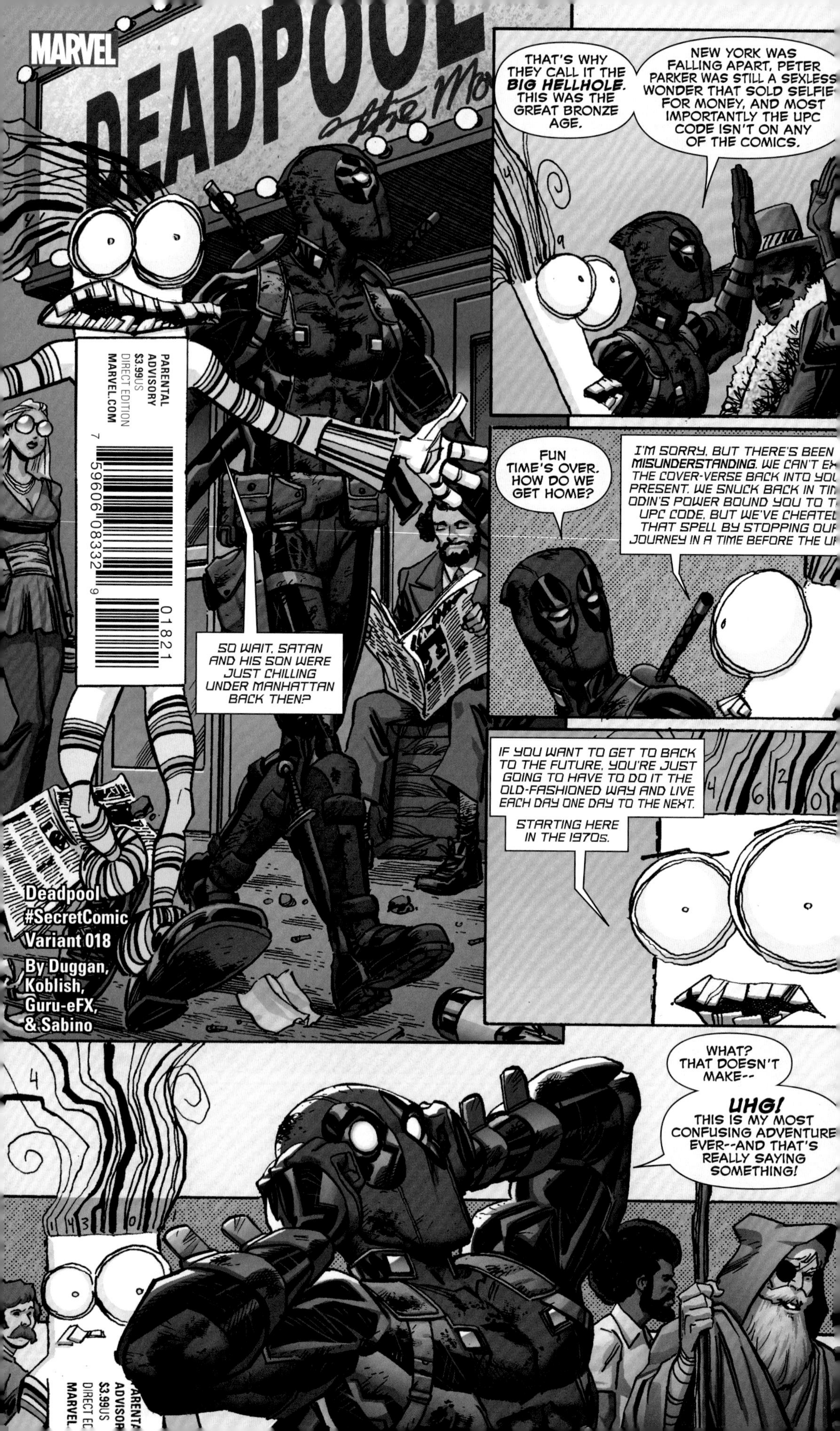
MARVEL
DEADPOOL
THAT'S WHY THEY CALL IT THE BIG HELLHOLE. THIS WAS THE GREAT BRONZE AGE.
NEW YORK WAS FALLING APART, PETER PARKER WAS STILL A SEXLESS WONDER THAT SOLD SELFIE FOR MONEY, AND MOST IMPORTANTLY THE UPC CODE ISN'T ON ANY OF THE COMICS.
PARENTAL ADVISORY
$3.99US
DIRECT EDITION
MARVEL.COM
SO WAIT, SATAN AND HIS SON WERE JUST CHILLING UNDER MANHATTAN BACK THEN?
FUN TIME'S OVER. HOW DO WE GET HOME?
I'M SORRY, BUT THERE'S BEEN MISUNDERSTANDING. WE CAN'T EX THE COVER-VERSE BACK INTO YOU PRESENT. WE SNUCK BACK IN TIM ODIN'S POWER BOUND YOU TO T UPC CODE, BUT WE'VE CHEATED THAT SPELL BY STOPPING OUR JOURNEY IN A TIME BEFORE THE U
IF YOU WANT TO GET TO BACK TO THE FUTURE, YOU'RE JUST GOING TO HAVE TO DO IT THE OLD-FASHIONED WAY AND LIVE EACH DAY ONE DAY TO THE NEXT.
STARTING HERE IN THE 1970s.
Deadpool #SecretComic Variant 018
By Duggan, Koblish, Guru-eFX, & Sabino
WHAT? THAT DOESN'T MAKE--
UHG! THIS IS MY MOST CONFUSING ADVENTURE EVER--AND THAT'S REALLY SAYING SOMETHING!
PARENTA ADVISOR $3.99US DIRECT ED MARVEL.

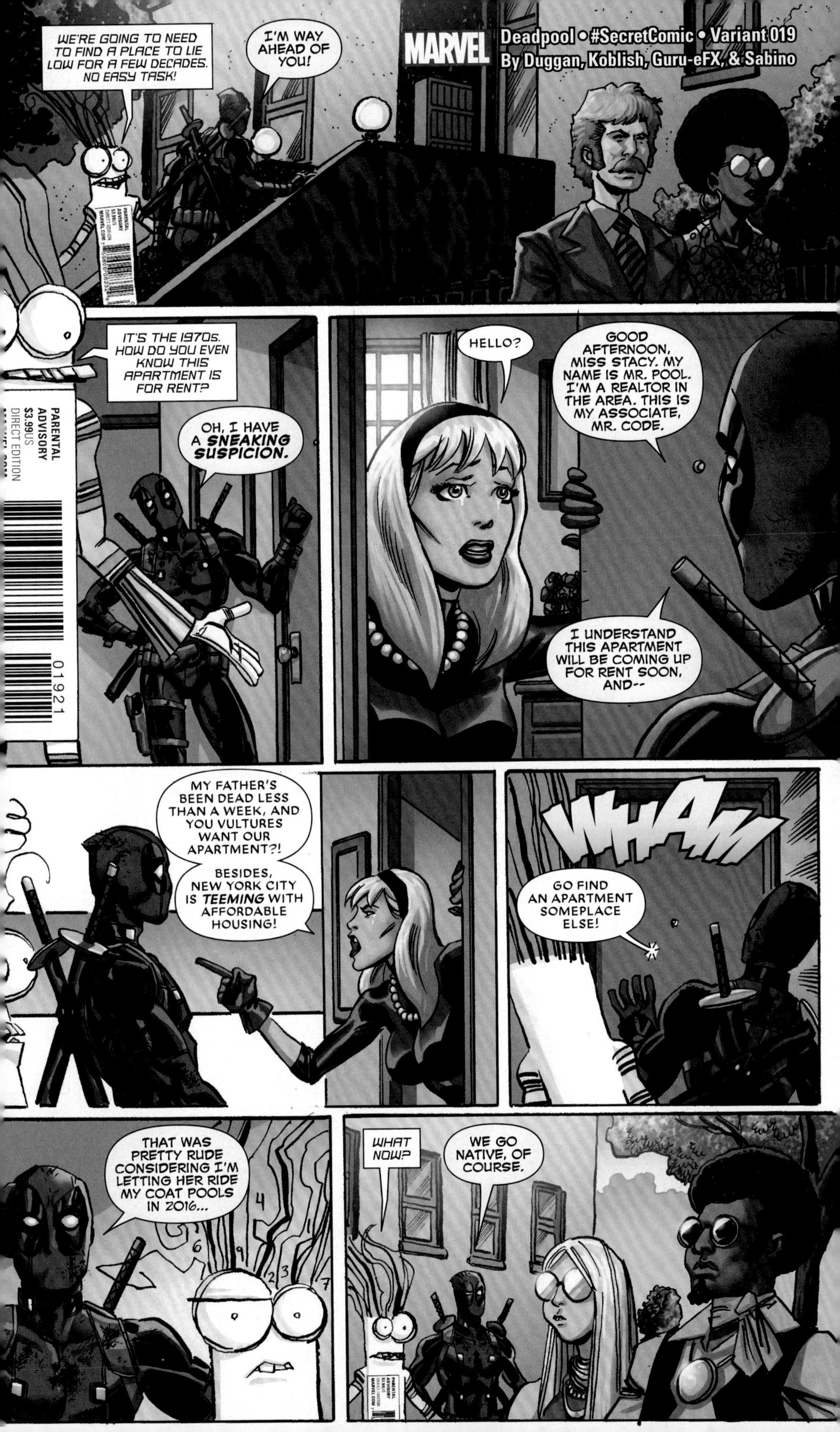
MARVEL
Deadpool • #SecretComic • Variant 019
By Duggan, Koblish, Guru-eFX, & Sabino
WE'RE GOING TO NEED TO FIND A PLACE TO LIE LOW FOR A FEW DECADES. NO EASY TASK!
I'M WAY AHEAD OF YOU!
IT'S THE 1970s. HOW DO YOU EVEN KNOW THIS APARTMENT IS FOR RENT?
OH, I HAVE A SNEAKING SUSPICION.
HELLO?
GOOD AFTERNOON, MISS STACY. MY NAME IS MR. POOL. I'M A REALTOR IN THE AREA. THIS IS MY ASSOCIATE, MR. CODE.
I UNDERSTAND THIS APARTMENT WILL BE COMING UP FOR RENT SOON, AND--
PARENTAL ADVISORY
$3.99US
DIRECT EDITION
MY FATHER'S BEEN DEAD LESS THAN A WEEK, AND YOU VULTURES WANT OUR APARTMENT?!
BESIDES, NEW YORK CITY IS TEEMING WITH AFFORDABLE HOUSING!
WHAM
GO FIND AN APARTMENT SOMEPLACE ELSE!
THAT WAS PRETTY RUDE CONSIDERING I'M LETTING HER RIDE MY COAT POOLS IN 2016...
WHAT NOW?
WE GO NATIVE, OF COURSE.

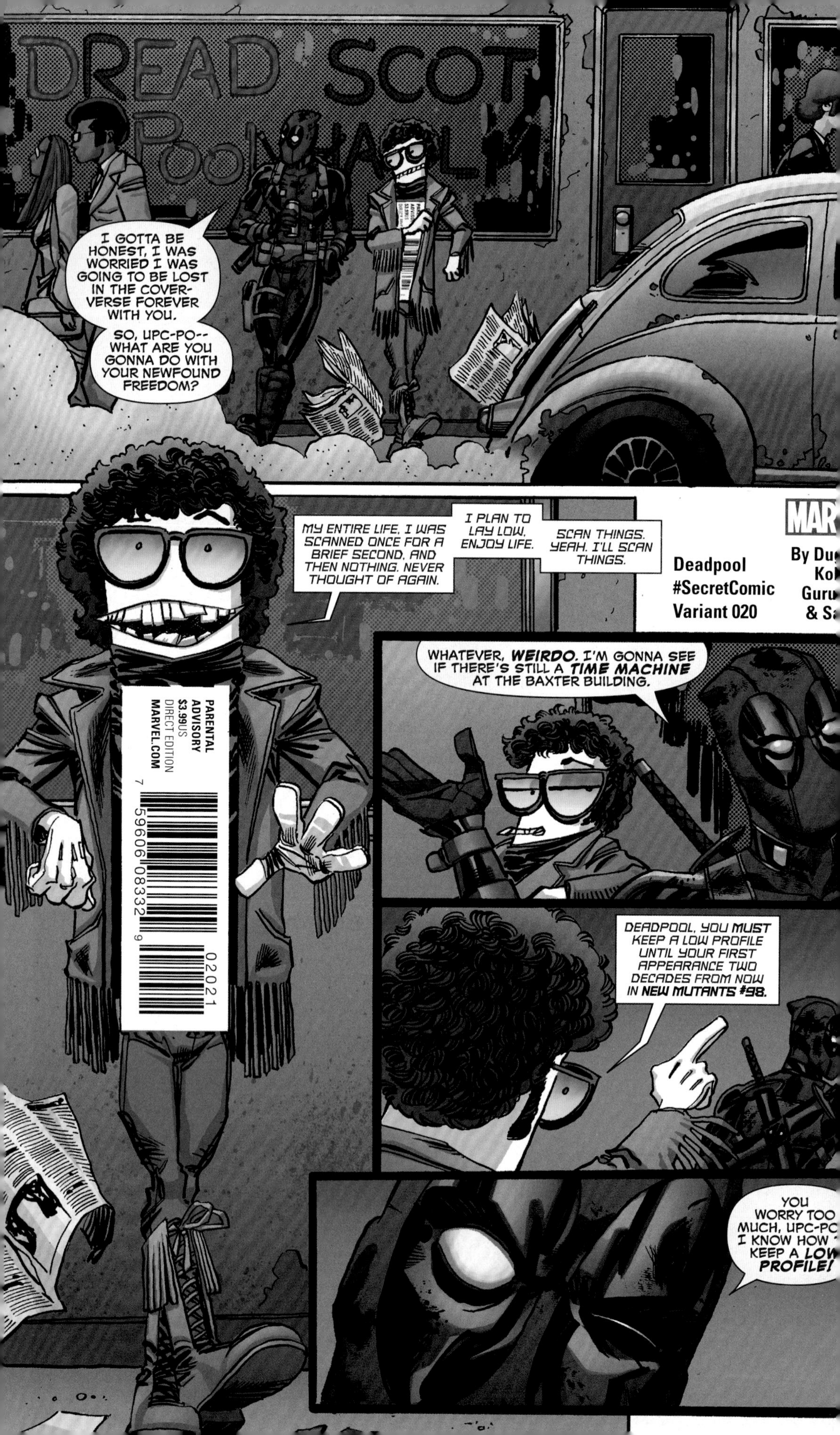
DREAD SCOT POOL HALL
I GOTTA BE HONEST, I WAS WORRIED I WAS GOING TO BE LOST IN THE COVER-VERSE FOREVER WITH YOU.
SO, UPC-PO-- WHAT ARE YOU GONNA DO WITH YOUR NEWFOUND FREEDOM?
MY ENTIRE LIFE, I WAS SCANNED ONCE FOR A BRIEF SECOND, AND THEN NOTHING. NEVER THOUGHT OF AGAIN.
I PLAN TO LAY LOW. ENJOY LIFE.
SCAN THINGS. YEAH. I'LL SCAN THINGS.
Deadpool #SecretComic Variant 020
PARENTAL ADVISORY $3.99US DIRECT EDITION MARVEL.COM
WHATEVER, WEIRDO. I'M GONNA SEE IF THERE'S STILL A TIME MACHINE AT THE BAXTER BUILDING.
DEADPOOL, YOU MUST KEEP A LOW PROFILE UNTIL YOUR FIRST APPEARANCE TWO DECADES FROM NOW IN NEW MUTANTS #98.
YOU WORRY TOO MUCH, UPC-PO I KNOW HOW KEEP A LOW PROFILE!

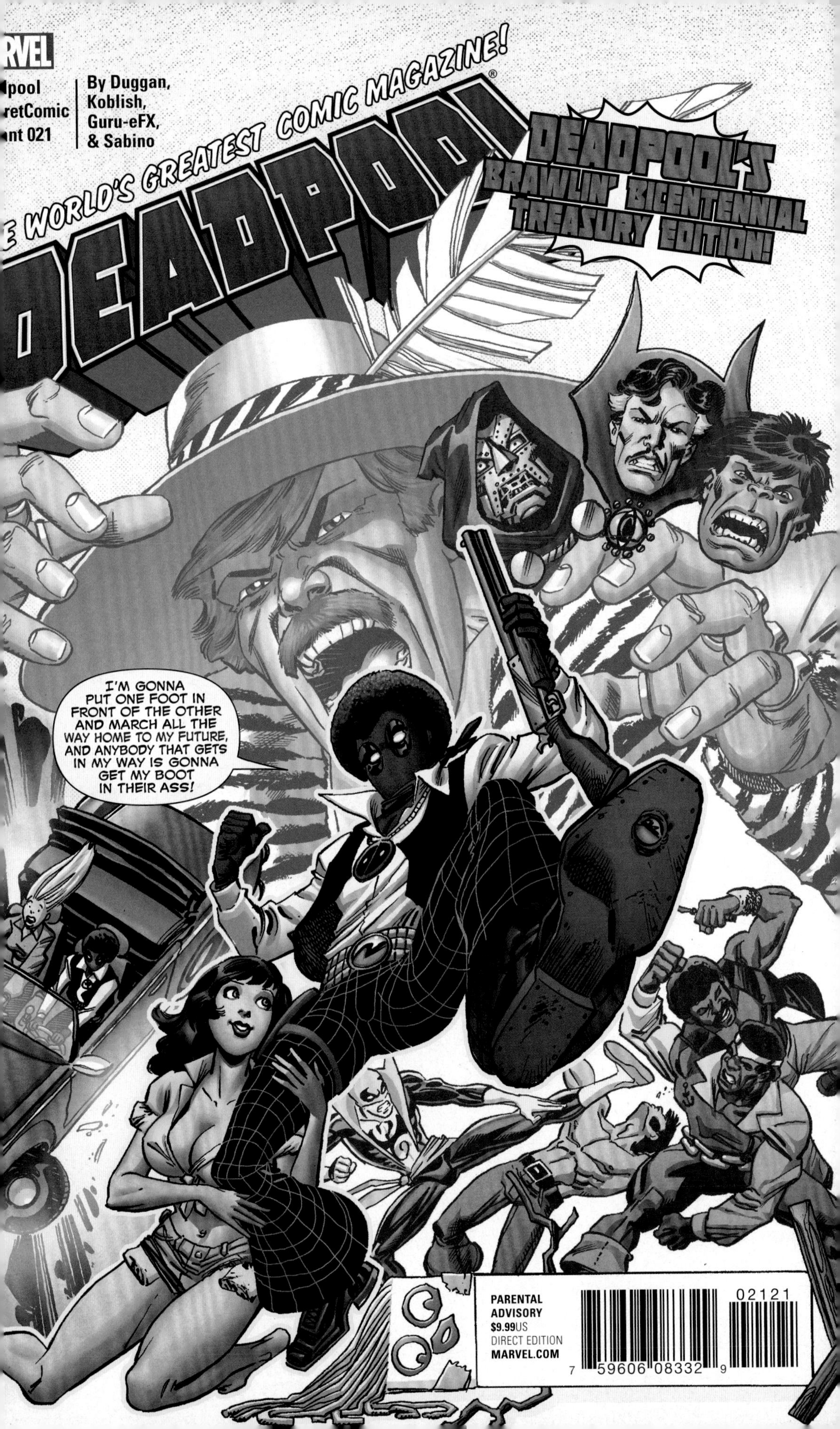

MARVEL
Deadpool
SecretComic
Variant 021
By Duggan,
Koblish,
Guru-eFX,
& Sabino
THE WORLD'S GREATEST COMIC MAGAZINE!
DEADPOOL®
DEADPOOL'S
BRAWLIN' BICENTENNIAL
TREASURY EDITION!
I'M GONNA PUT ONE FOOT IN FRONT OF THE OTHER AND MARCH ALL THE WAY HOME TO MY FUTURE, AND ANYBODY THAT GETS IN MY WAY IS GONNA GET MY BOOT IN THEIR ASS!
PARENTAL
ADVISORY
$9.99US
DIRECT EDITION
MARVEL.COM

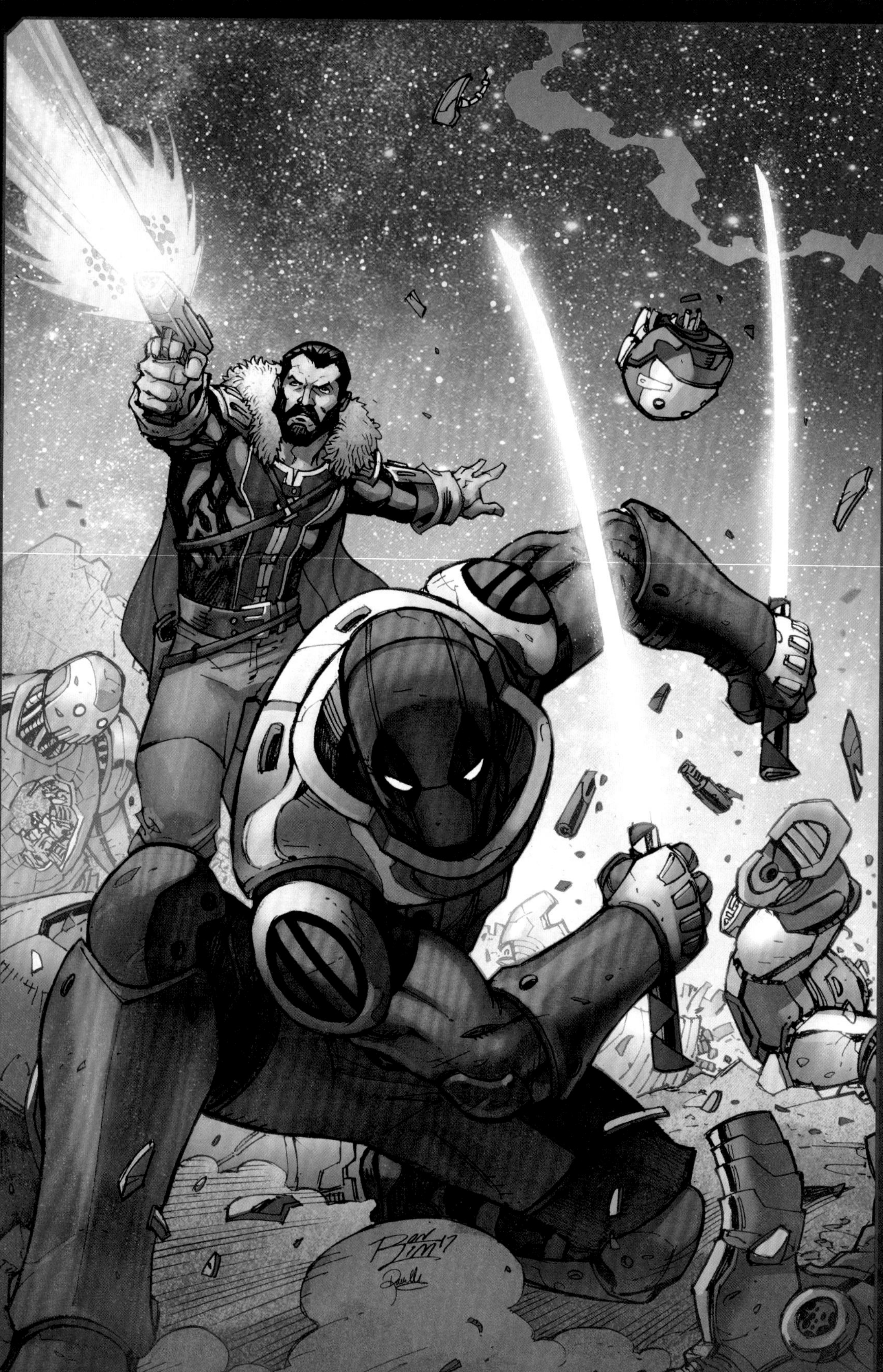

#30 variant by RON LIM & RACHELLE ROSENBERG

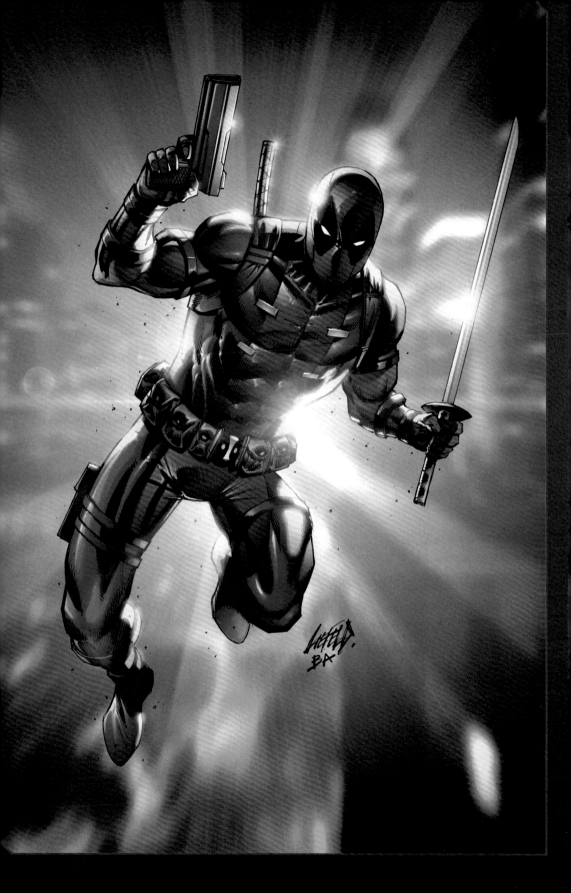

#30 variant by ROB LIEFELD & JESUS ABURTOV

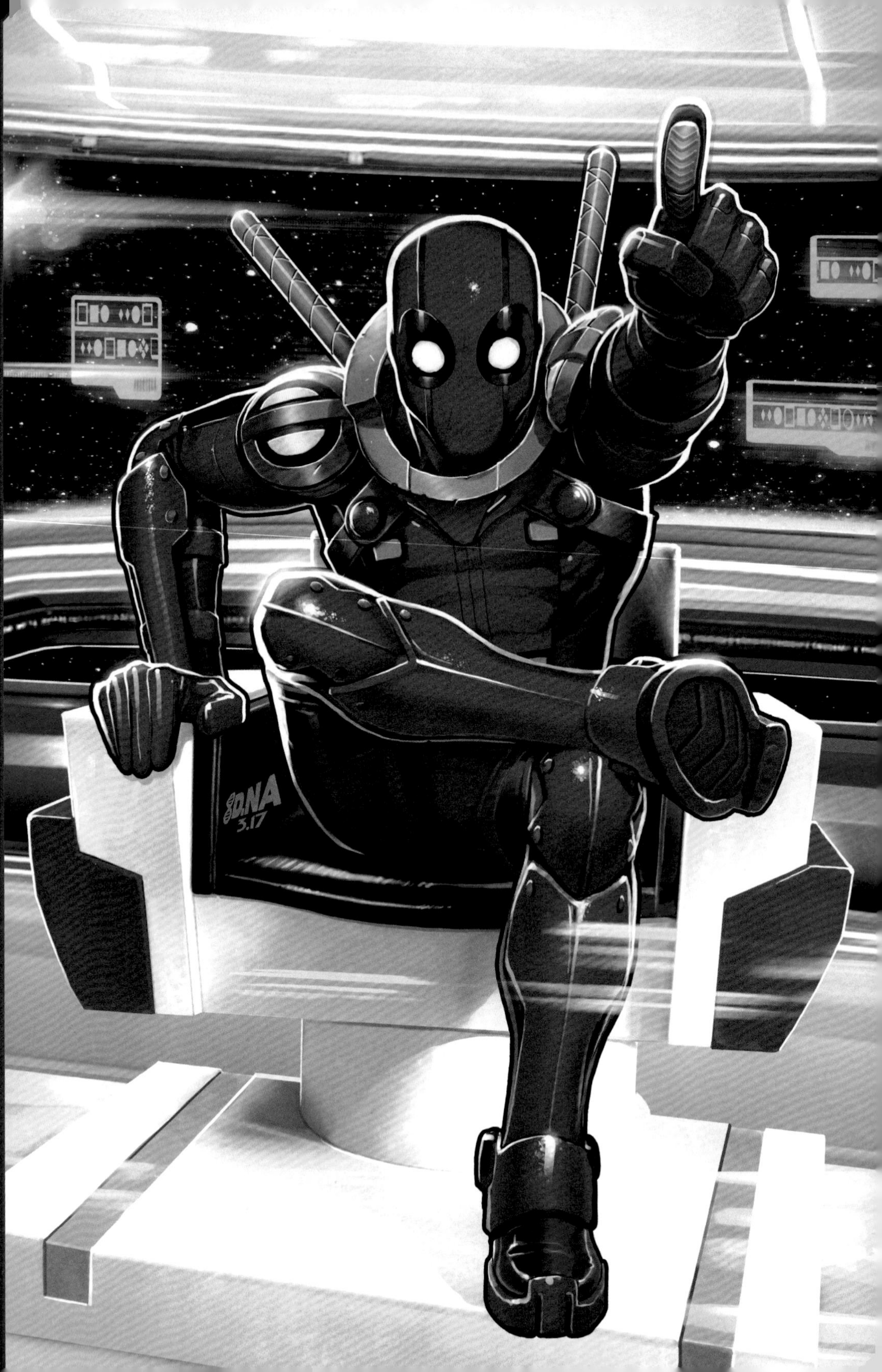
D.NA
3.17

IKE HAWTHORNE

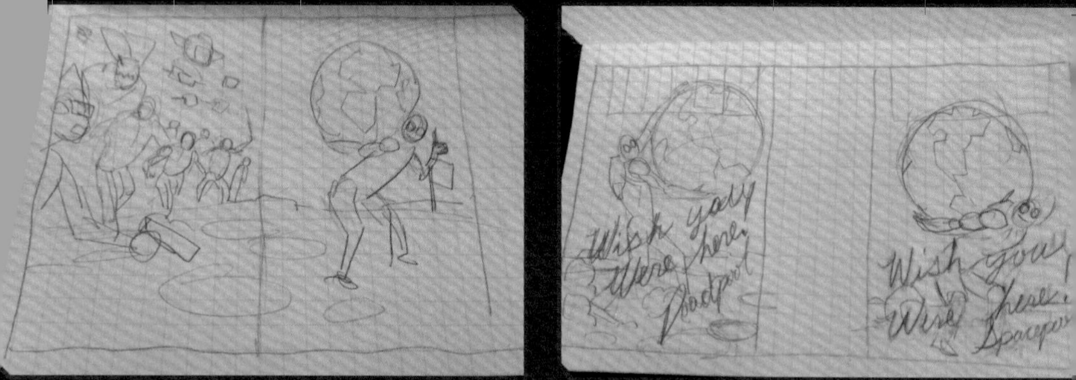

#30 variant cover sketches by DAVID NAKAYAMA

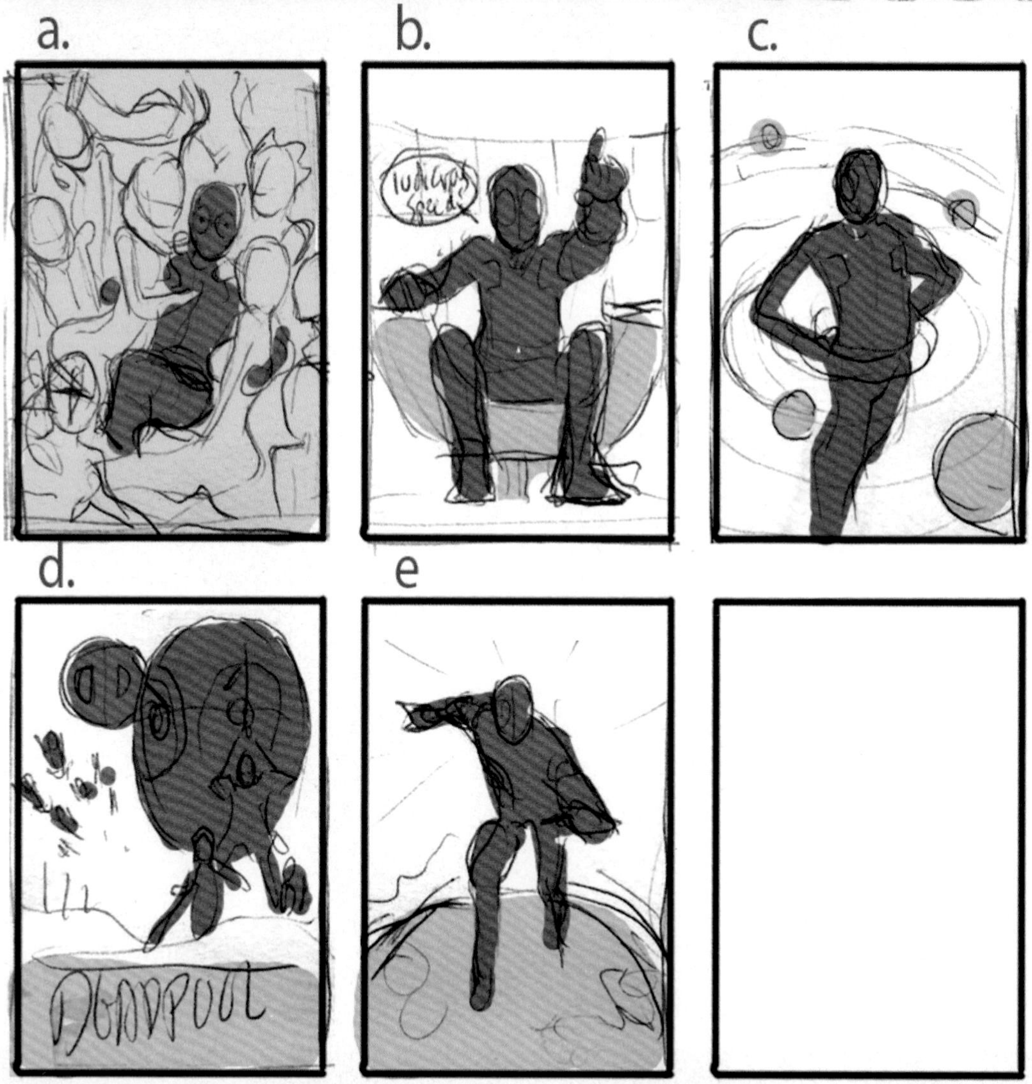
a.
b.
c.
d.
e

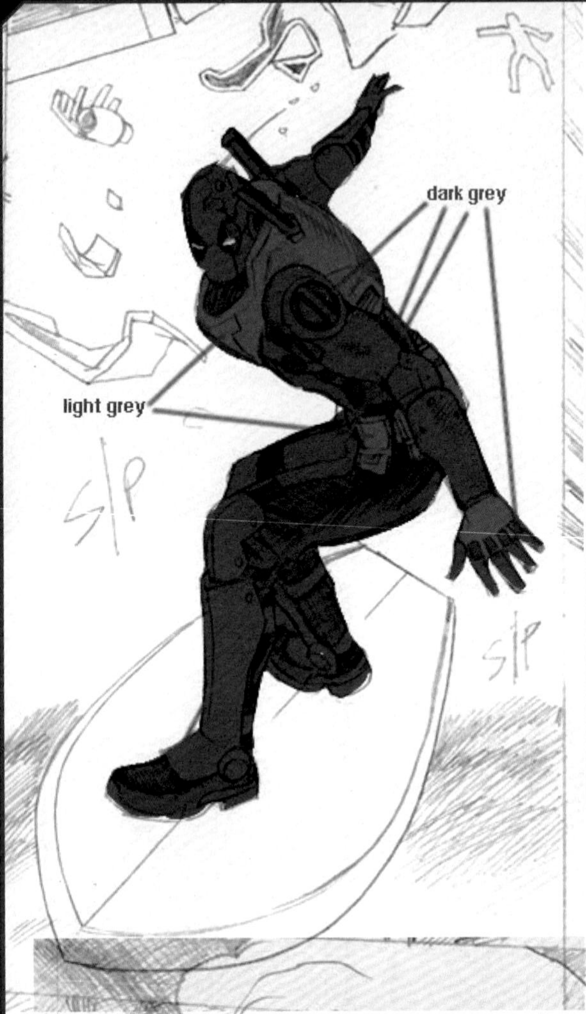
dark grey
light grey

Emphasis on red and black: omit the brown bits from DP's normal suit. DP is going into the dark to do dark things, I'd like him to look the part. Also, I want the design to constantly be contrasting red against black/grey, which defines the form better.

Mike

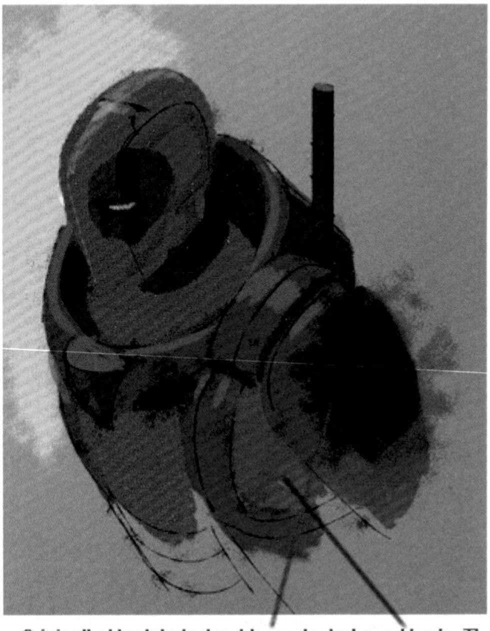

Originally I had dark shoulder pads, but a red body. The red arms/shoudler against the dark/black torso creates a better contrast silhouette. Reads better, and fits the normal DP design.

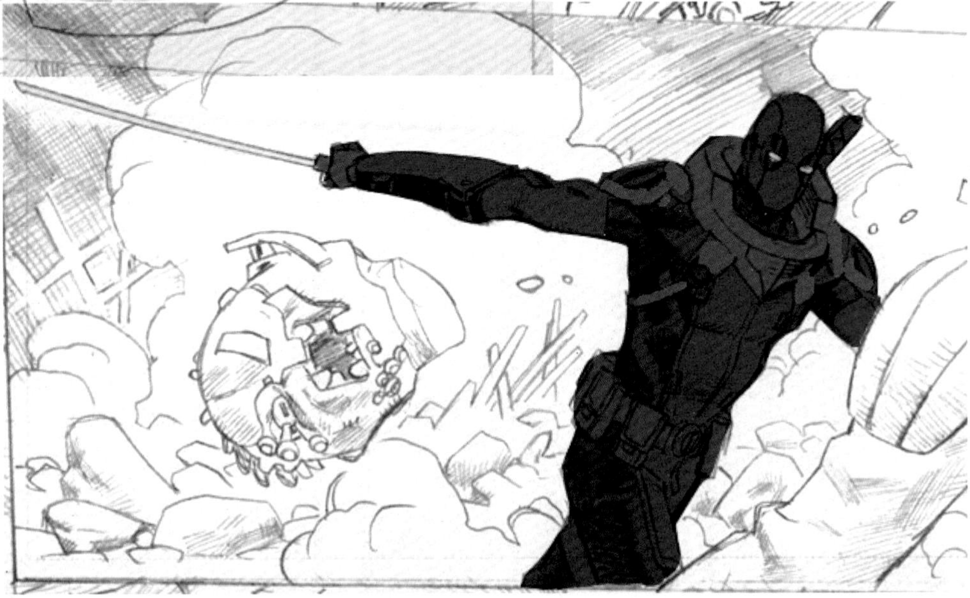